Evaluating
Medical Tests

In loving memory of three men very dear to me:
My grandfather, Benjamin Danielecki;
my father, Stanley Chmura;
and my uncle, Alexander Carpp

Evaluating Medical Tests

OBJECTIVE AND QUANTITATIVE GUIDELINES

Helena Chmura Kraemer

SAGE PUBLICATIONS
International Educational and Professional Publisher
Newbury Park   London   New Delhi

ⓒ 1992

For information address:

SAGE Publications, Inc.
2455 Teller Road
Newbury Park, California 91320

SAGE Publications Ltd.
6 Bonhill Street
London EC2A 4PU
United Kingdom

SAGE Publications India Pvt. Ltd.
M-32 Market
Greater Kailash I
New Delhi 110 048 India

Printed in the United States of America

Library of Congress Cataloging-in-Publication Data

Kraemer, Helena Chmura.
    Evaluating medical tests: Objective and quantitative guidelines/
Helena Chmura Kraemer.
        p.   cm.
    Includes bibliographical references and index.
    ISBN 0-8039-4611-2 (cl).—ISBN 0-8039-4612-0 (pbk.)
    1. Diagnosis—Methodology—Evaluation—Statistical methods.
    2. Function tests (Medicine)—Evaluation—Statistical methods.
    I. Title.
        [DNLM: 1. Bayes Theorem. 2. Diagnosis. 3. Discriminant Analysis.
    4. Evaluation Studies. 5. Models, Statistical. 6. Multivariate
    Analysis. 7. Sensitivity and Specificity. WB 141 K882e]
    RC71.3.K73 1992
    616.07′5′072—dc20
    DNLM/DLC   92-7999

92 93 94 95 10 9 8 7 6 5 4 3 2 1

Sage Production Editor: Astrid Virding

Contents

List of Statistical Notations:
Commonly Used Names and Symbols

Name	Symbol	Pages
True Positive	TP = % positive test and diagnosis	26-27, 29, 46, 54
True Negative	TN = % negative test, negative diagnosis	26-27, 29, 46, 54
False Positive	FP = % positive test, negative diagnosis	26-27, 29, 46, 54
False Negative	FN = % negative test, positive diagnosis	26-27, 29, 46, 54
Prevalence	$P = TP + FN$, $(P' = 1 - P)$	14-17, 27, 54
Level of Test	$Q = TP + FP$, $(Q' = 1 - Q)$	21-22, 27, 46, 77-82
Sensitivity	$SE = TP/P$	27, 32-33, 41, 54, 63-95
Specificity	$SP = TN/P'$, $P' = 1 - P$	27, 32-33, 41, 54, 63-95
Predictive value of a positive test	$PVP = TP/Q$	27, 33, 46, 96-113, 233
Predictive value of a negative test	$PVN = TN/Q'$, $Q' = 1 - Q$	27, 32-33, 46, 96-113, 233
Efficiency	$EFF = TP + TN$	27, 33, 46, 54, 114-130
Receiver Operating Characteristic Curve	ROC	71-91, 100-102
Quality ROC	QROC	75-91, 100-102, 123-129, 284
Quality and Cost ROC	QCROC	140, 145-149, 284
Kappa coefficients:	$\kappa(1, 0) = (SE - Q)/(1 - Q)$ $\kappa(0, 0) = (SP - Q')/Q$ $\kappa(0.5, 0) = \dfrac{(EFF - PQ - P'Q')}{(1 - PQ - P'Q')}$	10-12, 14-15, 34, 40, 47, 55, 66, 75-77, 99, 103-113, 115-116, 119-123, 135, 138, 233, 246-247, 280, 283

Foreword

This volume is a truly unique contribution on the evaluation of medical tests. The author, Dr. Kraemer, is adept at clear writing and thoughtful reasoning. This reader—a nonstatistician—could follow the conceptualization, the logical steps to evaluate the problem, and nearly all of the mathematics as well.

As a clinician, I found this work to be a refreshing confirmation of the need for careful clinical thinking before testing. Dr. Kraemer both logically and mathematically has demonstrated that the appropriate use of medical tests requires clearly framed key questions *before* a judicious, logical sequence of testing. Is the test to screen for diagnosis? Is it to establish the diagnosis clearly? Is it to clearly exclude or to definitively make the diagnosis? These questions lead to issues of true positives and negatives, and false positives and negatives. What actions are to follow if the test is positive or negative? What next tests will there be? What treatment options follow from answers to these questions, surprisingly, affects both what test properties are sought and whether or not to conduct the test at all! In addition, the use of test batteries for diagnosis and prognostication, as well as the relative costs and benefits of tests is discussed in language that nonmathematicians can clearly grasp.

For researchers, graduate students, medical students, residents, and statisticians, this book is a gold mine. It provides the statistical underpinnings and specific recommendations for evaluating the performance of laboratory tests. Issues of sample definition, blinding, defining the "gold standard" against which the test is to be evaluated, and the definition of test procedure are all dealt with in a succinct, straight-forward style.

The reader is led to understand both the conceptualization and computation of sensitivity, specificity, predictive value, and test efficiency, as well as the assumptions that underlie and affect these results. The logical basis and statistical options for evaluating multiple tests in sequence or in test batteries, and the evaluation of prognostic tests are detailed.

Each chapter moves from defining the real life issue surrounding a particular aspect of test evaluation, to the logical assumptions underlying the issue, to the mathematical formulations needed, then to illustrations with real data from various studies, and finally to a succinct summary of issues. Dr. Kraemer very usefully illustrates each key point with case study examples, which not only helps to make the point clear, but also helps clinicians understand the application in practice of the points made and helps researchers and statisticians see the practical consequences affected by their efforts. As such, it is the most readable statistically based book I have encountered.

Finally, a third group of readers—policymakers, health economists, and health service researchers—will find this book to be of extraordinary value. It not only takes the reader through the practical issues of how to assess the performance of a test in terms of diagnosis and prognosis, but it also provides a guide to the essential element of weighing the costs and benefits of the test to the patient and physician. The good news is that more tests are not necessarily better for patients—even if resources are unlimited. Even better, the least costly tests may in many circumstances be the best. The new high-technology tests may play a key role, but are most likely of optimal use in selected situations. It provides a logically argued, mathematically justified basis for medical test cost containment without reducing the quality of care to patients.

In sum, this volume is a pleasure to read. It succinctly combines carefully reasoned conceptualization with the mathematical methods for addressing test evaluation problems. With clinically relevant, illustrative examples, it draws on the author's extensive experience and research in biomedical statistics. It should be required reading for medical students and practitioners. It is invaluable to researchers and statisticians, and it provides a logical, scientific basis for efforts at medical cost containment. It is a classic!

—A. JOHN RUSH, M.D.
BETTY JO HAY DISTINGUISHED CHAIR AND PROFESSOR
DEPARTMENT OF PSYCHIATRY
UNIVERSITY OF TEXAS SOUTHWESTERN MEDICAL CENTER
DALLAS, TEXAS

Preface

This book is written with a concern for patients and for the physicians who make clinical decisions about patients. However, it is not specifically written to be read by either patients or by clinicians, but, rather, by those researchers and policymakers concerned with the evaluation of medical tests used to make clinical decisions for patient care and for research use.

What initially aroused my curiosity about the topic of medical tests was an experience familiar to many. A few years ago, in the process of changing medical insurance coverage, my husband and I underwent complete physicals. At the start we knew we were generally healthy, with a few aches and pains characteristic of our age. We could well afford to lose a few pounds and get a bit more exercise.

Over the course of several days, we had complete health histories taken, evaluations of signs and symptoms, and physical examinations. We were sent to the laboratory for a battery of blood and urine tests, and arrangements were made for obtaining a stool sample for further tests. Then we were sent for a chest X-ray, for me a mammogram, a resting EKG, and, for him, an exercise stress test and a glucose tolerance test, and, finally, for me, a pelvic sonogram and a uterine biopsy. Eye exams, including tests for early detection of glaucoma, and dental exams, including X-rays, completed the process.

The verdict was that we were generally healthy. Our aches and pains were completely normal, typical of someone our age. We could afford to lose weight and to get more exercise.

In total, the examinations and the tests cost many hundreds of dollars, some paid by us, and some covered by health insurance. The cost of health insurance, of course, was paid by us indirectly and by our respective employers.

Was it worth the cost to be assured that we were in fact as healthy as we thought? If such assurance were the outcome, it probably would be worth the cost.

What made this experience different was that at that time I was consulting or collaborating in several research projects concerned with certain medical tests (exercise stress tests, dexamethasone suppression test). In the course of that work I had been reviewing the medical research literature on medical test evaluation, including evaluations of some of the very tests we experienced. I well knew that there is little assurance of health from negative medical tests. The types of blood, urine, stool, and tissue tests used are not without error. Which lab one uses and which technician actually runs the tests influence how well the test is done and how accurate the results. At best, the standards for these tests are set high to prevent "false alarms." Thus a negative test result is seldom complete assurance of absence of whatever disorder the test is meant to detect. There were questions being raised in the medical literature at the time about the value of mammography. The exercise stress test was controversial, particularly when used, as in this case, for an asymptomatic patient. The interpretation of the EKG and of the X-rays and sonogram have some degree of subjective error. Two experts evaluating the same test results do not necessarily come to the same conclusion.

In the years since I became interested in medical test evaluation, I have seldom discussed the issue without someone offering some amusing, dramatic, or disturbing anecdote about their own experience with medical testing, and none suggest complacency on the state of the art. The cover story of the *U.S. News & World Report* (November 23, 1987) issue titled "Are We Hooked on Tests?," expresses many of the same concerns I will in this treatment of the subject, summarizing "In short, more Americans are being pricked and prodded, scoped and scanned, and the cost is steep—sometimes life itself" (p. 61). Over these years, the problem of the lack of quality of medical tests has become, if anything, more serious, and the solution is not in sight. This is not merely a statistical issue, or merely a medical issue, it is a national policy issue of the greatest importance.

The problem has become particularly salient, because many of the tests now in routine use are relatively new, and new, high-technology tests are proliferating. When my parents were my age, they were faced with a far more limited battery of available tests. To investigate the possibility of heart disease a generation ago, only history, signs, symptoms, and physical examination were used. At that time, the EKG was not in routine use, and the exercise stress test was unknown. At present, the EKG at a cost of about $50, and the exercise stress test at a cost of about $200 would routinely be used. A generation from now, when my children are my age, will the test used be scintigraphy, ventriculography, magnetic resonance tests, each at a cost of $1,000 or more, or some even more invasive or costly tests? Will one of these tests replace the resting EKG and the exercise stress test, or will they all just be added to the list as these tests have been added to the list of a generation ago?

More important, is it unequivocally true that the next generation will be more assured that whatever tests are run accurately assess their medical conditions, more assured than I am now or my parents were then?

These are, of course, issues that have received widespread attention. It is surprising, however, how frequently these concerns lead to one of two results. Either it is recommended that medical insurance companies refuse to pay for certain tests, in which case the patient bears the onus of the resolution of the problem. Alternatively, the clinician is implicitly or explicitly reprimanded for ordering unnecessary or poor-quality tests. There has been speculation that it is the "money-grubbing" clinician who is at major fault here. I disagree with both these attitudes.

I am not a clinician faced with deciding which tests to run or how to interpret the test outcomes or which clinical decisions to make on that basis. But I empathize with their situation. They cannot afford to avoid using the standard medical tests. If they were not to call for a mammogram, and a patient were later to die from a malignancy that, detected earlier, could have been cured, they would be subject to accusation of "malpractice." The legal definition of malpractice is phrased in terms of what is "good medical practice." If "good medical practice" includes the use of some possibly worthless medical test, the clinician must order it, whatever his or her own personal and professional opinion of the test may be.

Furthermore, it is no more within the purview of the clinician to decide which tests are or are not valid, how each should be conducted, or for which patients, as it is to decide which drugs or medical devices are effective and safe, indicated, or contraindicated for which patients, and in what dosages or at what level. The FDA is mandated to oversee the licensing of drugs and medical devices both to protect patients and to provide guidelines for clinicians. No such protection exists for the "marketing" of medical tests. "Marketing," I think, is the accurate word, for the cost of medical tests, as estimated in the *U.S. News & World Report* (and other reports are similar), "represents $1 of every $3 of the nation's $450 billion health-care bill" (p. 60). I am not as sanguine about the role of hospital and clinic administrators, the role of manufacturers of high-tech instrumentation for medical testing, the role of academic researchers for whom discovering a new medical test means publications, fame, and other rewards, as I am about the role of clinicians.

Patients and their physicians suffer the brunt of the problems associated with the range, choice, inaccuracy, and costs of medical tests, but the solution to these problems does not lie in their hands. It lies in the hands of those medical researchers who devise new medical tests, evaluate them, and recommend for or against their clinical use, and in the hands of biostatisticians such as I, who are involved in the process.

Many of the papers and books written to date on the methods of evaluating medical tests have been written by medical and public health researchers whose orientation to such problems is that of the purveyor of medical tests. That signals a conflict of interest. I have both a different professional and personal orientation. First of all, my research area is biostatistics, specifically that area dealing with the *methods* of evaluation of the quality of medical tests and diagnoses, with no commitment, positive or negative, about any particular test. Second, my point of view is close to that of the consumer of medical tests, i.e., the patient or the clinician representing that patient, not of the purveyor.

The views of the purveyor and consumer are not irreconcilable, but they are different. The purveyor focuses on the masses, the other on the individual. The background, knowledge, and experience of the medical or public health researcher and that of the biostatistical researcher, both interested in the quality of medical tests and diagnoses, are directed to the same goal, but may lead along different paths.

In my approaches to this subject I have been strongly influenced by a comment by Dr. Alvin Feinstein (1967):

Mathematics has no value in helping us understand nature unless we begin by understanding nature. To start with mathematical formulations and to alter nature so that it fits the assumptions is a procrustean nonsequitur unfortunately all too prevalent in contemporary "science." What emerges is tenable and sometimes even elegant in mathematics, but is too distorted by its initial assumptions to be a valid representation of what goes on in nature. I therefore prefer to work from the inside out, rather than from outside in: as a clinician trying to find whatever mathematics fits clinical medicine, rather than as a mathematician pouring clinical phenomena into a preconceived mathematical mold. (p. 16)

Again, I am not a clinician, but nevertheless I have tried to work "from the inside out," studying data from many medical research studies to see which mathematical models are supported by those data and which are not.

Current methods of evaluation of medical tests frequently depend on theoretical assumptions that are not supported by empirical results. The most common reason for such assumptions is to simplify the mathematics. Such assumptions are generally not made by mathematicians who have no need for such simplification, but, rather, by radiologists, pathologists, or pharmacologists or others involved in the application of medical tests. The costs of such simplifications are often inaccurate and misleading results. A biostatistician can only examine whether the behavior of the test will be adversely affected if what is claimed does not exactly hold (robustness of results). Whether the conclusions reached by a pharmacologist, a radiologist, or a pathologist, on the one hand and the biostatistician on the other agree or not depends on how closely the *data* support the contentions of medical experts.

In the following presentation, theoretical models are necessary, as they always are in making inferences from data to populations. However, the models that will be used will be motivated and supported by real, not hypothetical, examples. It is, I feel, vital to the future evaluation of medical tests that it be based on a *systematic*, a *completely objective*, and *empirical* methodology, and not anyone's subjective opinion.

I have a unique advantage over those who have earlier presented their approaches. They went first. I am in a position to incorporate and develop upon all they have discovered in the approaches I suggest. I have tried to do so. Bernard of Chartres is quoted (and Newton several centuries later) that "we are like dwarfs on the shoulders of giants, so that we can see more than they, and things at a greater distance, not by virtue of any sharpness of sight on our part, or any physical distinction, but because we are carried high and raised up by their giant size." There is no study discussed here from which I have not learned something new and valuable. When I criticize some of what has been done, it is with a knowledge that Monday morning quarterbacking is much easier than calling the plays on Saturday. I know that the last word on objective and quantitative medical test evaluation will not be said here. I hope and expect that others will build on what I do, in the course of which they will undoubtedly find much in my work, too, to criticize.

Acknowledgments

It has been at least 10 years since the first stirrings on the material contained in this book began. For many years I did not recognize that these were "stirrings." As a result, many more colleagues and friends were instrumental in helping me understand the problem and to finding ways of dealing with it than I can specifically enumerate here. I apologize for the omission and fully acknowledge my debts to them.

My first real exposure to this problem came with simultaneous research problems arising in connection with the evaluation of two quite different medical tests in two different areas. The first was the research into the dexamethasone suppression test (DST) for identification of a presumably biological subtype of depression, which was being done in the Mental Health Clinical Research Center (Dr. Philip Berger) and the other into the exercise stress test for identification of those with coronary artery disease (Dr. Robert DeBusk). As it happens, both these tests, then and now, are controversial, which, for my purposes, was an ideal situation. I owe a great deal of thanks to both of these investigators for asking all the right questions and demanding convincing answers, not merely convenient ones.

In connection with the Mental Health Clinical Research Center projects, I would also like to thank Sue Thiemann, who was my "right hand" for so many years, and who either did or checked many of the calculations done here, and Ellen Bush, now completing medical school, but who, as a research assistant then, helped enormously, not only in compiling the relevant research literature on the subject, but also in long discussions on what was going on in that literature that proved so confusing.

In connection with the DeBusk project, in addition to Bob himself, who was invaluable in helping me view the problem from a clinical perspective, I would also like to thank Dr. Charles Dennis (now at University of California, San Diego) for his help and insights. Finally, very special thanks are due to Dr. Ghassan Ghandour, who produced a program to do the analyses discussed here. While most of the numerical analysis presented in this book were done laboriously with no special computer software support, more recent applications have been facilitated by Ghassan's excellent program.

I would also like to thank Dr. John M. Harris, Jr., who, while a Clinical Scholar at Stanford, immersed himself in this problem from a different perspective from mine. Our discussions at that early stage were instrumental in my formulation and approach to the problem. His study, "Diagnostic Tests and Hodgkin's Disease," discussed in Chapter 5 is the only study I have included as an example in which there was any personal communication with the author. This was a deliberate decision on my part in order to focus on what is *reported*, not on what was *intended*, in a medical test evaluation. It is also why none of the many medical test evaluations I have personally had any involvement with are used here as illustrations. I made the exception for the Harris, Tang, and Weltz (1978) study only because Skip himself brought the problems in his study to my attention. His was the only among many studies exhibiting the same problem that presented data fully enough to gain insight into its resolution. That was probably because Skip, himself, was very aware of the problem.

Since these first applications with the DST and the exercise stress test, many clinical researchers have been generous with both time, interest, and their data to put these methods to test. While their data and their results are not used in the following presentation, I cannot overstate the value of these experiences and the discussion in connection with these projects in clarifying and expanding the material presented here. Thanks then also to:

Dr. Bryna Siegel (now at University of California at San Francisco), whose interest is to assess the quality of diagnostic criteria for autism; Dr. A. John Rush and Dr. Christine Gullian (University of Texas, Dallas) who executed what may be the definitive study to assess the quality of the dexamethasone suppression test for a subtype of clinical depression. After reviewing some 300 published reports on the DST, I found that not one of them, in my opinion, is free from some major methodological flaw. Reviewing the Rush et al. study was a pleasure, and being presented with the data set a joy; Dr. W. Stewart Agras and Dr. Robert Berkowitz (the latter now at University of Pennsylvania), whose interests include the development of prognostic tests for identification of young children who are at risk of developing obesity by their teen years, as well as prognostic tests to identify those in weight loss programs likely to succeed; all the participants in the field trials for DSM IV, particularly, Dr. Allen Frances, who have given me the opportunity to try out these methods in conjunction with their efforts, crucial to future directions in psychiatry; Dr. Victor Denenberg and Dr. Evelyn Thoman at the University of Connecticut, whose enthusiasms and insights opened new perspectives into the use and potential of these methods; Drs. Raquel and Reuben Gur at the University of Pennsylvania, whose application of these methods to differentiation of clinical and normal populations on the basis of perception of affect in faces, is an intriguing, novel, and very important application; at the Stanford Center for Research in Disease Prevention (SCRDP), Dr. Steve Fortmann, Dr. Joel Killen, and Ann Varady, who are trying to develop prognostic tests for identification of those likely to quit smoking, and they seem to be succeeding far better with those methods than has been achieved to date.

I would like especially to thank Dr. Darrell Wilson, who did the final review of the manuscript and, among other things, tried valiantly to make me sound more like a clinician. While I did learn, perhaps once and for all, that clinicians do not capitalize diseases or tests (hence coronary artery disease not Coronary Artery Disease, and exercise stress test not Exercise Stress Test) I'm afraid Darrell undertook a hopeless task. To a clinician, I suspect I will still sound "foreign." However, I learned a great deal from Darrell, and his efforts, I'm sure, at least decreased my "foreignness" to future readers.

I owe special thanks to my daughter, Stacey, who, very early in the process, undertook to learn to use WordStar in order to retype the early drafts of the first half dozen chapters into a computer format better suited to the task and then instructed me in the rudiments of its use and in the principles of file management. When I later lost Chapter 5, the lessons she taught me about backing up *every* file *every* time truly sank in.

My thanks, too, to Jerri Rudnick who patiently took my drafts and put her professional touch to typescript and tables.

Finally I owe thanks to my tolerant and patient family: To my husband Art, and daughters Stacey and Karen. Not only have they tolerated my one-track mindedness on this issue over much too long a period of time, but they have also, in numerous and untold ways, aided and abetted the process.

1

Introduction

Medical costs are rapidly escalating. A substantial portion of these costs is for medical tests for purposes of diagnosis, prognosis, or of monitoring response to treatments. "Dubiously costworthy respiratory therapy, diagnostic radioisotopes, electroencephalography, and cobalt therapy involve excesses of $995 million. . . . [W]e can add the CT scanner for another $200 million, . . . savings from the elimination of excess clinical lab tests probably would amount to another $4.0 billion" (Menzel, 1983, p. 12).

As Robin (1984) has stated:

> Some general nonspecific laboratory tests are included in the workup— usually a blood count, a urinalysis, some chemical measurements of the blood; not uncommonly, a chest X-ray; and quite commonly, an electrocardiogram. The nature of these tests and their number are established by tradition, by general usage, and by convenience. Their value for most patients has not been established. There is also an economic incentive at work—it is customary to overcharge for laboratory work. Data on the effectiveness of nonspecific laboratory studies in patient care, however, are scant. What is more important, individual doctors, not knowing the risks versus benefits, often order them routinely. (p. 28)

According to Nash (1985): "[A] growing body of medical research suggests that more than a quarter of the tests currently being performed are unnecessary and/or inappropriate and, moreover, yield results that are often inaccurate and misleading" (p. 47). What is more, Nash continues: "the incidence of iatrogenic disease is rising, in part because of the increasing availability of sophisticated and complex medical technology in the form of ever-new tests" (p. 12).

Former Secretary of Health, Education and Welfare Joseph A. Califano, Jr., participated in an investigation of the overwhelming medical costs paid under Chrysler Corporation coverage of its employees, an investigation that "revealed a level of unnecessary care, inefficient practices, overutilization, fraud, and abuse that appalled Lee Iacocca and all Chrysler management. It provided solid evidence of wasteful spending of health benefit dollars and of diminished quality of care provided to people Chrysler insured" (Califano, 1986, p. 18). Specifically, Califano reported that: "Chrysler-insured patients got more than a million laboratory tests, more than five for every insured man, woman, and child, at a cost of $12 million. Chiropractors increased over the prior year their diagnostic X-rays almost 15 percent for each employee. The Michigan Blues were billed an average of $10,000 annually per chiropractor, just for X-rays" (p. 18). Califano conveys a bleak warning:

> If we don't change the system, prepare to live in an America where the annual health care bill will hit a trillion dollars in the early 1990s and continue to double every six or seven years after that; where the cost of health care makes our automobiles and steel and other products so expensive that American industry can't compete in a global marketplace; and where government rations health care and bureaucrats issue hundreds of pages of regulations that determine who lives and who dies. (p. 8)

The newspapers carry articles almost daily about testing for AIDS, about testing for drug use, not just among athletes, but in the government and in industry as well. Medical tests are no longer limited to use by physicians supposedly for the health and well-being of their patients. They now influence the fabric of social interaction in many other areas as well.

The concerns expressed in the comments above reflect an almost universal dismay among those who have studied the problem from policy perspectives. This dismay results from: (1) the astounding cost of medical testing; (2) the fact the tests used, even the most familiar and common ones, are inaccurate, misused and misleading; (3) that such tests are used unnecessarily; and (4) they can be dangerous to the patients on whom they are used, either because of inherent risks in high-technology tests, or because of the consequences of their inaccuracies.

The evaluations of medical tests or comparisons between tests in terms of their qualities are based on statistical methods. However, there is justification to the statements reported in *The Lancet* ("The Value," 1979) that: "The assessment of diagnostic methods belongs to the backwoods of clinical research. New treatments are submitted to thorough testing, and books are written on the methodology of the controlled therapeutic trial; but no standards have been fixed for the assessment of diagnostic methods" (p. 809).

Yet there have been whole books and a prodigious number of papers written on these issues. Even an entire medical journal (*Medical Decision Making*) has been devoted to such issues. Any justification there is to the critique is not due to a paucity of proposals for dealing with such problems.

There exist at least three well-developed approaches to such problems: The Signal-Detection approach; the Bayesian approach; the Multivariate Discrimination approach. Each has its strengths, its weaknesses, its advocates, and opponents; however, the results of applying the three types of approaches in one study of a medical test may produce diverse outcomes. Applying the same approach to multiple studies of the same medical test may produce even more diverse outcomes. Multiple evaluations of the same medical test, however done, are more likely than not to end with a characterization of the test as "controversial."

As a result, medical tests frequently go into common clinical use without convincing documentation of their value. In absence of convincing documentation that a new medical test makes older tests unnecessary, new tests are simply added to the physicians's repertoire, and all may be applied to the same patient. In the course of time, not only may each test become more costly, but, in addition, the number of tests that can be ordered for a patient is ever increasing, and may include many that are of little value or that are redundant. Of greatest concern are the newest tests based on high technology, which involve enormous cost and often some risk to the patient.

Here I am concerned with the *statistical* evaluation of medical tests. In reviewing the statistical aspects of the various medical test evaluation methods and some of the many actual evaluations of medical tests, two facts emerge. First, medical terms are used in defining the statistical approaches with no precise definition and, consequently, in ways that differ from study to study. Secondly, the statistical assumptions underlying the various approaches are rarely precisely stipulated and rarely checked for empirical validity. Even more rarely does the robustness of the statistical outcomes to deviations from such assumptions enter consideration. These facts alone may account for many of the conflicting results that appear in the medical literature.

Accordingly, much of what follows is not new. I attempt to define certain statistical terms in ways consistent with their medical usage to articulate the assumptions that either seem to be made or need to be made to apply the current approaches. The models and approaches that result integrate many different approaches and extend the strengths of each.

Some of what follows is new and might be regarded as controversial, since it is contrary to what is sometimes now claimed. Every aspect of this approach is motivated, not by hypothetical examples, but, rather, with one or more examples of real medical tests as used on real medical patients in studies presented in respected and peer-reviewed medical journals. If such claims are to be questioned or disputed, questions and criticism should be based on *empirical* evidence, not on what has been said, what one believes, or what one hopes to be true. There are consequences of any statistical model necessary to a clear understanding of how the statistical outcomes of medical test evaluation can be interpreted. If the model is based on unsupported theory and not on real data, the consequences and the outcomes may also apply only in theory and not to real patients or tests.

Some of what is presented is meant to be provocative, to initiate and stimulate serious consideration of the issues involved. In presenting such materials, I have expressed views in the first person singular to differentiate these comments from presentations of what I would consider provable or documentable facts. What I say in these sections is based on my evaluation of empirical evidence, but I am signaling that I, myself, am not convinced by the evidence.

Examples from the medical literature will be presented to illustrate the principles or methods. Only those medical details necessary to explicate the statistical evaluation appear, and the original references are cited in which the medical details are elaborated. Not all examples used produce results concordant with their original presentation. This is necessarily so, for the approaches suggested here are meant to resolve the conflicting results that appear in the medical literature. Such conflicts cannot be resolved by agreeing with all sides.

2

Disorder and Diagnosis

The Disorder

Everyone knows what the difference is between a disorder and a diagnosis! Perhaps so, but in surveying the medical research literature on medical test evaluation, I have found that the distinction is not always clearly acknowledged, and a lack of clarity about the distinction may produce serious error.

A disorder (used generically for disease, condition, illness, dysfunction etc.) represents, according to *Blakiston's Gould Medical Dictionary* (1972): "A disturbance or derangement of regular or normal physical or mental function" (p. 453). The disorder is a characteristic of a patient. At any point in time, either the patient has the disorder, or the patient does not.

Moreover, in all evaluations of medical tests the disorder represents a *fixed* characteristic of the patient during the "period of testing": the time from the decision to have the patient undergo the test to the time at which all information pertinent to the evaluation of the test response has been obtained. A patient cannot both have the disorder and not have it at one and the same time, nor does he have the disorder at 8 a.m., recover by noon, and relapse by 8 p.m.. Such a situation would confound all approaches to medical test evaluation. This leads to the first assumption:

5

ASSUMPTION 1 (CONSTANCY OF THE DISORDER)
The period of testing must be defined so that throughout this period the patient either has the disorder or does not.

After the period of testing, a patient who had the disorder may recover, either spontaneously or in response to treatment. After the period of testing, a patient who was free of the disorder may incur the disorder. However, the period of testing must be a relatively short time—an hour, day, week, or month—during which the patient remains in a fixed clinical status vis-à-vis the disorder.

The test can only reflect the patient's status during the period of testing. No test can respond to characteristics of the patient that do not yet exist or to events that have not yet occurred, hence the second basic assumption:

ASSUMPTION 2 (PURPOSE OF MEDICAL TESTING)
The purpose of a medical test is to help determine whether or not a patient has a specific disorder *during the period of testing.*

Precision is essential in defining a disorder and distinguishing the disorder from a diagnosis of a disorder. The quality of a medical test depends on how well its results correspond to the presence or absence of a *disorder*; however, the evaluation of the quality of a medical test depends on how its results correspond, not to the disorder per se, but, rather, to a *diagnosis* of that disorder.

The Diagnosis of the Disorder

The *diagnosis,* as defined in *Blakiston's Gould Medical Dictionary* (1972) is "The art or the act of determining the nature of the patient's disease. A conclusion reached in the identification of the patient's disease" (p. 433). The diagnosis represents an attribute, not of the patient, but, rather, of the diagnostician or the diagnostic process in response to the patient. In many cases the diagnosis expresses a physician's subjective belief that the patient has the disorder, a belief that may, or may not, be warranted. Succinctly stated, a disorder is what the patient has; a diagnosis is what the physician gives him.

There have been many studies of the reproducibility of various diagnostic procedures (Koran, 1975) confirming what is well known: A second or third diagnostic opinion does not always confirm the first opinion. During the period of testing the patient may have both a positive and negative diagnosis at one and the same time (from different diagnosticians), and, if evaluated several times during the period of testing, may have a positive diagnosis at one time, and a negative diagnosis at another (even from the same diagnostician).

For this reason, when a patient has complaints that one physician cannot find a cause or cure for, there is good reason to seek a second opinion. When a patient is given a diagnosis that would require radical treatment such as surgery, radiotherapy, or chemotherapy, it is well worthwhile to obtain a second or even a third opinion. The value of a second medical opinion, both among physicians and among patients, is widely accepted.

Because a first, second, or third diagnosis, no matter how expert each may be, do not necessarily agree, it cannot be assumed that the *diagnosis* of the disorder is a constant during the period of testing, even if the disorder itself is. Such an assumption is contrary to empirical evidence and is usually easily contradicted by obtaining two "blind" diagnoses for each of a series of patients during the period of testing and comparing them. Some will almost inevitably be discordant.

For example, the diagnosis of coronary artery disease in medical test evaluations is frequently based on coronary angiography. Yet there have been several studies demonstrating interobserver variability in reading angiograms. In one such study on the concurrence of two expert evaluations of coronary angiographs, the agreement was said to be about halfway between chance and perfect (Detre, Wright, Murphy, & Takaro, 1975). Coronary angiography results have proved their clinical value, and interdiagnostician disagreement does not invalidate that value. Diagnosis of coronary artery disease based on coronary angiography may be called a "gold standard." Such a term, however, should not be taken to mean that the diagnosis is infallible, but only that it is considered one of the best diagnostic procedures known to date of this disorder. Some other diagnostic procedure, perhaps even a test currently under evaluation, may become the gold standard 10 years from now.

In fact, any diagnosis that depends on laboratory tests, on subjective interpretations (including those on autopsy), or on patient report, has some risk of error. The error may be due to the instrumentation, to some fault in the instrument or poor calibration, to poor training, carelessness, or human error in the assessors, to mislabeled samples or reports, and/or to misreporting or inconsistency in what patients say or do. Almost all diagnostic procedures include one or another of these elements. Much as patients wish it of their physicians, and much as physicians hope for it of themselves, infallibility is not currently within the reach of medical diagnosticians and probably will never be.

Diagnostic and Prognostic Tests

By my definition of the "period of testing," all the results pertinent to the evaluation of the test are obtained during the period of testing. The diagnosis, however, may be obtained either during the period of testing or in a specified period of time afterward, which is called the "follow-up period."

If the diagnosis is obtained during the period of testing, the test is here called a "diagnostic test." If the diagnosis is obtained during a follow-up period, it is here called a "prognostic test." In short, the test's label reflects the timing of the *diagnosis* in the evaluation study.

In medical test evaluation, the same test may be evaluated in one study as a diagnostic test and in another as a prognostic test. An exercise stress test, for example, may be evaluated as a diagnostic test against a concurrent diagnosis of coronary artery disease (the disorder) based on coronary arteriography in one study (Patterson et al., 1982), and as a prognostic test in another using a diagnosis based on the occurrence or non-occurrence of serious cardiac events during a one-year follow-up in another (Theroux, Waters, Halphen, Debaisieux, & Mizgala, 1979). In either case, the disorder of interest is some sort of coronary artery disease in the patient during the period of testing (Assumption 2). In one case the diagnosis of that disorder was defined in terms of whether or not the patient is recognized as having that disorder during the period of testing (diagnostic test). In the other it is defined by whether or not certain sequelae of that disorder did or did not occur during the follow-up period (prognostic test). Both are valid diagnoses of a disorder and valid bases for evaluation of a medical test for that disorder.

The Basic Model

To capture both the variability of the diagnosis and the relationship of diagnosis to disorder, I define the parameter p_i for each patient (labeled i) as the probability that patient i will get a positive diagnosis. For a diagnostic test, p_i represents the probability that one diagnosis, randomly chosen from all the independent repeated ("blinded") diagnoses that might have been made during the period of testing, is positive. For a prognostic test, p_i is the unknown risk of the diagnosis during the follow-up period.

For a diagnostic test, one can estimate p_i by obtaining multiple independent (blinded) diagnoses for patient i and computing the proportion positive. Several data sets describing such results appear in Figure 2.1. Three of the diagnostic procedures described there are based on what is often called "hard evidence": photofluorograms (Yerushalmy, 1956), gastroduodenal X-ray (Etter, Dunn, Kammer, Osmond, & Reese, 1960), and pathologists' classification of tissue slides (Kraemer, 1982). The remaining one is a psychiatric diagnosis, schizophrenia, often characterized as "soft" data, because it is based on subjective interpretation of patients' behavior. For the photofluorogram there were 8 independent readings per patient; for the gastroduodenal X-ray there were 3; for tissue classification 12; for schizophrenia, 6. What is listed on the x-axis is the percentage of the multiple readings per patient that was positive. Thus 0% on the x-axis represents complete agreement on a negative result and 100% complete agreement on a positive result. On the y-axis is the percentage of the total patients with that degree of agreement. In all four illustrations, there were few, if any, complete positive agreements (100% positive); the most common situation here appears to be complete negative agreement (0% positive). Since 0% and 100% positive represent absolute reproducibility, it can be seen that none of the diagnoses is absolutely reproducible, even those based on "hard evidence." Moreover, these distributions are quite different from one another. Generally, they tend to be roughly U-shaped or J-shaped (either forward or backward facing), but sometimes, as in the case of tissue classification or schizophrenia, there is a hint of a minor internal peak or two.

In contrast to such distributions that can be seen in "real life," are the type of hypothetical distributions seen in Figure 2.2, seldom seen

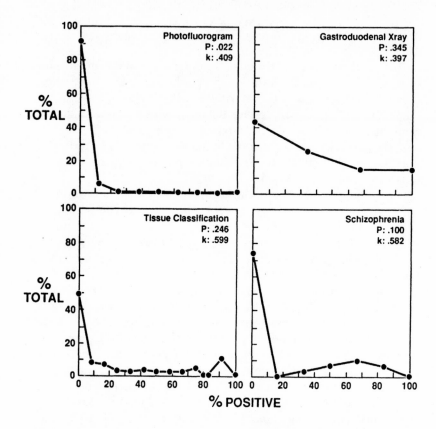

Figure 2.1. Four "real-life" cases showing the distribution of the percentage positive diagnoses when multiple independent diagnoses per patient are obtained. *P* is the estimated prevalence, and κ the estimated kappa coefficient of reproducibility of the diagnosis used.

in real life but frequently the basis of medical test evaluations in the research literature.

First is a completely random or unreliable diagnosis, one that can be generated by ignoring the patients and using a coin, a die, or a random number table to generate diagnoses. The values of p_i for all patients in the population are concentrated at one value here at 40%. Such a diagnosis is seldom seen in real life because by the time a decision procedure reaches a stage where clinicians are likely to

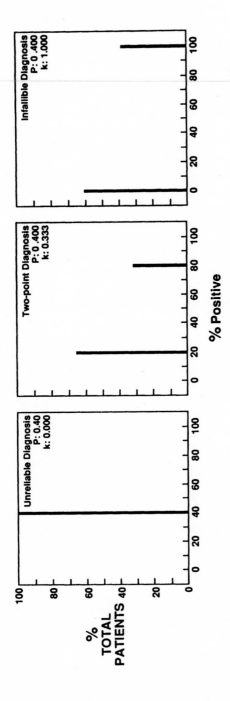

Figure 2.2. Three hypothetical cases showing the distribution of the percentage positive diagnosis when multiple independent diagnoses per patient are obtained with random decision making (unreliable diagnosis), with an assumed two-point diagnosis, and with complete reproducibility (infallible diagnosis). P is the prevalence and κ the kappa coefficient of reproducibility of the diagnosis in each case.

consider it a "diagnostic procedure," it is usually considerably better than tossing a coin or die.

Second is the opposite extreme: a completely reproducible or infallible diagnosis, in which every patient has a value of p_i that is either zero or one. If the diagnosis has any relevance to the disorder, those with $p_i = 1$ (100%) are clearly those with the disorder, and those with $p_i = 0$ (0%) are those without the disorder. That such a distribution is seldom seen in nature is an empirical fact demonstrated in studies such as those cited by Koran (1975) or that reported by Detre et al. (1975) and many others. Yet assumption of such a distribution often underlies medical test evaluation, slipping in under statements that say "Patients with the disorder," when what is precisely meant is "Patients with a positive diagnosis."

Finally, the third hypothetical example is a two-point distribution in which p_i can take on only two values between zero and one. Those with the disorder are thought to be those with the high value of p_i, and those without the disorder are thought to be those with the low value of p_i. The distributions seen in Figure 2.1 demonstrate that this two-point distribution is at least not universal, and may, in fact, be very rare.

It is possible to test whether an observed distribution differs significantly from a two-point distribution (Kraemer, 1982), and in most real-life cases where the sample size was adequate, the distributions do show significant deviation from a two-point distribution. The assumption of such a two-point distribution, however, produces very simple mathematics and is frequently used in the medical research literature at least as a first-order approximation to the truth.

In general, the true distribution of p_i is unknown, is not estimated, nor need it be estimated, in the course of medical test evaluation. It cannot be forgotten, however, that such an underlying distribution exists, that it has characteristics such as those illustrated by the examples in Figure 2.1 and not generally those in Figure 2.2, and that the results of evaluation of a medical test against such a "gold standard" will be influenced by the character of this distribution.

Among patients with the disorder, the magnitude of p_i may reflect stage or severity of the disorder. Among patients without the disorder, it may reflect the strength of risk factors for later development of the disorder.

Now, a most vital assumption:

ASSUMPTION 3

The diagnosis of the disorder used to evaluate a medical test must be clinically valid.

By this I mean that of two patients i and j, if $p_i > p_j$, patient i is more likely to have the disorder than is patient j. Thus, those most likely to have a positive diagnosis are also, by this requirement, most likely to have the disorder.

For a particular disorder, there may be many clinically valid diagnoses. Any one of these may be used in evaluating a test for that disorder. The evaluation outcome will depend on which one is used. For now what must be emphasized is that any question of the clinical validity of the diagnosis for the disorder that is used in evaluating a medical test produces at least an equal question of the validity of any of the outcomes of the evaluation of that test.

For example, the disorder of interest in the evaluation of the dexamethasone suppression test (DST) as used in psychiatry, is variously thought to be primary or endogeneous depression, or melancholia. There are various well-accepted diagnostic systems available to diagnose these disorders. Most widely used are the St. Louis and New York Research Diagnostic Criteria (RDCs) and the DSM-III (Diagnostic and Statistical Manual) or DSM-III-R. When any of these systems are used, the clinical validity of the diagnosis would be accepted with little question.

In one study of the DST (Carroll et al., 1981), however, a clinical diagnosis was chosen in preference to these systems. The development and justification for this diagnosis appeared in an earlier paper by the same research group. The Carroll et al. (1980) paper states: "In attempting to compare the validity of various clinical and research classifications we have used the DST as an independent validating criterion. [T]he DST results strongly validated the clinical diagnoses rather than the RDC diagnoses of these cases" (p. 190). In short, the clinical diagnosis was selected because it corroborated an as yet unproved test, the DST. Then the quality of the DST was assessed by how well it corroborated the clinical diagnosis. Needless to say, the DST fared well in the process; however, this particular evaluation of the DST cannot be accepted as valid simply because the diagnosis used was of questionable clinical validity.

The Prevalence and Reproducibility
of the Diagnosis

For patients drawn from a population:

$$\text{Mean } (p_i) = P; \quad (P' = 1 - P);$$

$$\text{Variance } (p_i) = \sigma_p^2;$$

$$\kappa_D = \sigma_p^2 / PP',$$

The parameter, P will be called the "prevalence," specifically of a positive diagnosis, in the population. The parameter σ_p^2 is a measure of the heterogeneity of the p_is in that population. The parameter κ_D, the "reproducibility of the diagnosis," is a kappa coefficient (Bloch & Kraemer, 1989; Kraemer, 1979; Kraemer & Bloch, 1988). The prevalence, P, and the reproducibility coefficient, κ_D, will figure prominently in evaluations.

If multiple blinded diagnoses were obtained from each of a sample of subjects from a population, the proportion of positive diagnoses among all the diagnoses done, $\hat{P}$, is an unbiased estimator of the prevalence, P. Estimation of P can be done from as few as one diagnosis per patient. In most cases, that is what is done.

Attached to each of the cases in Figures 2.1 and 2.2 are the estimates of values of the prevalence, P. What P represents is the "center of gravity" of the distribution.

To estimate κ_D, on the other hand, one needs two or more "blinded" diagnoses per patient. To estimate κ_D, compute the proportion of positive diagnoses for each subject, $\hat{p}_i$, which is an unbiased estimate of the true value p_i. Then the mean of the estimates $\hat{p}_i$, $\hat{P}$, as noted above, estimates the prevalence P. In addition, one computes the sample variance of the $\hat{p}_i$, S_p^2. Then, if there are m diagnoses per subject:

$$\hat{\kappa}_D = \frac{mS_p^2}{(m-1)\hat{P}(1-\hat{P})} - \frac{1}{(m-1)}$$

which estimates the reproducibility coefficient, κ_D (Fleiss, 1981).

It is rare to find studies that use more than two separate diagnoses per patient. The cases shown in Figure 2.1 are unusual and valuable exceptions. Most studies of reproducibility use only two diagnoses per patient, the minimum required. In that case, the above estimator can be simplified. It can be shown that for two diagnoses per patient, the above is equivalent to:

$$\kappa_D = \frac{\%\text{Observed Agreement} - \%\text{Chance Agreement}}{100\% - \%\text{Chance Agreement}},$$

where % Chance Agreement is computed from the estimated prevalence by:

$$\%\text{Chance Agreement} = [\hat{P}^2 + (1 - \hat{P})^2] \cdot 100\%.$$

Estimates of κ_D are also attached to the cases of Figures 2.1 and 2.2. The coefficients are far from the value 1 (or 100%), which would be associated with perfect reproducibility. Moreover, they are not uniformly higher for the diagnoses based on "hard" rather than "soft" evidence. In general, the wider and deeper the J-shape, the larger the kappa coefficient.

The more repeated diagnoses per patient and the larger the sample size of patients on which the estimates are based, the more precise the estimators will be. Measures of precision of these estimators are available, for these estimators have been extensively studied and discussed in the statistical literature (Fleiss, 1971, 1981; Kraemer, 1979, 1980). Standards for assessing their magnitude have also been suggested (Landis & Koch, 1977): A kappa above 0.8 might be considered "almost perfect," between 0.6 and 0.8 as "substantial," between 0.4 and 0.6 as "moderate," 0.2 to 0.4 as "fair," and below 0.2 as "slight" or "poor." These standards correspond to the magnitudes of kappas found for real diagnoses applied to real patients (Koran, 1975), and serve well as general, but not absolute, guidelines.

High- and Low-Risk Populations

It is convenient to refer to "high-risk" and "low-risk" populations. Populations of clinics or hospitals that specialize in treatments of the disorders of interest are "high-risk" populations. College students or the population of patients coming for routine physicals are "low-risk" populations. Older populations or those in lower socioeconomic groups may be "high-risk" populations for certain disorders. Because of the requirement of validity of the diagnoses, high-risk populations will have a higher prevalence, P, than will low-risk populations, regardless of which valid diagnosis is used. However, with one diagnosis a high-risk population may have an prevalence of 0.9, with another diagnosis it may be 0.3, both for the same disorder. The terms *high risk* and *low risk* are relative, not absolute.

Pre- and Posttest Risk, Prevalence, and Incidence: Confusing Terms

The terms *pretest risk, posttest risk* and *incidence*, commonly used in medical test evaluations, are not used here and the term *prevalence* is used with some trepidation. About the terms *prevalence* and *incidence*, Galen and Gambino (1975) say: "It is unfortunate that we are saddled with words that lack sharpness, but as much as we'd like to dispose of these words they are so established in the special literature of public health that we cannot eliminate them" (p. 10). These words will continue to be widely used, but their use in defining this model could prove confusing.

Testing or diagnosing a patient does not change whether or not the patient has the disorder. What is changed is the physician's *subjective* assessment of whether or not the patient has the disorder. The terms *pretest risk* and *posttest risk* are commonly used to signify such subjective probabilities of the disorder. To adopt these terms here would be imprecise, for the probabilities (risks) defined here are not *subjective* probabilities, nor are they related to the disorder, but, rather, to a diagnosis of the disorder, a different matter.

Similarly, the terms *incidence* and *prevalence* commonly refer to the occurrence of the *disorder* in the population. According to Assumption 1 of the constancy of the disorder during the period of testing, the incidence of the disorder during the period of testing is zero, since no new cases of the disorder can arise during the period of testing. The prevalence *of the disorder* during that time remains unknown, for all that is quantified in the course of medical test evaluation concerns the *diagnosis*, not the *disorder*.

The term *prevalence*, P, here refers to the occurrence of positive diagnoses in the population. By using various different valid diagnoses for the same disorder in the same population, one may arrive at different values of P. The choice of which of several valid diagnostic procedures is used does not affect how many people in the population actually have the disorder during that period of time. For all these reasons, P is not what is usually meant by prevalence or incidence or pretest risk of the disorder. It is the risk of a positive diagnosis, no more and no less.

Summary

A *disorder* is what a patient has; a *diagnosis* is what a physician believes a patient has. The disorder is assumed to be constant during the period of testing for each patient; the diagnosis may vary from one physician to another, from one time to another within the period of testing. A second or third diagnostic opinion will not always agree with the first. Furthermore, there are frequently different clinically valid diagnostic procedures for one and the same disorder. Which procedure the physician chooses to use does not alter whether or not the patient has the disorder, but can, of course, alter the diagnosis.

The purpose of a test is to detect whether or not the patient has a certain disorder during the period of testing, but the evaluation of a test is based on how well the test result corresponds, not to the disorder, but, rather, to a diagnosis of the disorder.

The model that expresses these facts assigns each patient a certain risk of a positive diagnosis (p_i). The mean value of p_i over patients in a population is the *prevalence* of the diagnosis (not the disorder), denoted P, and the reproducibility of the diagnosis is measured by the parameter κ_D, a kappa coefficient. This parameter equals 0% for random decision making and 100% for absolute reproducibility.

It is fundamental to valid evaluation of a medical test that the clinical validity of the diagnosis to be used is medically accepted. Such validity forges the sole link between evaluating a test against a diagnosis and drawing inferences from these results as to the performance of that test against the disorder.

3

Definition: Test Protocol, Response, Referent

A medical test is defined by specification of its protocol, its response, and its referent.

The *protocol* of a medical test instructs the user what exactly is done to or elicited from patients during the period of testing. If a test requires that the patient be drug free for a period of time, or fast overnight, or that he drink a quart of water in a 4-hour period, if there is an administration of some drug in some dosage at some specified time, if blood or urine samples are to be drawn at specified times and processed in certain ways, all this must be specified in the protocol.

For example (Carroll et al., 1981), one protocol for the dexamethasone suppression test (DST) specified that the patient was an inpatient during the period of testing. At 11:30 p.m. patient received 1 mg dexamethasone. Blood samples were drawn at 8 a.m., 4 p.m., and 11 p.m. the following day. Another protocol specified that the patient received 2 mg dexamethasone. A third protocol specified that the patient was an outpatient, received 1 mg dexamethasone at 11:30 p.m. with a single blood drawing at 4 p.m. the next day. Finally, yet a fourth protocol specified that the patient was an outpatient, received 2 mg dexamethasone at 11:30 p.m. with a single blood drawing at 4 p.m. the next day.

These are four *different* tests, even though each might be called a dexamethasone suppression test (DST). Such tests may have quite different accuracies (and did) as well as quite different costs. The data from the evaluation of these four tests cannot validly be pooled without first ascertaining whether the changes in protocol produce differences in test performance.

Patient i's *response* to a test is defined mathematically as a vector in multidimensional real space, x_i. That is, the test response is a *list* of quantitative or qualitative bits of information elicited from or about the patient during the period of testing. The components of that list may be measured in any way: dichotomies (e.g., yes/no or male/female), 3-, 4-, or 5-point scales (e.g., poor, moderate, good), or measures on a continuum (e.g., age). In fact, a component may even be measured at the nominal (categorical) level (e.g., race: white, black, Asian), but this type of response seems to be quite rare. Definition of the test response is an integral part of the definition of the test. Any information elicited from the patient during testing that may be of importance in determining whether or not the disorder is present may be included as a component of the test response at the discretion of the test proponent.

In the DST with the above protocols, for example, for the two inpatient protocols, the response was a three-dimensional vector containing the plasma cortisol levels as assayed from the three blood samples by the competitive protein-binding method (Carroll et al., 1981). For the two outpatient protocols, the response was a one-dimensional vector containing the single plasma cortisol level assayed from the 4 p.m. blood sample. In any of these protocols, the age and gender of the patient, what psychotropic drugs the patient was using and in what dosages, and other such information that might have been pertinent to the diagnosis of the disorder might have been included as part of the test response. None of these, in fact, was. Specification of the test response is part of the specification of the test and is the prerogative of the test proponent; however, any change in the definition of the test response, may result in a different test.

It should be noted that the word *response* is used in a very generic sense. That is, it may be a simple observation about the subject (gender, race) or a clinical assessment of the subject's behavior or a recording of a patient's report (report of signs and symptoms), or a reading of an X-ray or other image, or the result of an assay applied to a tissue sample from the patient. Any bit of information from or about the subject, however protocol dictates it be obtained, is here called a *response*.

The *referent* of a test is a rule that classifies each possible value of x_i, the test response, as "positive" or "negative." The referent must also be specified in defining the medical test.

A DST, for example, could consider a patient positive (a) if the maximal of three cortisol levels (in the inpatient protocols) exceeded 5 μg/dl, or (b) if the 4 p.m. cortisol level (in any of the protocols) exceeded 5 μg/dl. The "cut-off" point could, in fact be 2, 3, 4, or 6 rather than 5 μg/dl.

The term *referent value* has been used in this context by Galen and Gambino (1975) and others. Their usage of the term *referent value* tends to connote a univariate response, whereas, *referent*, as it is here used, may be based on a multivariate test response. That extends the possibilities.

For example, one referent might be to declare a test positive if *either* the 8 a.m. value exceeded 3.5 μg/dl *or* if the 4 p.m. value exceeded 5 μg/dl. Such an "and/or" rule is somewhat more complicated than reducing the test response to a single response (maximal reading or average), but may produce a better test.

Discussion of appropriate or desirable referent values frequently involve definitions of what is or is not a "normal" value, i.e., a value that typifies a patient free of the disorder. In what follows, it is suggested that how one defines who is "normal" or what response is considered "normal" may be immaterial. The ideal referent, the one toward which we are aiming, is one that best distinguishes the patients with the disorder from those without the disorder in the clinical population of interest. How this referent relates to what characterizes a hypothetical "normal" patient, if such a patient could be defined and found, may differ from one clinical population to another. To put a great deal of effort into defining and finding the normal patient and to studying what it is that characterizes the normal patient may be wasted effort in medical test evaluation, vital though it may be in other medical research areas.

The Basic Model

The parameter q_i represents patient i's probability of a positive test. As in defining p_i, what is meant is that if the patient could be independently tested multiple times during the period of testing, the probability that one, randomly chosen of these test responses would be classified positive, is q_i. The distributions of q_i for various tests in a population are similar in general to those shown for p_i in Figure 2.1. (It must be remembered that today's "test" may become tomorrow's "gold standard." Thus there must be a symmetry in what mathematical assumptions are applied to each.)

For patients in a specified population, I define the *level* of the test as Q, where

$$Q = \text{Mean}(q_i).$$

I define the *correlation of test* and *diagnosis* as the product moment correlation coefficient, ρ, between p_i and q_i over the patients in the population of interest. Finally, I define a *legitimate test* as one with $\rho > 0$, and a *random test* as one with $\rho = 0$.

Hereafter, I will restrict consideration only to legitimate or random tests. This restriction poses no limit on the referents, for if $\rho < 0$, the excluded case, one need only reverse the referent and assign a "positive" result to those who previously were "negative" and vice versa to make the test legitimate.

The restriction of consideration to random and legitimate tests guarantees that patients with a positive test, in general, are at least as likely to have a positive diagnosis as those with a negative test. Since, by Assumption 3, a positive diagnosis is assumed to be associated with the presence of the disorder, this forges the necessary link between a positive test, a diagnosis of the disorder, and the presence of the disorder itself.

Summary

A medical test is defined in terms of its protocol, its response, and its referent. The protocol defines exactly what the patient must do, or what must be done to the patient, during the period of testing. The response is a list of information elicited from the patient during the period of testing that might be used to reach a test decision. The referent is a rule that specifies which responses will define a positive test, that which might suggest the presence of the disorder.

Each patient has a certain probability of a positive test, q_i. The mean value of this probability over the patients of a population is called the "level" of the test, denoted Q. The "correlation of test and diagnosis" is defined as the product moment correlation coefficient between p_i and q_i over the patients in the population, and denoted ρ. A "legitimate" test is one with $\rho > 0$, a "random" test one with $\rho = 0$.

4

Families of Test Referents

Definitions: Base and Family

In evaluating a test, one might restrict consideration to a single referent, or might wish to consider several possible referents for the same test protocol and response. To deal with the problem of evaluating multiple referents for a single protocol and response, I will consider a "family" of referents defined on a "base."

A *base* is a specified set of referents. It may consist of only one referent, a finite number of referents, or an infinite number. For example, one way of defining the response to the DST is to measure the plasma cortisol level at 8 a.m. One might consider only one referent: cortisol level > 5 µg/dl. One might also consider a finite number: cortisol level $> 1, 2, 3, 4, 5,$ or 6 µg/dl. One might also consider a continuum: cortisol level $>$ any positive real number. Any one of these is an appropriate choice of base.

The "family" of referents defined on a base is a set of tests that includes:

1. each referent specified in the base;
2. the referent that assigns everyone a positive test result;
3. the referent that assigns no one a positive test result; and
4. all linear combinations of referents in the family.

To explain what exactly (4) means: If R and S are two referents in the family, then for any w, $0 < w < 1$, the rule that with probability w, R is used, and with probability $(1 - w)$, S is used, is a linear combination of R and S and, by definition, is included in the family.

Thus, for example, (2), (3), and (4) combined indicate that the referent that with probability w assigns a patient to a positive test result and with probability $(1 - w)$ assigns a patient to a negative test result, without any reference at all to the patient or to the test response, is in the family. This linear combination is simply that of using a random number generator to create test results, for example, random decision making. This set of tests is, by definition, included in every family of tests, specifically to define what a "worthless" test in the family looks like.

Once again, the definition of the base and hence of the family is the prerogative of whoever is proposing the tests. To some extent, its definition depends on practical consideration. For example, to define a test positive if the age of the patient exceeded 35.16357 years is silly. Age is never so accurately determined in clinical practice, and it would take a stretch of imagination to believe that a 5-minute error in time of birth could make all that much difference. Usually it suffices to choose referents that depend on knowing age accurately to the year for adults, to the month for infants or toddlers, and to the hour for newborns. Similarly if the plasma cortisol level assay is only accurate enough to determine level to 0.1 µg/dl, it would inadvisable to define the base as including cortisol level ≥ 3.512 µg/dl.

On the other hand, there is an advantage in selecting a reasonably large family. If attention is focused on only one referent (e.g., age > 35 years) and that one test seems poor, this may reflect a poor choice of referent rather than some deficit in the protocol or response. The same protocol and response with a base of referents such as "age" > 40, 45, 50, or 55 years, or even 40, 41, . . . years, might be a much better choice.

In a large study of the exercise stress test (Weiner et al., 1979), for example, the sole referent was defined as having a ST-segment depression > 1mm at .08 seconds after the J-point. When applied to women, this test seems far less accurate than when applied to men. Perhaps a better selection for women might be to define a positive test as ST-segment depression > 2mm? Because the investigators chose to report only the single referent, we cannot know. The investigators could, of course, find out from their original data. To choose only a single referent was their prerogative, but it leaves such questions unanswered.

A Special Family: Multiple Discriminant Rules

One case of special interest is that defined by several different types of multivariate discriminant approaches. The family of interest is one defined as:

$$w_1 \cdot x_{1i} + w_2 \cdot x_{2i} + \ldots > \text{real number,}$$

where w_1, w_2, . . . represent some system of weights that can be applied to the multiple test responses, x_{1i}, x_{2i}, . . . to obtain a "risk score" for subject i. What this procedure does is to reduce a multivariate test response to a univariate one, a "risk score."

The family of interest here is that obtained by varying the choices of the weights, w_1, w_2, . . . and then varying the real number that represents the cut-off point for the risk score. Analytic approaches such as Multiple Discriminant Analysis, Log-Linear Analysis, Logistic Regression Analysis, or Cox Proportional Hazards Model, are used to determine an optimal weighting of the components of the test response, and to test which of the weights are different from zero, i.e., ascertaining which of the test response components contribute to a linear prediction model.

In Chapters 12 and 13 I will return to examine such models and how they fit in the framework of medical test evaluation. Until then, such models represent one special type of family that might be considered and evaluated along with and/or rules and others.

Summary

Cases frequently occur where there is one protocol and response but several referents. To deal with this situation, I define a "base" of tests and a "family" of referents. The base includes any referents specified for inclusion. The family includes all tests in the base, plus the two null tests that give everyone a positive or everyone a negative test result, and finally all linear combinations of tests in the family.

5

Population and Sampling

.

Outcomes: True and False Positives
and Negatives

There are four possible outcomes to diagnosing and testing a particular patient. Both the diagnosis and the test might be positive ($D+$, $T+$): a "True Positive." Both the diagnosis and the test might be negative ($D-$, $T-$): a "True Negative." The result of the diagnosis and test might be discordant. If the diagnosis is positive and the test negative ($D+$, $T-$), this outcome is called a "False Negative." If a diagnosis is negative and the test positive ($D-$, $T+$), this outcome is called a "False Positive."

These terms, like prevalence, incidence, etc. are deeply ingrained in the test evaluation literature, and are convenient labels for the four possible outcomes. A problem will arise only if more is read into the terms than they are defined to mean.

A patient may have a disorder, but be mistakenly diagnosed negative. The diagnosis is, after all, not infallible. In this case the outcome of testing will be either a False Positive or a True Negative. If either label were to be interpreted as indicating that the patient is "really" free of the disorder, the effect of the original misdiagnosis is compounded. Of course, the same problem arises with a patient who does not have a disorder and is mistakenly diagnosed positive.

26

Table 5.1 Definition of the Outcome Probabilities, Prevalence, Level of Test, and Descriptive Statistics for Test Performance

		Test Result		
		+	−	
Diagnosis	+	TP	FN	P
	−	FP	TN	$P' = 1 - P$
		Q	$Q' = 1 - Q$	1

Prevalence = P = TP + FN
Level of test = Q = TP + FP

Sensitivity = SE = TP/P
Specificity = SP = TN/P'

Predictive value of a:
 Positive test = PV P = TP/Q
 Negative test = PV N = TN/Q'

Efficiency = TP + TN

To be precise, the True Positive, False Positive, False Negative, and True Negative labels describe the combined outcomes of diagnosis and test combinations, no more. They carry no necessary implication as to whether or not the patient has the disorder, nor whether the test result is right or wrong. In short, we cannot assume that the diagnosis is correct and the test wrong; the opposite may occasionally be true.

Within a population of patients, these four outcomes happen with certain probabilities, as presented in Table 5.1, denoted TP, FP, FN, and TN, corresponding to the initials of their respective labels. The entire process of objective and quantitative evaluation of medical tests is based on sampling patients, diagnosing and testing them, and estimating these probabilities or certain combinations of these probabilities, such as those listed in Table 5.1. With this information, the correspondence between the test results and those of the diagnosis is assessed.

A strong correspondence between a test and a clinically valid diagnosis demonstrates that the medical test, like the diagnosis, is a valid indicator of the presence of the disorder. On the other hand, a weak correspondence between the test and the presumably valid diagnosis suggests a weakness or invalidity of the test. Why the test is weak, whether because it was intrinsically a poor choice or because the protocol, response, or referent were poorly selected or the wrong population studied, will ultimately remain a matter of conjecture.

Blind Evaluation

A serious bias may arise in generating the data to estimate the probabilities of Table 5.1 if the diagnostician knows the results of the test before making the diagnosis, or the tester knows the results of the diagnosis before conducting and evaluating the test, or, finally, if either the test or the diagnosis are used to decide which patients are eligible or ineligible for inclusion in the sample for the evaluation.

The diagnosticians' prior knowledge of the test results may influence the diagnosis. How strong this influence might be depends on the diagnosticians' opinion of the value of the test result as an indicator of the presence of the disorder. If they feel that the test is worthless, they may simply discount the result in making the diagnosis. At the other extreme, if they have implicit faith in the test, the test may well completely determine the diagnosis. In such cases, there may appear to be a strong correspondence between the results of the test and diagnosis when, in fact, none truly exists except in the minds of the diagnosticians.

A similar situation arises when the testers know the diagnosis while conducting and evaluating the test. Any interaction between the testers and patients or any subjectivity in evaluating the test response may be influenced by the testers' prior knowledge of the diagnosis. The correspondence between test and diagnosis may then be completely determined by that prior knowledge rather than by any true correspondence between test and diagnosis.

For these reasons, in the objective evaluation of a medical test, the diagnostician must be blind to the test result and the tester blind to the diagnosis; and the eligibility for the evaluation study must be determined once and for all before either the test or the diagnosis is done. Having the recruitment and eligibility decisions, the testing, and the diagnosis done by separate staff is the safest course. To be sure, in the process of diagnosis, the diagnosticians may become independently aware of some of the possible test responses, or the testers, who might well be talented diagnosticians, may form their own independent opinions of what the diagnosis should be. That causes no problem, and is, in fact, to be expected. However neither should communicate to the other or have any opportunity of influencing the other in his decisions. The independence of the two judgments must be assured for the evaluation of the medical test to be a fair and objective one. Because of the imperfect reproducibility of both the diagnosis and the test, frequently the testers' opinion of what the diagnosis must be and the diagnosticians' opinion of what the test results should be will not coincide.

The Basic Model

That sets the scene: The test proponents define the disorder and select a valid diagnostic criterion for that disorder. They define the test protocol, response, and referent (or a family of these). They are then asked for one more specification: What is the population of interest? This is the population from which a sample must be drawn to estimate all the parameters of interest. Each patient has a certain probability of a positive diagnosis, p_i, and a certain probability of a positive test, q_i. Since the diagnosis and test are independently (blindly) done, the probability of a True Positive outcome for patient i is:

$$p_i \cdot q_i .$$

Over a sample of patients from a population, the probability of a True Positive outcome is:

$$\text{TP} = \text{Mean } (p_i \cdot q_i),$$

and this, in turn, is mathematically equal to:

$$\text{TP} = PQ + \rho \cdot \sigma_p \cdot \sigma_q .$$

Similarly, the probabilities of the other three outcomes are:

$$\text{FN} = PQ' - \rho \cdot \sigma_p \cdot \sigma_q ,$$

$$\text{FP} = P'Q - \rho \cdot \sigma_p \cdot \sigma_q ,$$

$$\text{TN} = P'Q' + \rho \cdot \sigma_p \cdot \sigma_q .$$

For a random test ($\rho = 0$):

$$TP = PQ,$$

$$FN = PQ',$$

$$FP = P'Q,$$

$$TN = P'Q'.$$

For a legitimate test ($\rho > 0$):

$$TP > PQ,$$

$$FN < PQ',$$

$$FP < P'Q,$$

$$TN > P'Q'.$$

Finally, for a test and diagnosis in perfect agreement, the ideal test, which is only possible when the level of the test is the same as the prevalence ($P = Q$):

$$TP = P,$$

$$FN = FP = 0,$$

$$TN = P'.$$

This collection of equations demonstrates that the probabilities of the four outcomes depend on which valid diagnosis is selected and what population is being evaluated (P, ρ), on how the test is defined and which population is studied (Q, ρ), and on the correlation between the test and diagnosis in that population (ρ). *Change the diagnosis, or change the test protocol, response, or referent, or change the population, and all the outcome probabilities may change.*

For example, in the CASS study (Weiner et al., 1979), the resting EKG proves of little value as a diagnostic test for coronary artery disease as diagnosed by arteriography in a clinic population with a complaint of chest pain. However, in a later study of patients who come into an emergency room with a complaint of acute chest pain

(Brush, Drand, Acampora, Chalmer, & Wackers, 1985), the resting EKG proved a valuable prognostic test to identify those who would later have in-hospital complications of acute myocardial infarction. These are two *different* populations and two related but *different* disorders. The fact that the resting EKG is to be recommended in one case and to be recommended against in the other is *not* in conflict unless one forgets for whom each test is intended and for what disorder.

For this reason, to specify which population is of interest in test evaluation and to sample that population appropriately are essential to valid medical test evaluation. Which population that should be, of course, depends on which population the test is ultimately intended to be used. Sometimes there is only one such population, and sometimes there are several.

In specifying a population, discussions of medical test evaluation frequently focus on prevalence. As noted above, however, we do not know the prevalence *of the disorder* in a population. We can only know or estimate the prevalence *of a positive diagnosis* of that disorder. That prevalence may change remarkably within the same population when one valid diagnostic criterion rather than another is used.

For example, Olefsky, Farquhar, and Reaven (1973) remarked that "depending upon the criteria used, the number of individuals with diabetes in a given population can vary from 0.5 to 24 percent" (p. 202). This is a phenomenon true for many different disorders and many different clinical populations.

A particularly vivid demonstration was presented in a study of the exercise stress test for coronary artery disease presented by Chaitman et al., (1981). In this study there were 8,157 patients in six subgroups defined by gender and type of chest pain (see Table 5.2). In each subgroup a diagnosis was based on coronary arteriography using four different criteria, each presumably a valid diagnosis of coronary artery disease. The prevalence among women with nonischemic chest pain ranged from 1% to 24%, for men with definite chest pain from 2% to 40%, depending on which diagnosis was used.

For that reason, the characterization of a population in terms of its prevalence alone does not suffice. In Table 5.2, for example, with one diagnostic procedure, the prevalence for men with probable angina and that for women with definite angina were both about the same, 82%-83%. In terms of any other diagnosis of the same disorder, these two groups are dissimilar: 66% versus 72%, 44% versus 53%, 22% versus 31%. If the similarity of these two groups in prevalence for one

Table 5.2   Prevalence for Six Clinically Defined Populations Using
Four Different Diagnostic Procedures and Using Coronary
Angiography for Diagnosis of Coronary Artery Disease

Gender	Type of Chest Pain	Some Abnormality	Number of Abnormal Vessels		
			>0	>1	>2
Male	Definite	97%	93%	72%	43%
	Probable	82%	66%	44%	22%
	Nonischemic	40%	14%	6%	2%
Female	Definite	83%	72%	53%	31%
	Probable	57%	36%	19%	8%
	Nonischemic	24%	6%	1%	1%

SOURCE: Chaitman et al. (1981)

diagnostic procedure had led us to believe that these groups were
completely medically similar, we might have been seriously misled.

No, a population should be specified in terms of its clinical characteristics and any inclusion or exclusion criteria considered appropriate. Ultimately the same criteria would be used for the clinical application of the test. This amounts to "packaging instructions" for the
test, when and if the time comes to "market" the test.

It should be no surprise that to evaluate a medical test in a specific
population requires a sample from that specific population, and that
results may not generalize beyond that population. There is no area
of clinical research in which a definition of the population and proper
sampling procedures are not vital to the validity of any conclusions.
Here, as in other areas of clinical research, where there is interest in
two or more different populations, similar in terms of prevalence or
not, test evaluation must be separately done for samples from each of
those different clinical populations. Whatever conclusions are drawn
from evaluation of a medical test in a specified population apply to
that population, and to the best of the knowledge gained from that
evaluation, *only* to that population. There is no guarantee that results
generalize further.

In the sections to follow, I will discuss several different sampling
options: naturalistic, retrospective, and prospective. To understand
when one would choose one, and when one would prefer another, a
bit of background statistical theory will be needed. In these next few

sections, we will need to be especially careful to distinguish population values from sample estimators of those population values. To do this I will, as I have earlier, append a "hat" to the estimators, e.g., $\hat{P}$ is a sample estimator of P. The notation is cumbersome and will fortunately be unnecessary in later chapters, when comments will apply both to population values and their estimators.

Descriptors of Outcomes: Sensitivity, Specificity, Predictive Values, and Efficiency

The basis of medical test evaluation lies in estimating the outcome probabilities or certain combinations of these probabilities. These combinations include descriptors of outcomes called *sensitivity, specificity, predictive values,* and *efficiency.* Such descriptors will be discussed at great length in later chapters, but will be briefly introduced here to facilitate discussion of sampling options (see Tables 5.1 and 5.3).

Sensitivity and specificity are conditional probabilities describing test performance with reference to the diagnosis. *Sensitivity* is defined as the probability of having a positive test result among those patients who have a positive diagnosis. *Specificity* is the probability of having a negative test result among those patients who have a negative diagnosis. In terms of the outcome probabilities:[1]

$$\text{Sensitivity} = SE = TP/(TP + FN) = TP/P,$$

$$\text{Specificity} = SP = TN/(FP + TN) = TN/P'.$$

The *predictive values* are conditional probabilities describing the performance of the diagnosis with reference to the test. Predictive Value of a Positive test (PVP) is the probability of having a positive diagnosis among those patients having a positive test. Predictive Value of a Negative Test (PVN) is the probability of having a negative diagnosis among those patients having a negative test. In terms of the outcome probabilities:
Predictive Value of a

$$\text{Positive Test} = PVP = TP/(TP + FP) = TP/Q,$$

Table 5.3   Calculation of Descriptive Statistics of the Exercise Stress
Test for Coronary Artery Disease in the Population of Males
with Definite Angina

		Test		
		+	−	
Diagnosis	+	473	81	554
	−	22	44	66
		495	125	620

$P = 554/620 = .894 \,(\pm .012)$ $SE = 473/554 = .854 \,(\pm .015)$
$Q = 495/620 = .798 \,(\pm .016)$ $SP = 44/66 = .667 \,(\pm .058)$

$TP = 473/620 = .763 \,(\pm .017)$ $PVP = 473/495 = .956 \,(\pm..08)$
$FN = 81/620 = .131 \,(\pm .014)$ $PVN = 44/125 = .352 \,(\pm.043)$
$FP = 22/620 = .035 \,(\pm.007)$
$TN = 44/620 = .071 \,(\pm.010)$

$EFF = (473 + 44)/620 = .834 \,(\pm.015)$
$\kappa(1, 0) = (.854 - .798)/.202 = (.352 - .106)/.894 = .277$
$\kappa(0, 0) = (.667 - .202)/.798 = (.956 - .894)/.106 = .583$

$\chi^2 = 620 \cdot .277 \cdot .583 = 100 \,(p < .001)$

SOURCE: Weiner et al. (1979)

Negative Test = $PVN = TN/(TN + FN) = TN/Q'$.

Finally, *efficiency* is defined as the probability that test and diagnosis agree:

Efficiency = $EFF = TP + TN$.

Now we can begin to discuss different ways we might sample in order to obtain valid and precise estimates of these various probabilities and descriptors, and to do so most cost-effectively.

Naturalistic Sampling

Conceptually the easiest sampling method, but frequently most difficult to do in practice, is Naturalistic Sampling. Here the evaluator decides how large a sample to gather, N_0, and takes a random or representative sample of that size from the population of interest. Each patient in the sample undergoes both diagnosis and testing.

For example, in Table 5.3 is an evaluation of the exercise stress test for coronary artery disease (Weiner et al., 1979). A sample of 620 ($N_0 = 620$) males with definite angina were sampled from a well-specified population (Weiner et al., 1979), and each underwent diagnosis and test with the results as reported in Table 5.3. Estimation of the outcome probabilities and descriptors are those one would intuitively use.

The proportion of patients who are observed to have a positive diagnosis is the obvious estimator of the prevalence. This estimator, denoted $\hat{P}$, is an unbiased estimator of the prevalence P. Its standard error is:

$$\text{Standard Error } (\hat{P}) = (PP'/N_0)^{1/2}.$$

The standard error itself can be estimated by substituting the estimate $\hat{P}$ into the above formula in place of P.

By *mean* and *standard* error of any estimator, we mean that if the sampling procedure (here N_0 randomly sampled from the specified population) and the estimation procedure were repeated over and over again, the mean of these repeated estimators would be P and their variance would be the square of the standard error. In saying that P is unbiased, I am saying that P does not consistently over- or underestimate P over repetitions. The standard error reflects the precision of the estimator, that is, how closely $\hat{P}$ estimates P.

In Table 5.3, for example, we find that the estimated prevalence is $554/620 = .894$ (sometimes reported equivalently as 89.4%). Its standard error is estimated as:

$$(0.894 \cdot 0.106/620)^{1/2} = 0.012 \text{ (or } 1.2\%).$$

Frequently this report is succinctly summarized as in Table 5.3 either as 0.894 ± 0.012 or $89.4\% \pm 1.2\%$.

In Naturalistic Sampling the proportion of the N_0 patients with positive test Q provides an unbiased estimator of the level of the test (Q). The precision of this estimator is reflected by:

$$\text{Standard Error } (\hat{Q}) = (QQ'/N_0)^{1/2}.$$

In Table 5.3, the estimate of the level of the test is $0.798 \pm .016$ or $79.8\% \pm 1.6\%$.

Each of the four outcome probabilities can be estimated by the proportion of the N_0 patients with the observed outcome: $\hat{TP}$, $\hat{FN}$, $\hat{FP}$, $\hat{TN}$. These are also unbiased estimators of their respective probabilities and their precisions are reflected by:

$$\text{Standard Error } (\hat{TP}) = [TP(1 - TP)/N_0]^{\frac{1}{2}},$$

$$\text{Standard Error } (\hat{FN}) = [FN(1 - FN)/N_0]^{\frac{1}{2}},$$

$$\text{Standard Error } (\hat{FP}) = [FP(1 - FP)/N_0]^{\frac{1}{2}},$$

$$\text{Standard Error } (\hat{TN}) = [TN(1 - TN)/N_0]^{\frac{1}{2}}.$$

In Table 5.3 these value are $0.763 \pm .017$, $0.131 \pm .014$, $0.035 \pm .007$, and $0.071 \pm .010$.

The efficiency, too, follows the same pattern. The proportion of the outcomes in which test and diagnosis agree is an unbiased estimate of the efficiency with a standard error given by:

$$\text{Standard Error } (\hat{EFF}) = [EFF(1 - EFF)/N_0]^{\frac{1}{2}}.$$

In Table 5.3 efficiency is estimated as $0.834 \pm .015$.

Thus far, it seems easy enough. To obtain quite precise estimators of the prevalence (P), the level of the test (Q), the four outcome probabilities, and the efficiency, one need only take a large enough sample size to bring their respective standard errors within limits. Playing about a bit with the common form of the standard errors, we find that every one of the standard errors above is less that $0.5/(N_0)^{1/2}$. One might begin to believe that one needs 25 patients to guarantee a precision of 10%, 100 patients to guarantee a precision of 5%, 2,500 patients to guarantee a precision of 1%. If 5% seems a small enough error, one might even begin to think that 100 patients is always enough for a medical test evaluation.

Unfortunately that is not the whole picture. The sensitivity (SE) can be estimated by the proportion of patients with a positive diagnosis who have a positive test $(\hat{SE})$ and the specificity (SP) by the proportion of patients with a negative diagnosis having a negative test $(\hat{SP})$:

$$\hat{SE} = \hat{TP}/\hat{P},$$

$$\hat{SP} = \hat{TN}/\hat{P'}.$$

However, $\hat{SE}$ is not an unbiased estimator of SE. Its mean is:

$$\text{Mean } (\hat{SE}) = SE(1 - P'^{N_0}).$$

The problem here is that with repeated sampling of N_0 patients, particularly from a low-risk population, there is some probability of obtaining a sample in which none of the patients has a positive diagnosis ($\hat{P} = 0$). Since the sensitivity cannot be estimated from such a sample, it must be discarded or some arbitrary rule must be made for what $0/0$ means, perhaps $0/0 = 0$ by definition. Whatever tactic is taken creates a bias in the estimator. In general, $\hat{SE}$ tends to underestimate SE.

For the estimator to have negligible bias, the sample size, N_0, must be large enough relative to the magnitude of the prevalence, P, to make the probability of obtaining a sample with no positive diagnoses negligible. As a result, a sample size that suffices in a higher-risk population may be totally inadequate in a low-risk one. What is more, the exact standard error of $\hat{SE}$ is a complicated expression involving SE, P, and N_0. In general, the exact standard error of $\hat{SE}$ exceeds:

$$[SE(1 - SE)/(N_0 \cdot P)]^{1/2}.$$

However, when the sample size N_0 is large relative to the magnitude of the prevalence, P, the above equation serves as an approximation to the exact standard error ($\hat{SE}$). On the other hand, when N_0 is small relative to P, the estimator of SE is biased, it lacks precision, and the sample estimator of precision itself is inaccurate. Everything is likely to go wrong at the same time.

Such statistical considerations begin to clarify that if the *combinations* of the outcome probabilities, such as sensitivity, are of interest, it is not enough to ensure only that N_0 is large on some absolute scale. There must be assurance that N_0 is large enough relative to P. In turn, that means that with a low-risk population, the sample size must be much larger than with a higher-risk population.

Similar considerations affect what happens to specificity and the predictive values. One might estimate specificity by the proportion of patients with a negative diagnosis who also have a negative test $(\hat{SP})$. The predictive value of a positive test is estimated by the proportion of those with a positive test also having a positive diagnosis $(\hat{PVP})$. The predictive value of a negative test is estimated by the proportion of those with a negative test also having a negative diagnosis $(\hat{PVN})$ (see Table 5.1).

Each of these estimators, like $\hat{SE}$, is somewhat biased, with a bias that depends on the size of the sample, N_0, and then on the size of P', Q, and Q' respectively. The bias is negligible only if N_0 is large enough relative to P', Q, Q'. Only then approximately:

$$\text{Standard Error } (\hat{SP}) = [SP(1 - SP)/(N_0 \cdot P')]^{1/2},$$

$$\text{Standard Error } (\hat{PVP}) = [PVP(1 - PVP)/(N_0 \cdot Q)]^{1/2},$$

$$\text{Standard Error } (\hat{PVN}) = [PVN(1 - PVN)/(N_0 \cdot Q')]^{1/2}.$$

In operational terms, if Naturalistic Sampling is to be used, not only must the total sample size, N_0, be large, but it must also be large enough to guarantee that the number of patients with a positive diagnosis, the number with a negative diagnosis, the number with a positive test, and the number with a negative test are all reasonably large. Thus the number in each marginal position of the 2×2 table of, for example, Table 5.1, must be reasonably large.

How large is "reasonably large"? A question such as this inevitably lacks a single, firm, unequivocal, and defensible answer. As a rule of thumb, I would recommend that no test evaluation be undertaken unless one can expect to see at least 10 patients in each of the marginal positions of Table 5.1, and the analysis of the results not be undertaken unless one actually sees at least 10 patients in each of the marginal positions. This rule would mean that the minimal sample size under any circumstances is 20, but that 20 subjects suffice only if both the prevalence and the level of the test are 0.5. When the prevalence is low, say 0.01, one would need at least 1,000 patients in a naturalistic sample, and if it were as low as 0.001, at least 10,000 patients.

With this rule of thumb, the estimators of sensitivity, specificity, and predictive values are likely to be reasonably unbiased, and the estimated standard errors reasonably accurate. With this rule, the estimator of sensitivity (or any of the other combinations) may not be as precise as you might like, but the standard error will fairly accurately tell you how imprecise it is.

Papers in the medical research literature that do not approach even this minimal sample size abound. For example, a study published in the *New England Journal of Medicine* reported results in which there were two patients with neuroblastoma in situ and one without, for the evaluation of P-Nuclear Magnetic Resonance (Maris et al., 1985). Such very small samples are particularly common for the high-cost, high-technology tests. The proliferation of extremely small sample sizes in medical research literature evidences the difficulties of obtaining the samples necessary to Naturalistic Sampling.

In the CASS study (Weiner et al., 1979), the necessary large sample size was achieved by a multi-center collaboration. This study, a portion of which was presented in Table 5.3, is an excellent model for medical test evaluation. The general population sampled naturalistically was that of patients presenting with chest pain who were to undergo angiography, excluding those with unstable angina, previous myocardial infarction, digitalis therapy, or the inability to complete the exercise stress test. That describes the overall population, then, to which the results of this evaluation apply.

But then, not only was this population as a whole examined, but, in addition, the results were presented in clinically relevant subgroups of the population. If only the total population had been evaluated, the exercise stress test would emerge either as a "good" or a "bad" test in that population. Subdividing the total by clinical characteristics such as gender and type of chest pain facilitated consideration of whether the test may be better (or worse) for certain types of patients than it is for others. From the medical consumer's point of view, this is vital.

If the test were excellent for men in general, but not as good for women with nonischemic pain (which seems to be the case), the preponderance of men in the population (and the sample) might lead to a conclusion that the test is excellent overall. Then those women, who constitute about 12% of that population, might undergo exercise stress testing unnecessarily.

On the other hand, a test might be very valuable only for some subgroup of the total population, perhaps a minority of the sample. If subgroups were not examined, such a test might be labeled worthless overall and discarded. That too, would be unfortunate for the minority group.

In Table 5.3 I demonstrated the results of diagnosing and testing the 620 male patients with definite angina. Are the estimators good? All the marginals exceed 10 (554, 66, 495, 125), the minimal level specified in the rule of thumb for initiating analysis. The estimated standard errors themselves seem to indicate precision of 1%-6% in all descriptive statistics. The estimators are reasonably precise; but is the medical test good? That is indeed the crucial question. We are, however, at this stage only prepared to deal with the more limited question as to whether the test is *legitimate* or not. To be good, a test must be at least legitimate, but many legitimate tests may not be good enough to recommend for general use.

The Two-by-Two Chi-Square Test

It was noted earlier in this chapter that if the test were random, then TP = PQ, FN = PQ', FP = $P'Q$, and TN = $P'Q'$. All these probabilities can now be estimated from a naturalistic sample, and we can compare TP with PQ, FN with PQ', etc. For a random test, these will correspond closely; for a legitimate medical test, they will be discrepant with TP greater than PQ, FN less than PQ', etc. The more discrepant these values are, the better the medical test. Assessing the discrepancies is the basis of the Chi-Square test.

This statistical test appears in every basic statistics textbook and in every computer statistical package and need not be discussed in detail here. Suffice it to say, that, to demonstrate that the medical test is legitimate, one computes a test statistic, χ^2, and compares its value with 3.84 (5% significance level), 6.63 (1% significance level) or 10.83 (0.1% significance level). If the value of the test statistic exceeds the designated value, it proves beyond reasonable doubt (as indicated by the significance level) that the medical test is a legitimate one.

There are many equivalent ways of expressing the test statistic, χ^2. The ones here presented are not the ones recommended for computational use, but are designed to provide some insight into how the test statistic reflects sensitivity, specificity, and predictive values. First we compute two indices labeled $\kappa(1, 0)$ and $\kappa(0, 0)$ defined:

$$\kappa(1, 0) = (SE - Q)/Q' = (PVN - P')/P,$$

$$\kappa(0, 0) = (SP - Q')/Q = (PVP - P)/P'.$$

It may not be immediately apparent that $(SE - Q)/Q'$ must be exactly equal to $(PVN - P')/P$, or that $(SP - Q')/Q$ must be exactly equal to $(PVP - P)/P'$. It is a mathematical fact that may be proved by expressing each in terms of the four outcome probabilities.

Later there will be intensive development and discussion of these two indices, $\kappa(1, 0)$ and $\kappa(0, 0)$. The numbers 0 and 1 within the parentheses will later be related to various cost-benefit factors that enter into the definition of the quality of a medical test. For now, it should only be noted that the relationships expressed in $\kappa(1, 0)$ and $\kappa(0, 0)$ are important in connecting the sensitivity and the predictive value of a negative test and connecting the specificity and the predictive value of a positive test, and that I am here using the quality indices only to define the test statistic for Naturalistic Sampling. That value is:

$$\chi^2 = N_0 \cdot k(1, 0) \cdot k(0, 0).$$

From this expression, we see that a demonstration of the legitimacy of a medical test requires that sensitivity and specificity both be large (one or the other alone does not suffice). Predictive values must both be large (one or the other does not suffice). Finally, a recurrent refrain, N_0 must be large. The rule of thumb minimal value presented earlier is designed to validate use of the test; it does not necessarily guarantee its power. The rule of thumb is minimal, not satisfactory, sufficient, optimal, or an overall recommended value.

In Table 5.3 we find that $\kappa(1, 0) = .277$ and that $\kappa(0, 0) = 0.583$. Thus $\chi^2 = 100$. Comparing this value with the reference points for the Chi-Square test, we find the result significant with level less than 0.1%. We conclude that, beyond reasonable doubt, the exercise stress test used for males with definite angina is a legitimate test for coronary artery disease.

In the CASS study there were actually six subpopulations, as well as the total population, and two different diagnoses. We can repeat the analysis that appears in Table 5.3 for each of these. A summary of the results appears in Table 5.4. The first line of this table repeats the results of the analysis done in Table 5.3.

There are a number of important points to notice in this summary. First of all, despite what is initially a large sample size, there is still

Table 5.4 Summary of Results for the Exercise Stress Test for Two Different Diagnoses (CAD: Coronary Artery Disease; MVD: Multi-Vessel Disease) of Coronary Artery Disease in Six Subpopulations and in the Total Population

Populations		N_0	P	Q	SE	SP	PVP	PVN	EFF	χ^2
CAD Diagnosis: Coronary Artery Disease										
Male	Definite	620	89%	80%	85%	67%	96%	35%	83%	100
	Probable	594	70%	61%	75%	74%	87%	56%	75%	126
	Nonischemic	251	22%	30%	54%	77%	39%	86%	72%	19
Female	Definite	98	62%	72%	85%	49%	73%	67%	71%	13
	Probable	240	40%	56%	76%	57%	54%	78%	65%	25
	Nonischemic	242	5%	30%	31%	73%	6%	95%	70%	NS
Total		2,045	58%	59%	79%	69%	78%	70%	75%	478
MVD Diagnosis: Multi-Vessel Disease										
Male	Definite	620	68%	80%	89%	39%	75%	63%	73%	68
	Probable	594	47%	61%	82%	57%	63%	79%	69%	101
	Nonischemic	251	6%	30%	80%	73%	16%	98%	74%	19
Female	Definite	98	39%	72%	90%	38%	48%	85%	58%	9
	Probable	240	22%	56%	83%	52%	33%	92%	59%	20
	Nonischemic	242	1%	30%	Insufficient Sample Size					
Total		2,045	39%	60%	86%	59%	57%	87%	69%	401

SOURCE: Weiner et al. (1979)

one subgroup (women with nonischemic pain, using multi-vessel disease (MVD) as the diagnosis) in which the sample size is inadequate for further analysis. Here, the estimated prevalence is only 0.8% (rounded to 1% in Table 5.4). For such a low-risk population using this diagnosis, one would need more than 1,250 patients (10/.008). Only 242 were sampled.

To say that 242 was an inadequate sample size may seem odd when a sample size of 98 in the same table was deemed adequate for other of the subgroups. Again it must be emphasized that what constitutes an adequate sample size is much larger for very low- or for very high-risk populations than it is for populations where the prevalence is moderate. As a result, there is no inconsistency in saying that in one (low-risk) population a sample size of 242 was inadequate, while in another (moderate-risk) population, a sample size of 98 was adequate.

Two different clinically valid diagnoses (CAD and MVD) for coronary artery disease were used. The results using one and then the other *in the same population* (males with definite anginal chest pain CAD versus MVD, for example) differ in all respects other than level (*Q*). Remember that changing the diagnosis changes the results, and the sensitivity, specificity, and predictive values and the results of the Chi-Square test characterize the correspondence between test and diagnosis and not that between test and disorder directly. However, if both are clinically valid for the same diagnosis, there must be a certain consistency in the inferences that result from evaluation, and Table 5.4 shows such consistency.

Change the population, however, and everything may change. There is no necessary consistency to the results. That the prevalence might change is expected. That the predictive values change from one clinical population to another is well known. That sensitivity and specificity change is frequently denied, but despite the denials, they do change. In Table 5.4 over the six subgroups, the sensitivities of the test evaluated against the diagnosis CAD range from 31% to 85%, the specificities from 49% to 77%—variation far beyond the chance level.

The Chi-Square tests in Table 5.4 (last column) indicate that except for females with nonischemic chest pain, the exercise stress test is a legitimate test. Care should be taken not to interpret χ^2 as a measure of how "good" the test is. The larger the χ^2, the less doubt that the medical test is legitimate, but legitimacy does not necessarily guarantee the quality of a medical test.

Retrospective Sampling

As seen in the CASS study, practical problems with Naturalistic Sampling arise when the population is a low-risk one. Then, as in the case of females with nonischemic pain in the CASS study reported in Table 5.4, necessary sample size grows inordinately large.

In addition, Naturalistic Sampling requires that every patient in the sample undergo both diagnosis and test. When the test is costly and risky, and, after all, yet of unproven value, there may be both financial and ethical reasons to restrict testing as much as possible. A sampling strategy designed to handle both these problems is Retrospective Sampling.

As before, a representative sample of size N_0 is drawn from the population and each patient is diagnosed. This sample is called the *screening sample*. As in Naturalistic Sampling, the proportion of patients diagnosed positive $\hat{P}$ is an unbiased estimate of the prevalence (P) with standard error:

$$\text{Standard Error } (\hat{P}) = [P(1 - P)/N_0]^{1/2}.$$

Then a random sample of size N_1 is drawn from among those in the screening sample with a positive diagnosis and a random sample of size N_2 from among those with a negative diagnosis. Only these $N_1 + N_2$ go on to be tested. By my rule of thumb, N_1 and N_2 must each minimally exceed 10, and must be such that the number of these $N_1 + N_2$ patients who go on to have a positive test, or who go on to have a negative test must also minimally exceed 10. However, $N_1 + N_2$ is generally much less than N_0.

Let's consider an example: Etter et al. (1960) studied cinefluorography and conventional spot-films each alone and then in combination as a test for duodenal ulcer. The diagnosis was based on "conventional fluoroscopy and the two technics just mentioned, by one of the radiologists participating in the study" (p. 766). The population included healthy white males primarily in their fifth and sixth decades who presented for a periodic health examination. The sample size (N_0 in our notation) was 245, of whom 50 were diagnosed positive. Thus from the screening sample:

$$\hat{P} = 50/245 = .204, \text{ or } 20.4\%.$$

All the patients with a positive diagnosis ($N_1 = 50$) and 86 randomly selected patients with a negative diagnosis ($N_2 = 86$) underwent testing. While 20.4% ($\hat{P} = .204$) of the screening sample had a positive diagnosis, 36.8% of the tested sample did. I will use the notation OP for the proportion of the subset tested who had a positive diagnosis: here OP = .368. Etter et al. (1960) took precautions to ensure the blindness of diagnosis and test:

> All identifying data were removed. Each of the three radiologists, independently and without knowledge of the clinical history or previous readings, read the spot films, then the cinefluorograms, and then the two concurrently. . . . Enough time elapsed between various readings of the films of the same individual so as to make recall a negligible factor. (p. 767)

The Etter et al. (1960) test protocol is well described. The test response has nine entries, three radiologists each using cinefluorography and spot-films alone and in combination, classifying the test positive if there was "Constant deformity without crater, crater with or without deformity" (p.767). Each entry was evaluated separately as a referent.

The proportion of the N_1 patients with a positive diagnosis having a positive test ($\hat{SE}$) is an unbiased estimator of the sensitivity (SE) with standard error:

$$\text{Standard Error } (\hat{SE}) = [SE(1 - SE)/N_1]^{1/2} .$$

The proportion of those N_2 patients with a negative diagnosis having a negative test ($\hat{SP}$) is an unbiased estimator of the specificity (SP) with a standard error:

$$\text{Standard Error } (\hat{SP}) = [SP(1 - SP)/N_2]^{1/2} .$$

That is all that can be estimated directly from the data. *It is not valid to estimate the predictive values or the efficiency or the outcome probabilities as if Naturalistic Sampling had been done.* However, all the other probabilities and combinations can be *indirectly* estimated using only estimates of P, SE, and SP. This is because, in the way the SE and SP are defined:

$$TP = P \cdot SE,$$

$$FN = P \cdot SE' \quad (SE' = 1 - SE),$$

$$FP = P' \cdot SP' \quad (SP' = 1 - SP),$$

$$TN = P' \cdot SP.$$

Thus the four outcome probabilities can be reconstructed from the knowledge of P, SE, and SP and can be estimated by substituting estimates of P, SE, and SP.

Moreover, the level of the test, the predictive values, and the efficiency can now be estimated using estimates of TP, FN, FP, TN, since:

$$Q = P \cdot SE + P' \cdot SP',$$

$$PVP = P \cdot SE/Q,$$

$$PVN = P' \cdot SP/Q'.$$

$$EFF = P \cdot SE + P' \cdot SP.$$

The estimators, $\hat{PVP}$ and $\hat{PVN}$, obtained by entering estimates of P, Q, SE, and SP in the equations above, are known as Bayes' estimators of the predictive values. This fact is frequently referred to in the medical literature of medical test evaluation. Bayes' Theorem is a classical mathematical theorem relating certain conditional and unconditional probabilities. Here the conditional probabilities are the sensitivity, specificity, and the predictive values, the unconditional probabilities are the prevalence and the level of the test. As a result, the estimation of the predictive values in a Retrospective Sampling study is a special application of Bayes' Theorem.

In the Etter et al. (1960) study, unfortunately, the sensitivities and specificities reported (nine sets) have questionable statistical validity. In this study, testers were allowed to defer a reading. When a set of films had one or more deferred readings, that patient was dropped from the sample. The original sample of 136 patients was reduced to 116, and the decision to exclude was obviously based on the testing.

Furthermore, the test results of the three testers using both techniques simultaneously were evaluated for consensus. There was consensus on 68 patients, and a joint review of the remaining 48 produced consensus on 36 more. The remaining 12 patients were then dropped from the sample. Thus the original sample of 136 patients was reduced to 104 (23.5% dropout).

What is more, the original diagnosis was then discarded and replaced with the consensus of the testers. The precautions taken in the study to ensure the blindness of diagnosis and test therefore were superfluous, since the consensus that replaced the original diagnosis obviously directly reflected the testers' opinions. The estimates of sensitivities and specificities reported then are of questionable validity for two reasons: first because of questionable sampling procedures, and second because of lack of blindness between test and the diagnosis used as the criterion.

In general, for Retrospective Sampling, the Chi-Square test statistic is:

$$\chi^2 = (N_1 + N_2) \cdot \text{WF} \cdot \kappa(1, 0) \cdot \kappa(0, 0)$$

where OP is the observed proportion of positive diagnoses OP = $N_1/(N_1 + N_2)$; (OP' = 1 – OP), OQ, the observed proportion of positive tests (OQ' = 1 – OQ), and WF is a weighting factor:

$$\text{WF} = (\text{OP} \cdot \text{OP}' \cdot \hat{Q} \cdot \hat{Q}')/(\text{OQ} \cdot \text{OQ}' \cdot \hat{P} \cdot \hat{P}') \,.$$

Since the size of N_1 and N_2 are arbitrarily set by the test evaluator, of course, OP does not estimate the prevalence, nor does OQ estimate the level of the test.

The larger the expected χ^2, the more powerful the statistical test, i.e., the more likely to detect the legitimacy of the medical test. Without any complex or detailed power analysis, but simply by examining the form of χ^2, we can ascertain the following facts:

1. For a fixed total sample size, $N_1 + N_2$, power is maximized if $N_1 = N_2$, i.e., if OP = 0.5.

2. For a fixed total sample size, $N_1 + N_2 = N_0$ and $N_1 = N_2$, Retrospective Sampling will generally yield a more powerful test than will Naturalistic Sampling. The exception is when the prevalence is 0.5. Then both sampling procedures yield about equally powerful results. For this reason, Retrospective Sampling becomes a more and more

appealing strategy the more the prevalence deviates from 0.5, i.e., very low- or very high-risk populations.

3. The costs of Naturalistic Sampling and Retrospective Sampling for the same situation may be very different. In Naturalistic Sampling, one selects N_0 subjects and does both the test and diagnosis on each. If the cost per test is $\$T$ and per diagnosis is $\$D$, the cost of obtaining the information in Naturalistic Sampling is:

$$N_0 \cdot (\$T + \$D).$$

In Retrospective Sampling, one samples N_0 patients and diagnoses each, but tests only $N_1 + N_2$ patients. The cost then is:

$$N_0 \cdot \$D + (N_1 + N_2) \cdot \$T.$$

If the cost of testing is great ($\$T$ large), and that of diagnosis small ($\$D$ low) there can be substantial savings in doing Retrospective Sampling, possibly with little loss of power.

At the risk of stating the obvious: The major limitation on Retrospective Sampling is that the test must be a diagnostic test, for the diagnosis must be made *before* testing is done.

Despite the problematic results of the Etter et al. (1960) analysis, this study ideally demonstrates the situation in which Retrospective Sampling might be preferred. If the study had been done using Naturalistic Sampling and the original sample size ($N_0 = 245$), there would have been 2,205 (9 · 245) readings necessary, a prohibitive investment of time. With Retrospective Sampling the number of readings was almost half as large, 1,224. The precision of the estimator of the sensitivity would have been unaffected, $N_1 = 50$). The precision of the estimator of the specificity would have been decreased somewhat, but would have remained satisfactory (standard error less than .054). In this case, using Retrospective Sampling represented less time and effort for the radiologists. In other cases it might also represent less risk and discomfort for patients. In any case, the cost incurred in obtaining such a saving in time, effort, risk, or discomfort is some degree of loss in the precision of one or the other estimators. But, as in this case, such a loss of precision might be quite acceptable given the reduction in cost.

For a valid statistical evaluation, there is no question in the Etter et al. (1960) study that the diagnosis should not have been changed midstream to reflect the consensus of the tests. It is rather more difficult to be so dogmatic about the propriety of dropping patients from the sample. Should films of poor quality (or, in general, uninterpretable diagnostic or test material) *not* be discarded? Does *any* dropout of patients, whatever the reason, invalidate an evaluation? Dropouts, planned or unplanned, are common problems in medical test evaluation, worthy of some discussion.

The Problem of Dropouts

When a population has been specified and a representative sample drawn from that population, any non-random dropouts may bias the sample, i.e., render it no longer representative of the population. Medical ethics, however, dictate that a patient may choose to withdraw from participation in a research study any time during the study. A few such dropouts, particularly random ones (unrelated to either test or to diagnosis) are not likely to do much harm. The larger the number of such dropouts, the greater the risk of ending the study with a biased sample and biased results. Test evaluators should exert every effort to retain patients in the study.

More serious risk of bias occurs if the researcher chooses to drop patients from the sample for reasons having to do with either the diagnosis or the test. This happened in the Etter et al. (1960) study—the patients did not choose to drop out, the researchers chose to drop them. That study, however, is not unique in this respect.

For example, Harris, Tang, and Weltz (1978) reported the evaluation of several "noninvasive" tests for staging patients with Hodgkin's disease. The disorders of interest were tumors of the abdominal lymph glands, the liver, the spleen, and the urinary tract. Diagnosis was based on results found at laparotomy. Harris et al. (1978) state: "If the literature is at all helpful, reports on the 'value' of noninvasive tests should describe in detail the composition of the patient series (e.g., the distribution of patients by age, sex, and presence or absence of symptoms, etc.)" (pp. 2390-2391). The population studied in this report was young men with Hodgkin's disease. Excluded were those with extra-nodal disease detected prior to laparotomy. Sampling was naturalistic, with a sample size of 108.

Table 5.5   Complete Reported Results of Diagnosis and Outcome for
Excretory Urography

Diagnosis at Laparotomy	Ureteral Deviation	Unsuspected Abnormal	Test Result Normal	Not Done	Total
Tumor	1*	11*	0	3	15
Normal	2*	6	47*	19	74
Not Diagnostic	0	0	0	0	0
No Tissue	2	0	12	5	19
Total	5	17	59	27	108

SOURCE: Harris et al. (1978)
NOTE: *Outcomes used in analysis by Harris et al. (1978)

The tests were lymphangiography, hepato-splenic scintigrams, and urography, tests described by the authors as "expensive, non-invasive diagnostic tests usually performed on Hodgkin's patients" (p. 2388).

Diagnosis and testing were not done blind. It is said that at laparotomy special attention was paid to nodes "in areas suggested by the lymphangiograms" and that "generally . . . the surgeon was unable to find nodal tissue in a patient with a negative lymphangiogram" (p. 2390). Consequently, the study may be biased because of non-blindness.

When the results were reported, the sample size for lymphangiograms was 73, for hepatic scintigram, 83, for splenic scintigram, 87, and for excretory urogram, 61. This means that between 19.4% (for the splenic scintigram) to 44.5% (for the excretory urogram) of the original sample of 108 were dropped. However, the Harris et al. (1978) study reported all the data in detail. We can continue to see what happened and what the effects might be. Consider the data in Table 5.5 for the excretory urogram.

There were apparently four, not two, results of the diagnosis: Tumor, Normal, Not Diagnostic, and No Tissue. When analysis was done, only the starred outcomes in Table 5.5 were used, i.e., "No Tissue" (19 patients) was completely excluded, and what a positive and negative test outcome was, changed with the diagnosis. It can be seen that the patients dropped were primarily those with negative diagnosis or test results. Consequently, the sample on which the

Table 5.6 Original and Modified Analysis of the Results of Evaluation
of Excretory Urography

a. Original Presentation				b. Amended Presentation			
	$T+$	$T-$			$T+$	$T-$	
$D+$	1	11	12	$D+$	12	3	15
$D-$	2	47	49	$D-$	10	83	93
	3	58	61		22	86	108

$P = 12/61 = .20$
$Q = 3/61 = .05$

$SE = 1/12 = .08$
$SP = 47/49 = .96$

$PVP = 1/3 = .33$
$PVN = 47/58 = .81$

$EFF = 48/61 = .79$

(Insufficient Sample Size)

$P = 15/108 = .14$
$Q = 22/108 = .20$

$SE = 12/15 = .80$
$SP = 83/93 = .89$

$PVP = 12/22 = .55$
$PVN = 83/86 = .97$

$EFF = 95/108 = .88$

$\chi^2 = 38.2 (p < .001)$

statistics were reported is from a higher-risk group than the population from which the original sample of 108 was drawn. What is more,
the results on which the analyses were based would indicate that the
excretory urogram is not a legitimate medical test, for the values of χ^2
expected by chance are almost exactly the values that were seen (see
Table 5.6).

To ensure the validity and objectivity of the conclusion, I would
argue that all 108 patients entered into the study should have been
included in the analysis, and to guarantee blindness, what a positive
test was (the referent) should have been defined without reference to
the results of the diagnosis. Exactly how this should have been done
is not a statistical decision, but, rather, a medical one.

From the medical consumer's point of view, it is of interest to ask
what the physician would do if he were to order a laparotomy for a
young man with Hodgkin's disease, and the laparotomy result were
to be "Not Diagnostic" or "No Tissue"? Would he ask the patient to
pretend that the procedure had never been done? Would he suggest
that the cost of hospitalization, surgery, anesthesia, the risks and
discomforts that the patient suffered in the process, are all to be
ignored? In effect, when such a patient is excluded from analysis in
the evaluation of the test, this is what happens: We pretend the patient
had not undergone the evaluation.

In fact, it is neither viable clinical practice nor viable research practice to simply "forget" such a procedure. In clinical practice, there would seem to be at least three viable options:

1. A further procedure is used to resolve whether or not the disorder is present and whether treatment should or should not be initiated, and this included in the definition of the diagnosis.
2. The positive diagnosis is given the benefit of the doubt, and for the ambiguous cases, treatment is initiated.
3. The negative diagnosis is given the benefit of the doubt, and for the ambiguous cases, no treatment is deemed necessary.

Whichever of these is most appropriate to the clinical situation is also appropriate to the research situation. Whether the definition of the gold-standard diagnosis is extended to include whatever is necessary to resolve the issue of the diagnosis, or the ambiguous results are de facto classified either as positive or negative diagnoses, whichever is to be given the benefit of the doubt. All patients tested and diagnosed are then included in the analysis of results.

In general, problems of exclusions should be dealt with in the a priori definitions of the population, the diagnosis, and the test protocol, and should not be based on the results of either the diagnosis or of the test. All patients who are unable or unwilling to participate in a research project, as well as those who are inappropriate in a clinical sense, should be excluded, but a priori.

For example, if an interview is part of the diagnosis or test, a psychiatric patient who is agitated, severely disturbed, unable to communicate, or hallucinating, should be excluded from the study. Such exclusion becomes part of the definition of the population, and part of the "packaging instructions" for the test.

If the diagnosticians are dissatisfied with the quality of the material presented to them, they might ask for more or better information. The honoring of such a request should be part of the specification of the diagnostic procedure. In the Etter et al. (1960) study, for example, any patient whose films were of such poor quality as to preclude decision, should have had new films taken. Alternatively, in the Harris et al. (1978) study, "Not Diagnostic" and "No Tissue" might be considered one possible diagnostic response: either a de facto positive one or de facto negative one.

Similarly, if there is irreparable technical deficiency in the test results, e.g., a poor quality film or a contaminated assay, an interrupted stress test, the test should be repeated. Again, that should be part of the protocol of the test.

In the Harris et al. (1978) study, for example, we might, naively, for purposes of illustration, choose to give the negative diagnosis the benefit of the doubt, classifying those whose diagnostic results were "Not Diagnostic" and "No Tissue" as a negative diagnosis. This results in the partition indicated in Table 5.5 and presented in column B of Table 5.6.

The contrast between the results in column a of Table 5.6, as reported by Harris et al. (1978), and those in column b of Table 5.6 are striking. The authors report a sensitivity of 8%, for example, while on the total sample, the sensitivity is 80%. The authors report a specificity 96%; the specificity on the total sample was 89%. The effect of the bias due to dropping out of patients is to exaggerate some qualities and to underestimate others. The Chi-Square test for Table 5.6, column a, shows no significant association between diagnosis and test. That in Table 5.6, column b, is significant at the 0.1% level. Thus there is no convincing evidence in the original report that excretory urography is even a legitimate test, while the amended presentation indicated that it is beyond reasonable doubt a legitimate test, perhaps even a "good" one.

The effects of dropping subjects, as can be seen from this demonstration, are not necessarily trivial. Such action may lead to rejecting a very good test or to proclaiming a very poor test good. Therefore, to the extent that it is within the power of the researchers to retain patients, *every patient included in the sample should be included in the analysis* (Swets & Pickett, 1982).

Prospective Sampling

Prospective Sampling is, in a sense, a mirror-image of Retrospective Sampling. A representative sample of N_0 patients is drawn from the population, the "screening sample," and each patient is tested (as in Retrospective Sampling, each was diagnosed). The proportion of patients with a positive test $\hat{Q}$ provides an unbiased estimator of the level of the test, Q. Its standard error is:

$$\text{Standard Error } (\hat{Q}) = [Q(1 - Q)/N_0]^{1/2}.$$

Then, a random sample of N_1 patients with a positive test, and a random sample of N_2 patients with a negative test are selected. As a rule of thumb, both N_1 and N_2 should exceed 10, and the number should be large enough to ensure that there will be at least 10 each with a positive and a negative diagnosis. Only these $N_1 + N_2$ patients, usually a number far less than the original N_0, undergo diagnosis.

The proportion of those with a positive test with a positive diagnosis ($\widehat{PVP}$) is an unbiased estimator of the predictive value of a positive test (PVP) with standard error:

$$\text{Standard Error } (\widehat{PVP}) = [PVP(1 - PVP)/N_1]^{\frac{1}{2}}.$$

The proportion of those with a negative test with a negative diagnosis ($\widehat{PVN}$) is an unbiased estimator of the predictive value of a negative test, PVN, with standard error:

$$\text{Standard Error } (\widehat{PVN}) = [PVN(1 - PVN)/N_2]^{\frac{1}{2}}.$$

With the estimators of Q, PVP, PVN, the four outcome probabilities can be estimated since:

$$TP = Q \cdot PVP,$$

$$FN = Q' \cdot PVN',$$

$$FP = Q \cdot PVP',$$

$$TN = Q' \cdot PVN'.$$

From these, the prevalence, the sensitivity and specificity, and the efficiency can be indirectly estimated since:

$$P = Q \cdot PVP + Q' \cdot PVN',$$

$$SE = Q \cdot PVP/P,$$

$$SP = Q' \cdot PVN/P',$$

$$EFF = Q \cdot PVP + Q' \cdot PVN.$$

The estimators of SE and SP here are also Bayes' estimators, based on the same mathematical theorem that yielded estimators of PVP and PVN from estimators of P, SE, and SP in Retrospective Sampling. While the Bayes' estimators of PVP and PVN from Retrospective Sampling are frequently mentioned in the medical research literature, the Bayes' estimators of SE and SP from Prospective Sampling are rarely mentioned.

The Chi-Square test for Prospective Sampling is:

$$\chi^2 = (N_1 + N_2) \cdot WF \cdot \kappa(1, 0) \cdot \kappa(0, 0)$$

where OQ is the observed proportion of those with a positive test

$$OQ = N_1 / (N_1 + N_2)$$

and OP the observed proportion of those with a positive diagnosis. Here the weighting factor WF is defined as:

$$WF = (OQ \cdot OQ' \cdot \hat{P} \cdot \hat{P}')/(OP \cdot OP' \cdot \hat{Q} \cdot \hat{Q}') .$$

Note that this weighting factor is the inverse of that used for Retrospective Sampling. Once again, OP does not estimate the prevalence, nor does OQ estimate the level of the test.

With respect to power and cost-efficiency, the situation is analogous to that in Retrospective Sampling. To reiterate in summary form:

1. Prospective Sampling yields greatest power for fixed total sample size if $N_1 = N_2$ (OQ = 0.5).
2. This will yield greater power than will Naturalistic Sampling with the same total sample size ($N_0 = N_1 + N_2$) provided the level of the test is not itself 50%.
3. The further the level of the test is from 50%, the greater the increase in power achieved by Prospective Sampling.
4. This strategy will be most cost-effective if the cost of the test is low and that of the diagnosis is high.

Prospective Sampling is a particularly appealing alternative for evaluation of a prognostic test where the diagnosis can be ascertained only after a followup of 1, 2, or even 10 years after the period of testing. The costs and difficulties of following patients over extended periods of time are enormous. When the prevalence is low, which is common in such studies, and the resources of the research group limited, which is almost universal in such studies, Prospective Sampling must be seriously considered. The major limitation to the use of Prospective Sampling, of course, is that it limits consideration to one and only one referent, i.e., not an extended family of tests.

For example, Wetzner, Kiser, and Bezreh (1984) report on the value of duplex ultrasound imaging. The disorder is atherosclerotic disease of the extracranial carotid circulation. The diagnosis is based on angiography, a positive diagnosis given to a patient with more than 60% stenosis. The protocol for the test is specified; the test response is a measure of the percentage stenosis as determined by duplex ultrasound imaging, with a referent of more than 60%.

No information is provided on the clinical characteristics of the population. However, there were 140 patients in the screening sample. Of these, 35 had a positive test result and thus:

$$\hat{Q} = 35/140 = .250 \text{ or } 25\%.$$

All of these 35 patients with a positive test ($N_1 = 35$) and 18 of the patients with a negative test ($N_2 = 18$) underwent diagnosis. That means that 66.0% of the sample ($QQ = .660$), as opposed to 25.0% of the population, had a positive test $\hat{Q} = 0.250$).

From the data, the estimated predictive values are:

$$P\hat{V}P = 33/35 = 0.943.$$

$$P\hat{V}N = 16/18 = 0.889.$$

Then

$$\hat{TP} = 0.250 \cdot 0.943 = 0.236,$$

$$\hat{FN} = 0.750 \cdot 0.111 = 0.083,$$

$$\hat{FP} = 0.250 \cdot 0.057 = 0.014,$$

$$\hat{TN} = 0.750 \cdot 0.889 = 0.667.$$

From these results we may compute that:

$$\hat{P} = 0.236 + 0.083 = 0.319,$$

$$\hat{SE} = \hat{TP}/\hat{P} = 0.236/0.319 = 0.739,$$

$$\hat{SP} = \hat{TN}/\hat{P'} = 0.667/0.681 = 0.979,$$

$$\hat{EFF} = \hat{TP} + \hat{TN} = 0.236 + 0.667 = 0.903.$$

The Chi-Square test statistic is 36.7, statistically significant at less than the 0.1% level. I would conclude that duplex ultrasound imaging is beyond reasonable doubt a legitimate test for atherosclerotic disease in that clinical population.

Except for the absence of a population definition, the results seem straightforward. However, the authors reported "a sensitivity of 0.94, a specificity of 0.88, and an overall accuracy (efficiency) of 0.92" (p. 507) which do not at all compare with the values of 0.74, 0.98 and 0.90 reported above. What here appears to have occurred was that the estimation procedure they used was that appropriate to Naturalistic Sampling, here applied to a case when Prospective Sampling was used. This produces invalid estimators. *Care must be taken that the estimators used are appropriate to the sampling method used.*

This study stimulates yet another interesting question. Reported in the Wetzner et al. (1984) study were 140 patients with 184 stenotic lesions. The distribution of results of the ultrasound diagnosis were there reported in terms of lesions, not patients. It appears, however, that when the sampling and analysis were done, the sampling units were patients, not lesions. What is the correct procedure?

The Sampling Unit

In another study of duplex ultrasound imaging (Garth, Carroll, Sommer, & Oppenheimer, 1983), there is a sample of 50 patients with 100 vessels. In one by James et al., (1982) there were 100 patients with 158 vessels. In both cases, the results were reported, and the estimates based on, the number of vessels, not the number of patients. Which is appropriate: patients, vessels, either or both?

From a medical consumer's viewpoint, the quality of the test should be determined as it is to be used, on the patient as a whole. A patient may have several carotid or coronary vessels, 2 eyes, 2 lungs, and 10 fingers and 10 toes. But it is the *patient* who has the disorder or not, who undergoes diagnosis, pays for the diagnosis, undergoes treatment, pays for treatment, and who may or may not recover. Whether the test is to be recommended or not should depend on its value for the patient as a whole, not for his right eye or his left index finger.

From a statistician's viewpoint, too, the unit of analysis should always be the patient. All the statistical analyses commonly used require that each entry in a table such as Table 5.1 be independent. When each comes from a different patient, no problem arises. However when the 2 vessels, 2 eyes, or 10 fingers or toes from the same patient are entered as if they were from different patients, the possible dependencies between them may well invalidate the statistical results. Consequently, the approach that Wetzner et al. (1984) utilized, using patients as the sampling unit, is the preferable one.

Pseudo-Retrospective Sampling:
An Invalid Approach

Naturalistic, Prospective, and Retrospective Sampling, properly done and analyzed, each lead to valid estimators of the outcome probabilities and to any combinations that might be of interest. They differ from each other in cost of execution, the calculation procedures used to estimate the outcome probabilities and pertinent combinations, and in the precision of the various estimators, not in the validity of the results. There is another quite common sampling method that runs a high risk of producing invalid results, one I will call "Pseudo-Retrospective Sampling."

In this strategy, a sample of size N_1 is drawn from a high-risk population, such as a hospital or clinic population. A sample of size N_2 is drawn from another, low-risk, population, such as a normal control population. Frequently these samples are matched in terms of age, sex, socioeconomic class, and other such demographic characteristics (mimicking case-control studies in epidemiology). No direct estimate of the prevalence in either population is obtained (as is obtained from the screening sample in the Retrospective Sampling procedure), but frequently some external estimates can be obtained from records or national studies for these or any other specified populations of clinical interest.

Each of the sampled $N_1 + N_2$ patients undergoes diagnosis and testing. Because of the way sampling is done, most of the positive diagnoses are found in the high-risk group, most of the negative diagnoses in the low- risk group. The results are then combined in one table and treated as if the sampling were retrospective. Using an external estimate of prevalence as one would in Retrospective Sampling use the estimate of prevalence from the screening sample, one may compute what purport to be Bayes' estimates of the predictive values.

The problems here are those encountered in epidemiology associated with Berkson's Fallacy (Berkson, 1946). In a nutshell, sampling a high-risk group and a low-risk group does not usually produce samples representative of the diagnosis positive and negative arms of any single clinical population. Matching procedures may render the sample even less representative and make the situation even worse. Since the sensitivity and specificity of a test may change from population to population, the estimates of sensitivity and specificity here obtained may be a biased estimate of the sensitivity in one population, the high-risk one, and a biased estimate of the specificity in the other, the low-risk population. In both cases, the bias results from the pooling of the results from two different populations. Furthermore, the external estimates of prevalence may themselves be biased estimates. Diagnostic procedures vary over place and time. A clinic or hospital record may not provide good enough gold standards for estimation of prevalence. National statistics are national in scope. The prevalence may vary from one locale to another, or one period of time to another, and be poorly estimated by national statistics.

Pseudo-Retrospective Sampling is an attractive idea. It is usually cheap and easy to implement. There have been several discussions of medical test evaluation that not only carry no warning about the possible biases inherent in this sampling procedure, but actually recommend it. Certainly this sampling procedure *may* produce the correct answers, but the chances are very high that it will not.

Galen and Gambino (1975) discuss a study by Rogers, Lyon, and Porter (1972) of a spot test for vanillymandelic acid and other guaiacols in the urine of patients for a disorder of neuroblastoma: "Nine of 13 cases of clinically apparent neuroblastoma (69%) were detectable by this test. Urine from 255 control subjects on unrestricted diets produced only one false positive reaction" (p. 72). Galen and Gambino (1975) ask: "Would we introduce this test in our laboratory? Should we introduce this test in our laboratory?" (p. 72) and then recommend against its use.

My own reaction is different: Because sampling was pseudo-retrospective, I believe no answer, positive or negative, should be based on this study. In particular, the cases in which there was clinically apparent neuroblastoma may not be representative of those with the disorder as yet undetected, and the "control" cases may not be representative of those within the same population who do not have the disorder. The clinical population in which such a test might be valuable would seem to be that in which patients are at risk, but not yet known from clinical signs and symptoms, to have the disorder. The result reported here is at best suggestive, a pilot study for future test evaluation studies, but no basis for deciding one way or the other about the proposed test.

Another example of the use of Pseudo-Retrospective Sampling, one with obvious policy relevance, is taken from the description of the enzyme immunoassay from Abbott Laboratories (1985) for the detection of antibody to HTLV III, the virus thought to cause AIDS. What is stated there:

At present there is no recognized standard for establishing the presence and absence of HTLV III antibody in human blood. Therefore sensitivity was computed based on the clinical diagnosis of AIDS and specificity and based on random donors. The Abbott studies show that: 1. Sensitivity based on an assumed 100% prevalence of HTLV III antibody in AIDS patients is estimated to be 98.3%; and 2. Specificity based on an assumed zero prevalence of HTLV III antibody in random donors is estimated to be 99.8%. (p. 13)

What was here estimated, then, was the level of the test among AIDS patients (98.3%) and the complement of the level of the test among blood donors (0.2%). If, in fact, the prevalence of HTLV III antibody in AIDS patients is 100%, as one would expect, then the sensitivity of the test *for AIDS patients* is 98.3%. If, in fact, the prevalence of HTLV III antibody in blood donors is 0% (unfortunately unlikely), then the specificity of the test *for blood donors* is 99.8%. However, we do not know the specificity of the test for AIDS patients, which is of little concern, but, we also do not know the sensitivity of the test for blood donors. That is of the greatest concern. This is a test designed for screening blood donations, and the sensitivity of this test *among blood donors* indicates what protection there is against transmission of AIDS via transfusion of blood from blood banks.

Summary

The questions that need to be answered to plan an objective and quantitative evaluation of a medical test, or to assess the quality of such an evaluation reported in the medical research literature, can now be compiled:

PLANNING AN EVALUATION

1. What is the disorder, how is it to be diagnosed in this study, and is that diagnosis valid?

2. What is the test (or family of tests) of interest in terms of protocol, response, referent (referents for a family)?

3. In what clinical populations is the test to be used? Is the sampling properly done to ensure a representative sample from that population? (If there are several such populations, such questions apply to each.)

Are there specific inclusion and exclusion criteria?

4. Is the sampling of the clinical population to be Naturalistic, Retrospective, or Prospective? If Naturalistic, how large is N_0 to be?

If Retrospective Sampling is to be used, be sure the test is being evaluated as a diagnostic test. How large is N_0 to be, and then how large are N_1 and N_2 to be?

If Prospective Sampling is to be used, be sure that one and only one test is being evaluated. How large is N_0 to be, and then how large are N_1 and N_2 to be?

In all cases, given what is known about the prevalence of the diagnosis in the population of interest, *will the sample sizes be large enough to yield at least 10 patients in each marginal position?*

EXECUTING AN EVALUATION

1. How are the blindness of the test and of the diagnosis to be assured?

2. What strategies will be used to minimize dropouts?

ANALYZING THE OUTCOME OF THE EVALUATION

1. What are the estimates of the prevalence, level, sensitivity, specificity, predictive values, efficiency, or any other measures of interest for the test? Were they properly estimated according to the rules

governing the sampling strategy used? Is the sample size large enough to yield reasonably precise estimates?

2. Does the Chi-Square test indicate that the test is, at the very least, a legitimate one?

Now we can begin to address the problem of finding "good," not merely "legitimate," tests.

Note

1. It should be noted that the abbreviation SE or se is sometimes elsewhere used for "standard error." In this presentation "standard error" will be spelled out and SE used as an easy mnemonic abbreviation for sensitivity.

6

Sensitivity and Specificity:
The Signal Detection Approach

Problems with Sensitivity and Specificity

Sensitivity and specificity were briefly introduced in Chapter 5. The sensitivity is the probability that a patient with a positive diagnosis will have a positive test result. The specificity is the probability that a patient with a negative diagnosis will have a negative test result. These represent clear, intuitively appealing, and, as we saw in Chapter 5, easily estimated descriptors of the performance of the test relative to the diagnosis.

While it is well known that "good" tests have high sensitivity or high specificity and preferably both, there remain problems with the unambiguous interpretation of these descriptors.

It is not unknown that the statistical testing of a medical test indicates that a test with 99.9% specificity is not even demonstrably legitimate. The too-facile explanation for this is that the statistical significance depends on factors other than the quality of the medical test. Perhaps in such cases the sample size was not sufficient to yield enough power to detect the legitimacy of the test?

It is not unusual that a clinician who has long used a medical test and considers it highly dependable in guiding his clinical judgments will find that the evaluation of that test discloses a sensitivity of 50%

or a specificity of 70%, figures that seem quite low. Alternatively, a clinician will use a medical test because it has been reported to be highly sensitive or highly specific in evaluation, only to find that it does not seem to work at all well in practice.

The facile explanation in such cases is that the subjective impressions of the clinician, as applied to relatively limited sets of patients, and perhaps using the test not precisely the way it should be used, may be wrong.

Such facile answers came all too easily to me at least, until the day I was asked to consult on a comparative evaluation of two computer algorithms used for continuous EKG monitoring in the Coronary Care Unit (CCU). Here the disorder was a life-threatening abnormal heartbeat pattern. The diagnosis was to be based on expert evaluation of printed EKGs. The test was based on continuous computer monitoring of the EKG from patients in the CCU, a positive test determined by the algorithm's detection of a pattern designated as life-threatening. Both algorithms under evaluation without question represented legitimate tests. The issue was to compare the two, and the criterion of excellence chosen was specificity. One term used to describe this criterion was the "false alarm" rate (1-specificity). The false alarm rate would have to be kept low, it was explained, in order not to hassle the CCU nurses. In fact, the false alarm rate was sometimes called the "hassle factor."

Imagine the CCU patient, having survived a myocardial infarction and still having life-threatening heart irregularities. He is assured that sensors on his chest continually monitor his heart. Any life-threatening abnormality would be detected and help would be summoned immediately. For the monitoring system and for the services of the nurses and doctors who would be summoned in such an emergency situation, he (or his insurance coverage) will pay well over $1,000 per day. Well worthwhile under the circumstances, one would think. However, what would you imagine his reaction would be if he were told that the monitor selected to provide this costly but essential protection is chosen, not on the basis of which algorithm provides him the greatest protection, but, rather, on which one causes the least inconvenience to the nurses?

Realistically, with any algorithm, there will be some, however rare, false alarms. The sensor may pull loose, or there might be some electrical abnormality on the line. The one and only way to ensure a zero false alarm rate is, obviously, to pull the plug on the monitoring system. Then it can never hassle the nurses, but, of course, it provides no protection to the patient either!

That insight expresses a simple statistical fact. For any disorder, any diagnosis, any test, and in any population, it is always possible to have 100% specificity: Give everyone a negative test result. It is similarly always possible to have 100% sensitivity: Give everyone a positive test result. A test with 100% specificity may not be a legitimate test, nor need a test with 100% sensitivity be a legitimate test.

Sensitivity and specificity are uncalibrated measures of test quality, measures with a variable zero-point and scale. The problem with interpreting these measures is similar to the one met were I to report: "The temperature outside is 40 degrees." Does that mean it is hot or cold? If the scale on which I measured temperature were Fahrenheit, a winter coat might be advisable; it the scale were Celsius, a winter coat might be very uncomfortable indeed.

My report that the temperature is 40 degrees is not fully informative unless I also give some indication of the scale on which I measured that temperature: Fahrenheit (32 at freezing and 212 at boiling); Celsius (0 at freezing and 100 at boiling), or some other thermometer calibrated in less standard fashion (10 at freezing and 40 at boiling? 40 at freezing and 100 at boiling?). In the same way, reporting the magnitudes of the sensitivity and specificity is not fully informative unless some indication of the scale on which they are measured is specified.

When a test with 99.9% specificity is found not to be legitimate, the fact is that it may not be legitimate: 99.9% may not be high enough. When the clinician finds a test useful to him or her in practice has "only" 50% sensitivity or "only" 70% specificity, those may be high figures, not low. Confusion arises because the test evaluations in the medical research literature frequently report sensitivity and specificity without giving any clue as to what the scale of reference might be. As a result, the clinician may well be correct that a test reported to have "high" sensitivity or specificity in the research literature is of no real help in practice. With such issues in mind, let us now examine sensitivity and specificity in more detail.

The Basic Model

Mathematically, sensitivity and specificity are expressed as:

$$SE = TP/P \qquad SP = TN/P'.$$

In terms of the basic model (Chapter 3),

$$SE = Q + \rho\sigma_p\sigma_q/P \qquad SP = Q' + \rho\sigma_p\sigma_q/P'.$$

Thus for a random test ($\rho = 0$), sensitivity (SE) equals the level of the test (Q), and specificity equals the complement of the level of the test ($Q' = 1 - Q$). For a legitimate test ($\rho > 0$), sensitivity exceeds the level of the test (SE > Q), and specificity exceeds the complement of the level of the test (SP > Q'). In any case, the ideal values of sensitivity and specificity are both 1.0, which may not always be an achievable value. For random or legitimate tests, the effective ranges of sensitivity and specificity do not extend from zero to 1.0. Sensitivity ranges from Q to 1; specificity ranges from Q' to 1. Any report of sensitivity and specificity of a test that does not also report its level gives no indication of the quality of the test.

The quality of sensitivity or specificity depends on where each lies within its effective range and is most succinctly expressed (as one would be converting temperature on whatever scale it was originally measured, to Celsius) with reference to that range:

$$\kappa(1, 0) = (SE - Q)/Q' \qquad \kappa(0, 0) = (SP - Q')/Q.$$

The sensitivity may well be 99.9%, but if the level of the test (Q) is also 99.9%, the sensitivity is of zero quality [$\kappa(1, 0) = 0$]. Randomly assigning positive diagnoses to 99.9% of subjects in a population yields a "test" also with 99.9% sensitivity. On the other hand, a specificity of 70% for a test with level 99% ($Q' = .01$), may be an outstanding test, perhaps close to the best that can ever be done.

The indices $\kappa(1, 0)$ and $\kappa(0, 0)$ originally defined in Chapter 5 in the computation of the 2×2 Chi-Square test statistic, measure the quality of sensitivity and specificity, thus *quality indices*. These quality indices do not necessarily replace sensitivity and specificity as descriptors of test performance. Just as one might choose to report temperature both in terms of Fahrenheit and of Celsius, one might choose to report both the sensitivity and specificity *and* their quality indices. However, to report sensitivity and specificity without somehow conveying their quality can be misleading (Kraemer, 1985).

The two indices $\kappa(1, 0)$ and $\kappa(0, 0)$ are so-called weighted kappa coefficients and, at the same time, are "attributable risks." In these statistical roles, both indices are familiar to segments of the statistical/

Table 6.1 Evaluation of the Folin-Wu Blood Test for Diabetes Done 3 Hours After the Test Meal (*Prevalence* = P = 12.1%)

Referent	P(%)	SE(%)	SP(%)	Q(%)	κ(1,0)(%)	κ(0,0)(%)
≥80	12.1	Insufficient Sample Size				
90	12.1	97.1	6.1	94.3	49.2	0.4
100	12.1	92.9	34.5	68.8	*77.2	4.8
110	12.1	81.4	67.8	38.2	69.9	15.6
120	12.1	68.6	86.5	20.2	60.7	33.1
130	12.1	60.0	94.3	12.3	54.4	53.5
140	12.1	57.1	98.2	8.5	53.1	78.8
150	12.1	48.6	99.6	6.2	45.2	93.6
160	12.1	42.9	100.0	5.2	39.8	**100.0
170	12.1	35.7	100.0	4.3	32.8	100.0
180	12.1	28.6	100.0	3.5	26.0	100.0
190	12.1	28.6	100.0	3.5	26.0	100.0

SOURCE: Galen and Gambino (1975) p. 107; Remein and Wilkerson (1961)
NOTES: [SE = Sensitivity; SP = Specificity; Q = Level of test]
*Optimally Sensitive Test: ≥ 100*mg/dl*, κ(1,0) = 77.2%
**Optimally Specific Test: ≥ 160*mg/dl*, κ(0,0) = 100.0%

medical research communities. There is considerable information in the methodological literature on their properties and uses. For the moment, however, let us focus only on their use in this context of medical test evaluation.

Table 6.1 presents data taken from Galen and Gambino's (1975) evaluation of studies originally done by Remein and Wilkerson (1961). The disorder is diabetes; the diagnosis was based on "criteria . . . established by a group of consultants and consisted entirely of the results of the 100 gram, 3-hour, oral glucose tolerance test" (p. 108). The sampling appears to be naturalistic, with a sample size for blood tests of 580, and for the urine tests of 515. The estimated prevalence in the sample on which blood tests were done was 12.1%, and in the sample on which urine tests were done was 11.8%.

Complete results for one of the several test protocols reported, the Folin-Wu blood test done 3 hours after the test meal, with referents based on cut-offs ranging from 80-190 mg/dl (i.e., the test result is abnormal if it exceeds 80, 90, etc.) appear in Table 6.1. When Galen and Gambino (1975) presented their results, they presented only sensitivity and specificity for each test, not its level. Thus the information necessary to judge its quality was not explicitly presented.

However, with the prevalence and the sensitivity and specificity for each test, it is an easy matter to recover the necessary information on level (see Chapter 5), since

$$Q = P \cdot SE + P' \cdot SP'.$$

The level of each test, then, appears in Table 6.1.

This illustrates a very common type of family: a "nested family." In a nested family, the tests can be listed in an order such that a patient positive on any test in the list is positive on all tests listed above it. Thus any patient positive when the cut-off is 190, is also positive when the cut-off is 180 or 170 etc.

For such a family, each successive test on the list must have a lower level. In Table 6.1, for example, the level drops from 94.3% to 3.5% as one goes down the list. It is also a mathematical certainty that each successive test on the list has a *lower* sensitivity and a *higher* specificity. In Table 6.1 the sensitivity gradually decreases from 97.1% to 28.6%; the specificity gradually increases from 6.1% to 100%. These patterns are a necessary mathematical consequence of the nesting of the tests.

If we were to choose the test with *maximal* sensitivity, we would always choose the first test on the list, whatever that might be. If we were to choose the test with *maximal* specificity, we would always choose the last test on the list, whatever that might be. The longer and more exhaustive the list, the more extreme the choice of referent. Ultimately the choice to maximize sensitivity would be to give nearly everyone a positive test result; the choice to maximize specificity would be to give nearly everyone a negative test result. Maximizing sensitivity or specificity amounts to "pulling the plug" on the test, i.e., not using it at all.

Galen and Gambino (1975) pose the question: "Of the . . . tests available, which is 'best'? Should we choose the test with the highest sensitivity, the highest specificity, the highest predictive value for a positive test, or the highest efficiency?" (p. 50). My answer, obviously not the one expected, is "No." The choice of "best" test should not be based on the magnitudes of sensitivity or specificity per se, but, rather, on their quality, that is, on $\kappa(1, 0)$ and $\kappa(0, 0)$.

Also listed in Table 6.1 are the values of the quality indices. Note that even with a sample size of 580, the referent using the cut-off 80 mg/dl could not be adequately assessed, since there were then fewer than 10 patients with a positive test. Beyond that, the test with optimal sensitivity is the one with the referent using the cut-off 100 mg/dl; the test with optimal specificity is the one with referent using the cut-off 160 mg/dl, since these are the tests with maximal $\kappa(1, 0)$ and $\kappa(0, 0)$ respectively.

The choice of optimally specific test here requires some further explanation. When two tests tie for optimal specificity, we propose that the tie be broken by any advantage in the quality of the sensitivity. In the same way, if two tests tie for optimal sensitivity, the tie is broken by any advantage in the quality of the specificity. Here, for example, all tests using cut-offs greater than 160 mg/dl tied in terms of the quality of specificity (all 100%), but the optimal test among these is the one with optimal sensitivity, namely 160 mg/dl. Two tests are of equal quality, therefore, only if they have exactly the same quality of sensitivity and specificity, and, in turn, that can happen only when they have exactly the same sensitivity and specificity.

In the full discussion of tests for diabetes presented by Galen and Gambino (1975), there were 136 different tests presented: four protocols (blood glucose measured by the Somogyi-Nelson method, or by the Folin-Wu method, urine glucose measured by the Clinitest, or Benedict's method), each at random hours and at 1, 2, and 3 hours after the test meal, and each with a set of nested referents. Sensitivities and specificities are presented for all the tests (sufficient information was presented to recover the levels).

As we did for the Folin-Wu 3 hours after the test meal (see Table 6.1), by computing the values of $\kappa(1, 0)$ and $\kappa(0, 0)$ we can find what the optimally sensitive and the optimally specific test is for each of the four test protocols, and at each of the selected times after the test meal. These results are presented in Table 6.2. Note that the test with optimal sensitivity is rarely (here never) the test with optimal specificity, and that the optimal referents differ depending on the type and timing of the test.

The issue can be pursued even further by identifying for each of the four test protocols, the optimal timing as well as the optimal referent (indicated by one or more asterisks in Table 6.2). Finally, the overall optimal tests (indicated by a double asterisk in Table 6.2) can be selected from *all* the tests.

The test with overall optimal sensitivity is the Folin-Wu test, at one hour after the test meal, with a cut-off of 80 mg/dl. There is an absolute tie for the optimally specific test between the Somogyi-Nelson

Table 6.2   Identification of the Optimally Sensitive and Specific Blood and Urine Tests for Diabetes

| Protocol | *Optimally Sensitive Tests* | | | *Optimally Specific Tests* | | |
	Referent mg/dl	κ(1,0)	κ(0,0)	Referent mg/dl	κ(1,0)	κ(0,0)
Somogyi-Nelson						
Random	80	73.9%	5.0%	190	19.3%	100.0%
1	90	*91.6%	6.7%	190	31.5%	100.0%
2	80	87.3%	3.5%	170	39.8%	**100.0%
3	80	72.7%	8.7%	140	38.3%	100.0%
Folin-Wu						
Random	110	69.6%	15.1%	170	31.3%	95.4%
1	80	**100.0%	1.2%	190	41.0%	96.4%
2	100	87.2%	3.5%	180	46.7%	96.8%
3	90	77.2%	4.8%	160	39.8%	*100.0%
Clinitest						
Random	1+	26.1%	71.9%	2+	20.9%	100.0%
1	1+	26.4%	51.6%	4+	19.1%	92.6%
2	trace	*40.0%	17.4%	4+	21.8%	80.1%
3	trace	34.6%	22.3%	3+	27.0%	*100.0%
Benedict's	Trace					
Random	1+	24.6%	27.1%	3+	17.8%	*100.0%
1	trace	39.8%	5.7%	3+	21.8%	80.1%
2	trace	*63.9%	4.0%	3+	31.5%	95.3%
3	trace	58.4%	7.0%	3+	26.8%	94.5%

SOURCES: Galen and Gambino (1975), p. 107; Remein and Wilkerson (1961)
NOTES: *, **: The optimally sensitive and specific tests for each of the four protocols, at different time points after the test meal, and identification of the optimal time for each test (* or **), and the overall optimal tests (**)

test at 2 hours with a cut-off of 170 mg/dl and the Folin-Wu test at 3 hours after the test meal with cut-off 160 mg/dl. (Both have sensitivity 42.9% and specificity 100%.)

In light of these findings, it is interesting to reevaluate the comments that are made by Galen and Gambino (1975) about these tests.

They point out that the Somogyi-Nelson test can claim greater chemical specificity than the Folin-Wu test, and they ask whether a test lacking chemical specificity also lacks diagnostic specificity. They conclude that this is so. Yet it can be seen in Table 6.2 that the referent that optimized the specificity of the Somogyi-Nelson test and that which optimized the specificity of the Folin-Wu test produced absolutely identical test performance.

Galen and Gambino (1975) pointed out that urine tests are less sensitive than are blood tests, and this comment is unequivocally supported in Table 6.2. The optimally sensitive urine test had a quality index of 63.9% compared to the quality indices for the optimally sensitive blood tests of 91.6% and 100%. In terms of the quality of specificity, the urine tests are also inferior to that of the blood tests. On all counts, blood tests would be preferred.

Galen and Gambino (1975) suggest that the referent level "to optimize the usefulness" of the Somogyi-Nelson test is based on the test 1 hour after the test meal with a referent of 160 mg/dl. From the present results, this choice neither optimized the sensitivity nor the specificity. In fact, in our later analyses, this test will prove not to be optimal in any sense. It is not obvious why Galen and Gambino (1975) selected this particular test.

The Receiver Operating Characteristic Curve (Test ROC)

Evaluating a family of tests with a base of 136 tests as was done above in the evaluation of the various tests for diabetes is not unusual. When a test is new, it is not usually known what the best referent might be. Examining a range of possible referents permits comparison of the qualities of such tests and the systematic and objective choice of the optimal referent. It is both prudent and cost-effective to do so.

In the above reevaluation of the tests for diabetes, this process was done analytically by computing the quality indices for each test and finding the ones with optimal sensitivity and specificity. The same process can also be done geometrically. Such a geometric approach forms the basis of the Signal Detection approach to medical test evaluation (Swets & Pickett, 1982).

Each test under consideration (one or many) can be located on a graph of sensitivity versus specificity, in what we will call the "ROC plane." In the illustration above, using blood and urine tests to diagnose diabetes, we would see a swarm of 136 points, which would be quite confusing to the eye of a novice at the use of this method. Let us instead begin with a somewhat simpler but equally interesting example, later to return to the diabetes tests.

Table 6.3 Evaluation of Duplex Ultrasound Scoring for Carotid Artery Stenosis

#	Referent[1]	P^2	Q	SE	SP	κ(1,0)	κ(0,0)
1	VR ≥ 1.5	34.8%	33.7%	80.6%	91.4%	70.8%	74.4%
2	SW ≥ 40	36.3%	52.8%	81.8%	63.8%	61.5%	31.4%
3	VR ≥ 1.5 or SW > 40	34.8%	58.4%	93.5%	60.3%	84.4%	32.0%
4	VR ≥ 1.5 and SW > 40	34.8%	26.9%	67.7%	94.8%	55.8%	*80.7%
5	AS ≥ 50%	41.0%	40.0%	70.7%	81.4%	51.2%	53.5%
6	AS ≥ 75%	41.0%	19.0%	39.0%	94.9%	24.7%	73.2%
7	MV ≥ 100	36.3%	27.5%	54.5%	87.9%	37.2%	56.0%
8	≥ 1 criterion	36.3%	61.6%	97.0%	58.6%	*92.2%	32.8%
9	≥ 2 criteria	36.3%	41.8%	81.8%	81.0%	68.7%	54.5%
10	≥ 3 criteria	36.3%	30.8%	66.7%	89.7%	51.9%	66.5%
11	+4 criteria	36.3%	13.2%	30.3%	96.6%	19.7%	74.2%

SOURCE: Garth et al. (1983), pp. 823-827.
NOTES: 1. Criteria:
  VR = Velocity Ratio
  SW = Spectral Width
  AS = Area Stenosis
  MV = Maximum Vinca
2. Prevalence estimates vary because of missing data.
*Optimally sensitive or specific test.

Nine tests were evaluated by Garth et al. (1983) and two more tests for which data were presented but which the authors did not explicitly evaluate. The disorder is carotid artery stenosis, the diagnosis based on arteriography. Sampling was naturalistic, with 52 patients. The population was defined as follows: "a history of transient ischemic attacks, cervical bruits, preoperative evaluation, prior stroke, and prior carotid endarterectomy" (p. 824). The test was duplex ultrasound scanning. The nine referents presented by Garth et al. (1983) and two more that could be evaluated (Test #3 and #4) on the basis of the data they presented, are listed in Table 6.3.

These same tests are presented geometrically in Figure 6.4. What is seen there, and what is typically seen, is a swarm of test points, all lying above the diagonal line extending from the upper left corner to the lower right corner of the ROC plane.

All tests must lie on or above the diagonal line simply because we restricted attention to random ($\rho = 0$) or legitimate tests ($\rho > 0$). (Any illegitimate test [$\rho < 0$] can be made legitimate by interchanging positive and negative test results.)

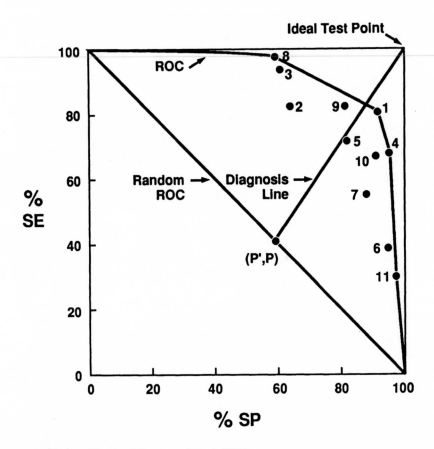

Figure 6.1. Duplex Ultrasound Scan ROC
SOURCE: Garth et al., 1983.

Now consider the family of tests with these 11 tests as the base. Included in this family by definition are the two "null tests," the test in which everyone has a positive test and the one in which everyone has a negative test. This includes in the family by definition the upper left-hand corner and the lower right-hand corner of the graph.

Included in this family also by definition are all the probability combinations of any two tests in the family (Chapter 4). What this means is that for any two test points in the specified set, including the null tests, all points on the line joining those two test points in the ROC plane, are also included in the family. As a result, the family of tests defined on the base (see Chapter 4) encloses an area of the ROC plane determined by joining all the test points in the base and the two corner points. The lower boundary of this area is always the diagonal line from the upper-left to the lower-right corners. This is called the "Random Receiver Operating Characteristic Curve," "Random ROC" for short. The upper boundary of this area is an irregular arc that I call the "Test Family Receiver Operating Characteristic Curve," "Test ROC" or merely "ROC" for short.

Within the particular set of tests (see Figure 6.1), there are several nested subsets: (3, 1, 4), (3, 2, 4), (5, 6) and (8, 9, 10, 11). If one focused on any one such nested subset, one would notice that each successive test point in that subset must lie below and to the right of the previous point. Again, this is a mathematical characteristic of *nested* families of tests. As a result, the ROC of any nested family of tests is a very well-behaved swarm of points, all in a more or less curved path leading from the upper-left corner to the lower-right corner of the graph.

When the Test ROC is defined in most current presentations of the Signal Detection approach (e.g., Swets & Pickett, 1982) discussion is limited to nested families of tests. Under that limitation, what I here describe as a "swarm" of points is usually described as a "curve" extending from the upper-left to the lower-right corners of the graph. Clearly the present definition of the Test ROC coincides with that definition for this limited type of family of tests, but the current definition has the advantage that it is more general. It is not limited to any particular type of family.

The optimal tests in a family of tests lie on the Test ROC nearest to the upper right-hand corner, the Ideal Test Point. Here these are tests #8, #1, #4, and maybe #11. This is so, because for any test that lies in the area between the Random ROC and the Test ROC, there must be one or more tests actually on the Test ROC with both greater sensitivity and greater specificity. Such a test on the ROC would then be preferred to one within that area.

It is not yet exactly clear which test or tests on the ROC one should choose as "optimal." Suggestions for identifying such tests in the early literature have been couched in terms of clinical costs and benefits that are frequently difficult to measure precisely (McNeil, Varady, Burrows, & Adelstein, 1975). We will return to this issue in detail in Chapter 9, but consider now an alternate geometrical approach that resolves a major part of this problem very easily.

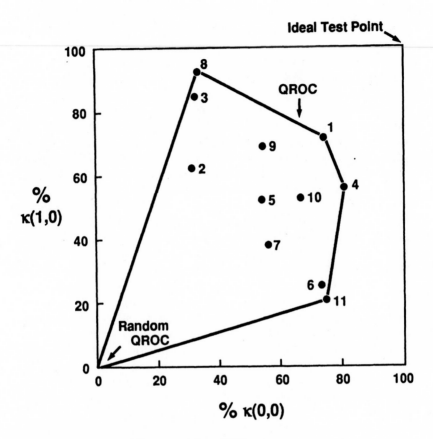

Figure 6.2. Duplex Ultrasound Scan ROC
SOURCE: Garth et al., 1983.

The Quality Receiver Operating
Characteristic Curve (QROC)

Every test under consideration (one or several) can also be located on a graph by its quality indices $\kappa(1, 0)$ versus $\kappa(0, 0)$, in what we will call the "QROC plane" (see Figure 6.2). Since we restrict attention only to random or legitimate tests, all the test points lie above and to the right of the point $(0, 0)$ which is called the "Random Quality

Receiver Operating Characteristic Point," "Random QROC" for short. The tests themselves, once again, form a swarm of points in the QROC plane.

By definition of the family, the point (0, 0) is always included in the family. The leaf-shaped figure obtained by joining all the test points in the base and the Random QROC we will call the Test "QROC." Most, but not all the tests in the test family lie within the Test QROC. The ones that are missing lie below and to the left of Tests #8 and #4, the highest and right-most test points in the QROC plane.

The transition from the Test ROC to the Test QROC can be visualized by imagining that a thread is run through the Random ROC in Figure 6.1 and pulled tight to draw all those random test points into a single point that becomes the Random QROC. Then the configuration is flattened out. The arc-shaped Test ROC thus translates into the leaf-shaped Test QROC in a one-to-one remapping. In the process all the tests in the base that lie on the Test ROC also lie on the Test QROC.

What advantage is there to this reshaping? The most salient is that it becomes very easy to identify the test with optimal sensitivity and that with optimal specificity. The test highest on the Test QROC is the one with optimal sensitivity (Test #8 in Figure 6.2); the test furthest to the right on the Test QROC is the one with optimal specificity (Test #4 in Figure 6.2). Later we will show that any test on the Test QROC between these two tests (e.g., Test #1) may lay claim to optimality on some basis, and one of these is the optimally efficient test (in this case, Test #1).

The test recommended by Garth et al. (1983) was, in fact, Test #1, i.e., the one that will later be shown to have optimal efficiency. Once again, the basis of their selection was not stipulated, but here we will be able to document their choice.

For a study based on Naturalistic Sampling, as this one was, the Chi-Square test statistic used to test the legitimacy of the test is:

$$\chi^2 = N_0 \cdot \kappa(1, 0) \cdot \kappa(0, 0) .$$

This identifies an interesting further advantage to the QROC over the ROC. What this indicates is that the statistic used to test the legitimacy of any test point is proportional to the area of the rectangle formed between the test point in the QROC plane and the Random QROC. The proportionality constant is the sample size in Naturalistic

Sampling (5.5) and the weighted sample size in both Retrospective (5.7) and Prospective (5.9) Sampling. Thus any point inside the QROC plane, i.e., not lying on either the x- or the y-axis will be statistically significant provided only the sample size is large enough. For this reason the statistical significance of the Chi-Square test statistic is not the best way to judge the quality of a test. For a fixed sample size, the tests that are "most statistically significant," i.e., those with the lowest p-levels, are those furthest away from the Random QROC, as logically must be true.

All Q-Level Tests

Those accustomed to think of the ROC as a smooth curve (for nested families) may tend to feel that the notion of a family of tests as a swarm in the ROC plane seems somewhat chaotic. Far from it: There are strict mathematical rules governing the behavior of this swarm (Kraemer, 1988).

Begin by defining the line connecting the point (P', P) on the Random ROC with the ideal point at $(1, 1)$ as the "diagnosis line" (see Figures 6.1 and 6.3). By definition of the sensitivity and specificity:

$$P \cdot SE + P' \cdot SP' = Q .$$

Geometrically this means that all Q-level tests evaluated in the population having prevalence P must lie on a line parallel to the diagnosis line and intersecting the Random ROC at the point (Q', Q) (see Figure 6.3). Q-level tests do not just scatter all over the place; they quite literally line up in the ROC plane. In Figure 6.3, for example, tests #4 and #7 lie on a line parallel to the diagnosis line, and thus must have nearly equal levels. In fact their levels are both about 27%.

If you were put a straightedge along the diagnosis line, all the tests with level (Q) equal to the prevalence (P) would lie on that straight line. If you were then to move the straightedge parallel to the diagnosis line upward, you would successively locate all the tests at higher and higher levels. Similarly, if you were to move the straightedge downward, you would successively locate all the tests at lower and lower levels. In short, if we were to define the north-south axis of the ROC plane by the diagnosis line's direction, the east-west

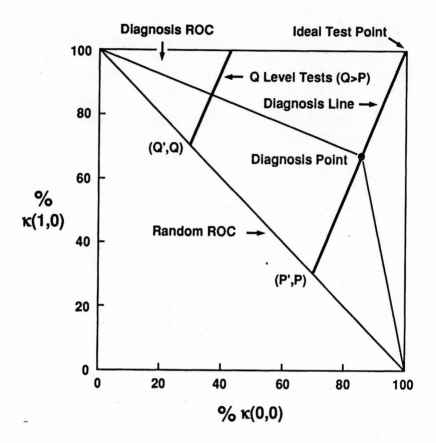

Figure 6.3. Geometry of the ROC

position of a test point in the ROC plane is determined by its level;
the north-south position is determined by its quality.

The problem is that the north-south axis is determined by the
prevalence, and thus by both the diagnosis and the population sampled. Its direction changes from one population to another. Without
the diagnosis line in the population being studied, to what extent the
position of a test point reflects its level and to what extent its quality
cannot be visually judged. That is the geometric counterpart of what
analytically was discussed by describing sensitivity and specificity
as uncalibrated measures.

In Figure 6.1, the diagnosis line was depicted. The prevalence in this population for this diagnosis was 41%. Thus the diagnosis line extends from (.59, .41) to (1, 1). As noted above, one can then see that Tests #4 and #7 must be the same level, a level less than 41% (about 27%) since they lie on a line parallel to the diagnosis line and below it. One can also see that the tests in order of level must be #8, #3, #2, #9, #5, #1, #10, #4 and #7, #6, #11. Tests #8, #3, #2, and #9 must have level greater than the prevalence of 41%; tests #5, #1, #10, #4, #7, #6 and #11 must have level less than the prevalence of 41%. But the only tests worthy of further interest are those within the set of the highest quality, those on the ROC, namely #8, #1, #4, and #11. A new insight: Each of these tests on the ROC must have a different level. Consequently, choosing the optimal test from among those on the ROC is tantamount to selecting the best level.

The behavior of tests in the QROC plane is equally orderly. From the above relationship:

$$P(SE - Q) + P'(SP' - Q) = 0,$$

or

$$PQ' \kappa(1, 0) - P'Q\kappa(0, 0) = 0.$$

Thus

$$\kappa(1, 0)/\kappa(0, 0) = P'Q/PQ',$$

The ratio $P'Q/PQ'$ is called the "odds ratio" of the marginal probabilities. The odds ratio equals 1 if and only if the level of the test equals the prevalence. When the level exceeds the prevalence, the odds ratio is above 1 and when prevalence exceeds level, the odds ratio is below 1.

Thus all Q-level tests lie on a line from (0, 0), whose tilt is determined by the relationship of the prevalence to the level of the test (see Figure 6.4). All tests with level equal to the prevalence lie on the main diagonal line, the diagnosis line. All tests with level greater than the prevalence lie above that line; all tests with level less than the prevalence lie below that line.

If you were to put a straightedge on the diagnosis line and pivot it upward, you would successively locate higher and higher level

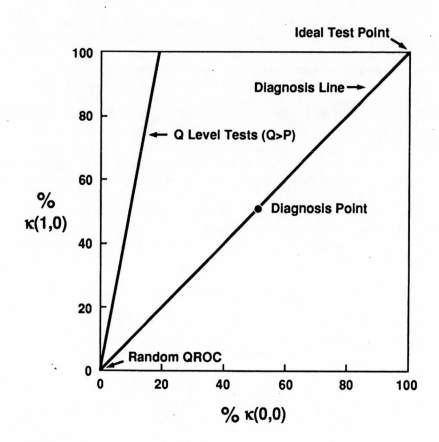

Figure 6.4. Geometry of the QROC

tests. If you were to pivot it downward, you would successively locate lower and lower level tests. In the QROC the angular distance from horizontal (or vertical) is determined by the relationship of level to the prevalence; the distance from the Random QROC, the point (0, 0), indicates the quality of the test.

Once again one could repeat the exercises done above with the ROC using the QROC in Figure 6.2 to show geometrically how one can recognize that two tests, like #4 and #7, are at the same level, how one can rank the tests in order of level, how one can recognize the tests with level higher than the prevalence and lower, and, finally, once

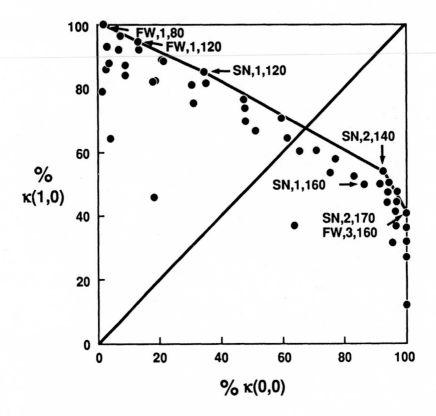

Figure 6.5. QROC of the Tests for Diabetes
SOURCE: Galen & Gambino, 1975.

again, where the optimal tests are on the QROC. In addition, one can quickly see the tests not likely to be significantly better than random (those near the stem of the QROC leaf). One can locate the optimally sensitive test (#8), the optimally specific test (#4), and all the other potentially optimal tests (#1).

Now no longer novices at examining the QROC, we can return to examine the 136 tests for diabetes considered earlier and by Galen and Gambino (1975). The tests are presented in Figure 6.5. (All are there, but not all are individually visible because of overlapping locations.)

The optimally sensitive test lies in the upper left-hand corner of the "leaf," the Folin-Wu test, 1 hour after the test meal, with a cut-off of 80 mg/dl. The optimally specific test lies on the far right, a tie between the Somogyi-Nelson test, 2 hours after the test meal, with a cut-off of 170 mg/dl and the Folin-Wu test, 3 hours after the test meal, with a cut-off of 160 mg/dl. Also on the QROC are three other tests: the Folin-Wu test, 1 hour after the test meal with a cut-off of 120 mg/dl; the Somogyi-Nelson test, 1 hour after the test meal with a cut-off of 120 mg/dl, and the Somogyi-Nelson test, 2 hours after the test meal with a cut-off of 140 mg/dl. These tests will be found to be optimal in a sense we have yet to define, but the Somogyi-Nelson test, 2 hours after the test meal with a cut-off of 140 mg/dl will, in particular, be found to be the optimally efficient test.

What is now particularly to be noticed is that the test selected as best by Galen and Gambino (1975), the Somogyi-Nelson test, 1 hour after the test meal, with a cut-off of 160 mg/dl, is well below the QROC (or the ROC). In no sense can it be an optimal choice within this family of tests for there are many tests even within the family with *both* better sensitivity and better specificity.

What Is a Good Test? The Diagnosis ROC, QROC

Back to the crucial question: When is a test a "good" one? Several partial answers have already been offered, and we can now finally pursue the question to its logical end.

1. A test that is on or near the Random ROC or the Random QROC is clearly *not* a "good" test, for by tossing a coin or using a random number table, any amateur can do as well in diagnosis or prognosis. More specifically, any test found not significantly better than a random one on a 2 × 2 Chi-Square test is not a "good" test, for it cannot even be empirically demonstrated to be legitimate. One definition of a "good" test, the very least demanding one, is that a test that does better than random decision making is a good test.

It is remarkable that many of the medical test evaluations in the medical research literature seem to be satisfied with this definition in that all that is demonstrated in documentation of the quality of a test is the statistical significance of the test. As shown above, any test that is even slightly better than tossing a coin, a die, or using a random number table, can be shown to be statistically significant merely by taking a large enough sample size. To a medical consumer whose life or well-being may depend on the quality of that test, that is simply not good enough.

2. A test that lies in the area between the Random ROC and the Test ROC, or equivalently in the area between the Random QROC and the Test QROC, is *not* a "good" test. In this case, there are demonstrably better tests even within the family. Demonstrably inferior tests are simply not good enough.

A slightly better definition of a "good test" is one that lies on the test family ROC. Unfortunately that may include tests that are not much better than random, for tests with very high or very low level will be on the ROC, not because of their quality, but because of their extreme level. Still not good enough, although many research reports that have used the Signal Detection approach to medical test evaluation seem to accept that type of definition.

3. A much better definition is that all tests on the test QROC between the optimally sensitive and the optimally specific tests are "good tests" provided they can be demonstrated to be legitimate. Yet this too is problematic. If the test family is based on information only slightly relevant to the diagnosis and disorder and the sample size is large, the *best* of such a set of tests may still be little better than random decision making. Still not good enough.

What would we ideally demand? Clearly what is needed is some clinically and statistically acceptable standard of what constitutes a "good test." Fortunately, that decision has already been de facto made, at least theoretically. In choosing a diagnostic procedure as the gold standard against which the tests are evaluated, that diagnosis has already been defined as a clinically acceptable definition of a "good test." What remains is to evaluate statistically the performance of this particular test in the same terms as we would evaluate any other test.

For this particular test (a test equivalent to the diagnosis), $p_i = q_i$ for all patients. Thus the prevalence equals the level of the test ($P = Q$) in any population. The correlation between the diagnosis and the test is, of course, perfect: $\rho = 1$, and the variances are the same ($\sigma_q = \sigma_p$). Thus the sensitivity and specificity in terms of the basic model are:

$$SE = P + P'\kappa, \qquad \kappa(1, 0) = \kappa,$$

$$SP = P' + Pk_D, \qquad \kappa(0, 0) = \kappa_D$$

where κ_D is the coefficient of reproducibility of the diagnosis. Since the level of this test equals its prevalence, it lies on the diagnosis line in both the ROC and QROC planes. More precisely, it lies on both those lines a distance from the Random ROC or QROC to the Ideal Test Point at $(1, 1)$ proportional to the coefficient of reproducibility of the diagnosis in that population, κ_D (see Figures 6.3 and 6.4).

The ROC of the family of tests based only on the diagnosis (a base of one test, the diagnosis itself) consists of two straight lines, one from $(0, 1)$ to the diagnosis point, and one from the diagnosis point to $(1, 0)$: the Diagnosis ROC (see Figure 6.3). The QROC of the family of tests based on the diagnosis consists of one straight line from $(0, 0)$ to the diagnosis point, coinciding with the main diagonal in the QROC plane (see Figure 6.4).

If the ROC of a family of tests under evaluation approaches or lies above the Diagnosis ROC, then there are tests in that family as good or better than the gold standard and thus unequivocally "good tests." The rule for the QROC is even easier: if the quality index of any test approaches or exceeds κ_D, that test is a "good test," in that its quality approaches or exceeds that of the diagnosis used as a gold standard.

These results require some orientation. The diagnosis point can only approach the ideal point with a near absolutely reproducible diagnosis. Koran (1975) reviewed a number of studies in which the reproducibility of various medical diagnostic procedures was assessed. Spitzer and Fleiss (1974) reviewed several psychiatric diagnostic procedures. Earlier in this book (Chapter 2), I presented three detailed examples of evaluation of certain diagnoses. This is far from a survey of the field, but what is seen there is typical.

Very few diagnoses have a coefficient of reproducibility exceeding .8. Diagnoses such as those based on EKG, X-ray, clinical evaluations of signs and symptoms, and subjective diagnostic opinions almost uniformly have coefficients of reproducibility below .8. The κ_D for the photofluorogram was .409, for gastroduodenal X-ray was .389, for pathologists' tissue classification was .591, for various psychiatric disorders ranged from .245 to .566. Detre et al. (1975) reported that the reproducibility of coronary angiography was about halfway between random and perfect, suggesting a κ_D of about .5.

Since the coefficient of reproducibility of the diagnosis serves as the target in the definition of a "good test," these values suggest what magnitudes of quality indices might be expected for "good" tests, now defined as those as good as the gold standard or diagnosis.

Such reasonable and realistic standards are essential. If tests whose ROCs do not closely approach the ideal point are labeled "poor," then very few tests, including the gold standards themselves will ever be found to be good tests. This creates a "Catch 22" situation. In those areas where diagnosis is poorest, the gold standards will be poor. Tests evaluated against these gold standards will have ROCs and QROCs that come nowhere near the ideal point, not because the tests are poor, but, rather, because the gold standard is nonreproducible. If the test evaluator does not consider this fact as a part of the evaluation, tests that are far better than the gold standard will be discarded. Then, when it is most vital to identify good new tests to supplement or to replace poor existing diagnoses, it will be least possible to do so.

While this has not been how medical test evaluations have been done in the past, this is not merely a theoretical answer. How would one *in practice* use this approach in finding the diagnosis point and the Diagnosis ROC and QROC?

For many diagnostic tests, the answer is relatively easy. Each patient (or a *random* subsample thereof) could be blindly evaluated for diagnosis twice during the period of testing, a second opinion on the diagnosis. From this information, the coefficient of reproducibility for the diagnosis can be estimated, located in the ROC or QROC planes, and the Diagnosis ROC and QROC drawn. This could then be used as a standard against which to evaluate the family of tests under evaluation.

Realistically, in some cases, obtaining an independent second diagnosis is not possible. For example, two full and separate coronary angiogram procedures per patient imposes an intolerable hardship on the patient. In this case a partial replication can be used: The entire procedure is not repeated, but each coronary angiogram is read twice, independently, by two diagnosticians. Since the major source of non-reproducibility is frequently in the reading, this serves as a viable alternative.

In some cases, particularly in the case of prognostic tests, even a partial replication is not possible. How can one ask a patient to repeat the same follow-up twice? In this situation, one could define a standard by using the best prognostic test known to date.

For example, one might use the best known test based on evaluation of signs and symptoms or the consensus prognosis of a panel of experts as a standard against which to compare the exercise stress test as a prognostic test for a coronary event during follow-up after myocardial infarction. Unless there are *no* known tests for the disorder and expert prognosis has *no* value in a particular situation, this type of strategy can always be applied. If, however, there were no known tests for the disorder and no valid clinical prognosis, then any legitimate test would be a "good" one.

To summarize: If all that is required in the evaluation of a medical test is the assurance that the test is better than random (a legitimate test), then all one needs to do is to demonstrate that the 2×2 Chi-Square test is significant (thus that the Test ROC arches higher than the Random ROC, or that the Test QROC loops away from the Random ROC.)

If all that is required is the selection of the optimal test within a family of tests, then all one needs to do is to obtain the QROC. The optimally sensitive, the optimally specific, and all the other tests eligible to be optimal in some as yet unspecified sense, are then easily identified.

If, however, one wishes assurance that the test is "good" in some stronger sense, the evaluator must provide some standard of how a "good" test will behave. A second independent diagnosis, a partially replicated independent diagnosis, or the best available test known to date for the disorder of interest, should be included in the evaluation. The ROC or QROC of this internal standard serves as a target for the ROC or QROC of the test under evaluation. There are, in fact, almost no published medical test evaluations that have done this.

What Is the Ideal Test? The Disorder ROC, QROC

Can a Test ROC really lie *above* the Diagnosis ROC, or a test quality index really *exceed* the coefficient of reproducibility, κ_D? Yes, it can, but there is an absolute upper limit to where a Test ROC and QROC can lie determined by the quality of the diagnosis in the population under study. It happens to lie above the Diagnosis ROC and QROC. However, this limit is theoretical, is usually unknown, and is difficult even to estimate. Its location bears on the issue of realistic evaluation, however. Let us, for this reason, pursue this essentially theoretical issue.

First of all, how can one improve on the gold standard? Easily: take two independent gold standards and classify the patient on the basis of the consensus of the two. There are here two possible referents. The patient might be classified positive: (1) if both are positive or (2) if at least one is positive. This defines a small nested family of tests with an ROC and QROC that will lie above the Diagnosis ROC and QROC.

One can then improve on that by taking three (or four or five, . . .) independent diagnoses per patient and classifying the patient on the basis of consensus. There are as many referents as there are repeated diagnoses: if all are positive, if all but one are positive, etc. For each number of repeated diagnoses (2, 3, 4, . . .) one can obtain an ROC or QROC, and each is successively higher than the last.

Eventually, however, as one increases the number of repeated diagnoses per patient, the ROC and QROC approach a limit defined as follows:

For any level Q, the test referent is defined:

$$q_i = 1 \quad \text{if} \quad p_i > C(Q),$$

$$q_i = w \quad \text{if} \quad p_i = C(Q),$$

$$q_i = 0 \quad \text{if} \quad p_i < C(Q),$$

where $C(Q)$ is the percentile of the distribution of the p_i in the population defined as:

$$\text{Prob}[p_i > C(Q)] + w\text{Prob}[p_i = C(Q)] = Q.$$

This limiting case is that obtained when a theoretically infinite number of independent repeated diagnoses per patient are obtained, and the patient is classified positive according to the proportion of positive diagnoses. This procedure identifies the proportion Q of the population most likely to have a positive diagnosis. By the way validity of the diagnosis was defined (Assumption 3 in Chapter 2), this must also identify those in the population most likely to have the disorder. For this reason, it is appropriate to call the upper limit the *Disorder ROC or QROC*.

In reality, of course, we cannot obtain an infinite number of repeated diagnoses per patient. It is hard enough to obtain two in order to find the Diagnosis ROC or QROC. However, in Chapter 2 we

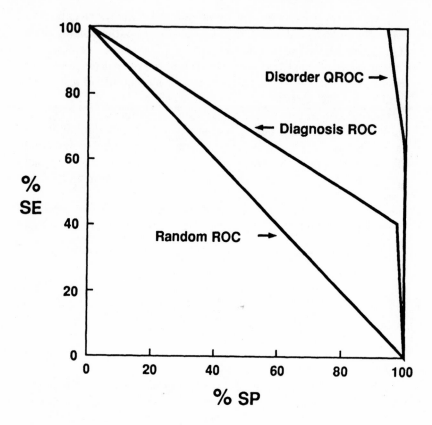

Figure 6.6. Photofluorogram ROC
SOURCE: Yerushalmy, 1956.

examined a few cases when a fairly large number of independent diagnoses were obtained and detailed information made available.

Yerushalmy (1956) reported eight independent evaluations of pho-tofluorograms. The estimated prevalence in that population was 2.2%, a very low-risk group, and the coefficient of reproducibility was .409, a moderately reproducible diagnosis. The estimated Diagnosis and Disorder ROCs and QROCs appear in Figures 6.6 and 6.7.

The point to be noted is that the ideal point, for most test evalua-tions, is beyond reach for diagnoses having the kind of prevalence and reproducibility that are typical. No test, for example (sampling

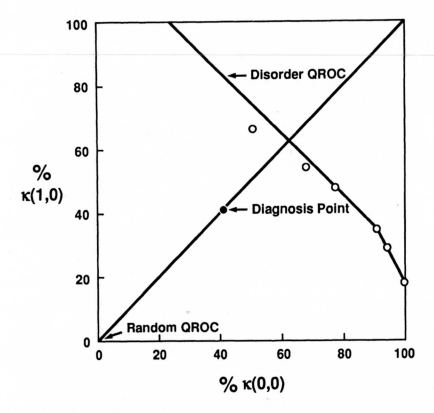

Figure 6.7. Photofluorogram QROC
SOURCE: Yerushalmy, 1956.

error aside), can achieve both a sensitivity and specificity of 95% evaluated against the diagnosis in the Yerushalmy study. Such a test point would be outside the Disorder ROC. The limitation is imposed not only by the quality of tests, but also by the quality of the diagnosis used as the gold standard.

Those familiar with Signal Detection results in the medical research literature may find this comment puzzling if not incredible. Many test ROCs reported in the literature seem to approach the ideal point closely, in direct empirical contradiction of the above assertion.

In reviewing the results that create this impression, it appears that many of these examples are theoretical, either hypothetical or computer simulations, not real situations with real patients and real data. Others describe real situations that are based on Pseudo-Retrospective Sampling and are thus quite possibly invalid. Finally, there are some diagnoses evaluated in moderate-risk populations having high enough reproducibility that such a result is possible.

To give an example: Speicher and Smith (1983) pose the following problem to their readers: If the sensitivity were 95% and the specificity were also 95% in a population with prevalence 0.5%, what would the predictive values of the test be? What the authors undoubtedly meant to do was to induce their readers to use a Bayes' estimator (see Chapter 5). However, in the way the problem is posed, the readers might well infer that these figures represent real tests, tests they are likely to encounter in practice, ones with a sensitivity and specificity of 95% in a population whose prevalence is as low as 0.5%.

Hypothetical examples, to be instructive and useful should mimic what is likely to be seen in the real world. This has not always been done in presentations of medical test evaluations, and such examples raise false hopes.

In fact, in low-risk populations such as those in Figures 6.6 and 6.7, because of: (1) the location of the diagnosis line very near the right border of the ROC plane, and (2) the difficulty in finding diagnoses with very high coefficients of reproducibility in a low-risk population, it is evident from the geometry of the situation that very few tests will have high sensitivity. In such a population it is easy to find tests with high specificity. One need only set the referent of a test so that the level is lower than the prevalence, and the specificity will be near 100%. For similar reasons, it is generally easy to find tests with high sensitivity in high-risk populations, but very difficult to find tests with high specificity. Whatever is rarer is harder to find: a positive diagnosis in a low-risk population, a negative diagnosis in a high-risk one.

Invalid sampling procedures (Pseudo-Retrospective Sampling in particular) create further problems. We noted above that it is easy to find high sensitivity in a high-risk population and to find high specificity in a low-risk population. Now, if one samples a clinical population (high-risk) to estimate sensitivity, and another low-risk population to estimate specificity, both values may well be very high. If one graphs such a sensitivity estimate against such a specificity estimate, the result is *not* a test point on the ROC plane. An ROC requires the sensitivity and specificity of a test in the *same* population. What does result, if mistaken as an ROC, looks remarkably good, frequently much better than any true ROC, and, in particular, much better than the ROC of the test in any *single* population in which it is likely to be used. When the test is one like a screening test for AIDS, the errors of using results from Pseudo-Retrospective Sampling to create ROC-like results may cost lives.

The Myth of the Constancy of Sensitivity and Specificity

The belief that the sensitivity and specificity of a medical test, and hence that the ROC of a test, remain constant as one moves from one clinical population to another with the same test and diagnosis, is a seductive belief. It is widely accepted among medical researchers and deeply rooted. I have been told that questions on the medical board exams in the past have required belief in the constancy of sensitivity and specificity to get the "correct" answer. The belief underlies many of the published evaluations of medical tests, even when the belief itself is not clearly articulated, and thus may be essential to the documentation of many of the medical tests currently in wide use. Thus it is vital that the issue be directly and unequivocally faced.

Because the belief often appears in conjunction with a statement of Bayes' Theorem, some medical researchers believe that the constancy of sensitivity and specificity is a mathematical fact, somehow part of Bayes' Theorem. How can Bayes' Theorem be wrong? The constancy of sensitivity and specificity is *not* a part of Bayes' Theorem. Bayes' Theorem defines a mathematical relationship among conditional and unconditional probabilities within a single population and has nothing specifically to do with medical tests. To question the constancy of sensitivity and specificity raises no question about the truth of Bayes' Theorem.

There are many published tables and nomograms that use Bayes' Theorem and purport to convert the (assumed constant) sensitivity and specificity to its predictive value of a positive test for populations having different prevalences (e.g., Fagen, 1975; Galen & Gambino,

1975). These tables and nomograms have limited utility. They can be used to compute the predictive value of a positive test for one population if the sensitivity, specificity, and prevalence are known in that population. They cannot be used in general to take the sensitivity and specificity in one population and make any projections as to what would happen in other clinical populations. The publication of such tables was based on the belief of the constancy of sensitivity and specificity.

To give an example: After the evaluation of the tests for diabetes discussed above, Galen and Gambino (1975) report that the original authors "Remein and Wilkerson caution against generalizing their findings to other populations," but immediately add "The general relationship, however, can be expected to remain true" (p.111). They then use the sensitivity and specificity calculated from samples from a population having a prevalence of about 12% to estimate the predictive values of other undefined clinical populations having prevalences of 1%, 3%, and 5% using the tables they provided. The original authors, however, were correct. The results should not be generalized, unless documentation is provided that the sensitivities and specificities, at least in these three other populations with prevalences of 1%, 3%, 5%, are the same as those in the population sampled and studied.

Many statisticians believe that the constancy of sensitivity and specificity is an empirical fact based on observation and experience within the context of medical test evaluation. When first I encountered medical testing research problems, I was told that it was a well-established fact. It took many puzzling experiences before I asked for the empirical documentation and found there was none. In fact, when systematic studies have been done (Hlatky et al., 1984; Hlatky et al., 1987) the results unequivocally indicate that sensitivity and specificity are not constants, that they change from one clinical population to another. We have seen some of these results in earlier chapters (see Table 5.4), and more will arise in future examples.

Nevertheless, it is all too easy to ignore or reinterpret evidence when it both runs counter to deeply held beliefs and, moreover, complicates evaluations. As a result, many responses to such evidence have included attribution of such results to inadequate sampling, subtle and unacknowledged variations in the diagnosis or in the test protocol or referent, inadequate sample size, inadequate analysis, etc. (Diamond, 1986; Swets, 1982). In short, the evidence is simply denied.

If the belief in the constancy of sensitivity and specificity were valid, the test ROC *would* remain constant for all population, the so-called ROC independence of prevalence. Thus if an optimal test were selected for one population, the same test would remain optimal for all. It would not matter whether one specified a relevant population, or how one sampled it. Any sort of sloppy sampling procedure would do, only provided that, once sampled, the diagnosis and test results for those sampled were carefully done. The population and sampling issues of Chapter 5 would be mere statistical quibbles.

The bottom line of these arguments must be the necessary and sufficient conditions that sensitivity and specificity of a test remains constant across all populations (Kraemer, 1987): (1) The diagnosis must be absolutely reproducible in all clinical populations ($p_i = 0$ or 1 for all patients), and (2) There must be absolute homogeneity in response to the test for all patients having a positive diagnosis ($q_i = A$ when $p_i = 1$) and for all patients having a negative diagnosis ($q_i = 1 - B$ when $p_i = 0$), where A and B are two fixed constants.

The sufficiency of the two conditions is easy to prove. If the conditions were true, then in any population, no matter how defined, the only patients with a positive diagnosis would have $q_i = A$. Thus the sensitivity in every population would be A. The only patients with a negative diagnosis would have $q_i = 1 - B$. Thus the specificity in every population is B.

The necessity of the two conditions requires a bit more effort. Suppose that the sensitivity were A in every population and the specificity B, but that one or the other of the two conditions above did not hold. To take one example, suppose there were patients with $0 < p_i < 1$ and $q_i > A$. Then in this population the sensitivity must exceed A. Suppose there were patients with $0 < p_i < 1$ and $q_i < A$. In this population the sensitivity would be less than A. Similarly, one can enumerate every case not covered by the two conditions and show that there would be a violation of the stipulation that the sensitivity is A and specificity B for every population. Thus if there were constancy, the two conditions must hold.

Empirical results indicate that there are very few absolutely reproducible diagnoses in the real world. Condition 1 above almost never holds. Even if there were a few absolutely reproducible diagnoses, the absolute homogeneity required by Condition 2 within each diagnostic group would preclude any variation due to stage or severity of the disorder or to individual differences in symptom expression.

What all this suggests is that medical test evaluation should be based on the assumption that sensitivity and specificity describe the performance of a test against a diagnosis *in the particular population being sampled*. If there is to be a claim that the sensitivity and specificity in one clinical population is the same (or approximately the same) as that in another, scientific integrity and medical ethics require that this claim be empirically documented.

Summary

Sensitivity and specificity are long-used and very familiar descriptors of medical test performance. The question that has been raised, however, is whether these descriptors of performance are also descriptors of quality. The answer appears to be negative. These are uncalibrated measures that reflect *both* quality and level. To what extent the magnitude of a sensitivity or specificity reflects level and not quality is not clear without further information.

For this reason I have suggested that sensitivity and specificity be calibrated so that the quality of sensitivity $\kappa(1, 0)$ be 0% and the quality of specificity $\kappa(0, 0)$ be 0% when the test performance is at the random level, and the upper limit (usually unachievable) for both be 100%. These measures can then be used to compare the tests within a family of tests or tests within the family against a criterion of excellence. With these measures, the optimally sensitive and optimally specific tests are simple to identify.

More simple yet is to graph the quality of the sensitivity and specificity for each test in the family in what was called a QROC. This represents an adaptation of the Signal Detection methods of medical test evaluation based on graphing the sensitivity and specificity for each test: the ROC.

Both the ROC and QROC follow strict geometric rules. A great deal of information on the performances of the tests in a family can be garnered from close visual scrutiny of the ROC and, more particularly, the QROC.

The Random ROC and Random QROC represent the worst of all possible medical tests: random tests. A "good" test is represented by the diagnosis used as the gold standard. Its location in the ROC plane or the QROC place is determined by the prevalence in the population and, especially, by the reproducibility of the diagnosis in the population of interest.

This observation finally resolves the problem of answering the fundamental question of whether the tests under evaluation are "good" tests or not. If their locations in the ROC or QROC plane are near or beyond the Diagnosis ROC or QROC, that unambiguously signals that they are good tests.

A test or tests evaluated against a gold standard can be located above the ROC or QROC of the gold standard itself, but there is a limiting ROC or QROC that is determined by the quality of the gold standard. Where this lies is theoretically known, but is difficult and often impossible to determine in practice. However, its location generally precludes obtaining a test very near the Ideal Test Point.

Estimation of the sensitivity and specificity and of the indices that indicate their quality depends on adequate sampling and estimation methods. As noted earlier, there is some flexibility. One can use Naturalistic, Retrospective, or Prospective Sampling, with the methods of estimation appropriate to each. One cannot use Pseudo-Retrospective Sampling without incurring a high risk of invalid results. Necessary and sufficient conditions for the validity of this sampling method include the perfect reproducibility of the gold standard, a rare occurrence.

Errors based on inadequate sampling and estimation are quite common in the medical research literature. It may well be that many of the medical tests in common use are there only because of statistical errors—a sobering thought.

7

Predictive Values:
The Bayesian Approach,
Risk Ratios, and Odds Ratio

Problems with Predictive Values

The predictive values of a positive test and of a negative test were briefly introduced in Chapter 5: the predictive value of a positive test (PVP) as the probability that a patient with a positive test has a positive diagnosis; the predictive value of a negative (PVN) test as the probability that a patient with a negative test has a negative diagnosis. As in the case of sensitivity and specificity, these are clear, intuitively appealing, and easily estimated descriptors of the performance of a medical test.

Generally, researchers interested in the development and documentation of a test seem to find sensitivity and specificity more appealing. On the other hand, clinicians and clinical researchers who are more interested in how the test can be used to characterize the patient or to make clinical decisions for the patient, seem to find predictive values more appealing. When information on test performance is presented by a test proponent to clinicians in terms of sensitivity and specificity, very often the immediate response is to use Bayes' Theorem to obtain predictive values.

Clearly a medical test can perform well only if it characterizes the patients well and vice versa. It does not make good common sense that the results obtained from the point of view of the test proponent and that of a clinician differ. Yet that often seems to be the case. Different conclusions as to the value of the test might be reached depending on whether the focus of interest is sensitivity and specificity on the one hand, or predictive values on the other. Such conflicting results are troublesome to a statistician as well as to a medical consumer.

Conflicting results aside, use of the predictive values presents few statistical problems. While predictive values, like the sensitivity and specificity, are uncalibrated measures, how to judge the magnitudes is well known and consistently applied in the medical literature. Unlike the situation with sensitivity and specificity, when comparing different tests against a single gold standard in a population, the optimal value of the predictive values and their maximal values coincide. As a result, the identification of the optimal test referent in a family of tests is less problematic than it is when using sensitivity and specificity. The predictive values vary from one clinical population to another, as do sensitivity and specificity, but that is well-known, unlike the situation vis-à-vis the putative constancy of sensitivity and specificity. As a result, the evaluation of medical tests using predictive values, from a statistician's viewpoint, is clear and straightforward.

From a consumer's viewpoint, there is one easily remedied problem. The focus of medical researchers in evaluating tests tends to be almost exclusively on the predictive value of a *positive* test (PVP). Galen and Gambino (1975), for example, present sensitivity, specificity, efficiency, and predictive value of a positive test, never mentioning the predictive value of a negative test. The same is true of other discussions of medical test evaluations.

A patient who undergoes a routine physical and is told that tests indicate that he is "healthy" should be able to have some confidence in the results. If the predictive value of a negative test were low, such confidence would be misplaced. Many disorders, such a cancer, are treatable only if detected early enough and deadly otherwise. Consequently, false negative results must be taken at least as seriously as false positive ones. Similarly, in AIDS blood screening tests, false positive tests are wasteful, but false negative tests, those indicated by low predictive value of a negative test, are deadly.

For such reasons, *both* of the predictive values will be given emphasis in the following presentation. Consideration will be very brief, for
it will rapidly become apparent that there is no fundamental difference between the Bayesian approach (predictive values) and the
results of Signal Detection methods (sensitivity and specificity), other
than calibration.

The Basic Model

Mathematically the two predictive values are expressed as:

$$PVP = TP/Q; \qquad PVN = TN/Q'.$$

In terms of the basic model (Chapter 3)

$$PVP = P + \rho\sigma_p\sigma_q/Q; \qquad PVN = P' + \rho\sigma_p\sigma_q/Q'.$$

Thus for a random test ($\rho = 0$), the predictive value of a positive test
equals the prevalence (P), and the predictive value of a negative test
equals the complement of the prevalence (P'). For a legitimate test, ($\rho
> 0$) the predictive value of a positive test exceeds the prevalence,
(PVP > P) and the predictive value of a negative test exceeds the
complement of the prevalence (PVN > P').

The usual statements in the medical literature take the form that
the posttest risk following a positive test (here PVP) should exceed
the pretest risk (here P), and that the posttest risk following a negative
test (here 1 – PVN) should be less than the pretest risk (P). Aside from
semantic problems inherent in using the terms pre- and posttest risk
(see Chapter 2), the results are completely consistent.

Once again, assessment of the magnitude of the predictive values
depends on their positions within the range of their values. Here the
effective range of the predictive value of a positive test is P to 1; that
of a negative test is P' to 1. This is somewhat simpler to deal with than
were the effective ranges of sensitivity and specificity, for here the
ranges are fixed once and for all by the population and the diagnosis.
In the case of sensitivity and specificity, they varied with the level of
the tests. When a family of tests is under consideration for a single
diagnosis in a single population, the predictive values all vary on the

Table 7.1 Evaluation of the Folin-Wu Blood Test for Diabetes Done 3 Hours After the Test Meal

Referent	Q(%)	PVP(%)	PVN(%)	κ(1.0)(%)	κ(0,0)(%)
80		Insufficient Sample Size			
90	94.3	12.5	93.9	49.2	0.4
100	68.8	16.3	97.2	*77.2	4.8
110	38.2	25.8	96.4	69.9	15.6
120	20.2	41.2	95.2	60.7	33.1
130	12.3	59.2	94.5	54.4	58.5
140	8.5	81.4	94.3	53.1	78.8
150	6.2	94.4	93.4	45.2	93.6
160	5.2	100.0	92.7	39.8	**100.0
170	4.3	100.0	91.9	32.8	100.0
180	3.5	100.0	91.1	26.0	100.0
190	3.5	100.0	91.1	26.0	100.0

SOURCE: Galen and Gambino (1975), p. 107; Remein and Wilkerson (1961)
NOTES: $P = 12.1\%$
*Optimal PVP: $> 160 mg/dl$, $\kappa(0,0) = 100.0\%$
**Optimal PVN: $> 100 mg/dl$, $\kappa(1,0) = 77.2\%$

same scale. As a result, the optimal predictive values are the maximal values. That prevents confusion.

Nevertheless, the quality of the predictive values continues to depend on where they stand within their range and are more succinctly expressed with reference to that range:

$$\kappa(0, 0) = (PVP - P)/P' \qquad \kappa(1, 0) = (PVN - P')/P$$

With that it becomes apparent that the quality of the sensitivity is exactly equal to the quality of the predictive value of a negative test. The quality of the specificity is exactly equal to the quality of the predictive value of a positive test. The apparent differences between sensitivity and specificity on the one hand, and predictive values on the other, are only a result of considering these values in their uncalibrated forms.

In Table 7.1 (taken from Galen & Gambino, 1975; Remein & Wilkerson, 1961) are presented the predictive values (Bayes' estimates) of the various referents for the Folin-Wu blood test, done 3 hours after the test meal: the same tests presented in terms of sensitivity and specificity in Table 6.1. The last two columns presenting quality indices are, of course, absolutely identical. The choice of the optimally sensitive test is the one with maximal predictive value of a negative test, that of the optimally specific test is the one with maximal predictive value of a positive test.

In Table 6.2 were presented the optimal tests for each of the various protocols based on optimizing sensitivity and specificity. If we were to select tests to optimize predictive values, the table would display exactly the same results except that the label "Optimal Sensitivity" would be replaced by "Optimal PVN" and "Optimal Specificity" by "Optimal PVP." Again the overall choice based on evaluation of the predictive values is absolutely identical. Such results allay the one statistical reservation about the Bayesian approach, that of the possible inconsistencies with other approaches resulting only from a different point of view. There can be no legitimate difference between conclusions based on proper use of Signal Detection methods and those on proper use of Bayesian methods. If one prefers to present sensitivity and specificity rather than predictive values as descriptors of test performance or vice versa or to present both, that should cause no discrepancies in conclusions of the evaluation process. The conclusions are based on the quality of these descriptive measures ($\kappa(1, 0)$ and $\kappa(0, 0)$), and the qualities are identical.

A Geometric Approach: The Test QROC

In the Signal Detection approach, each test could be located graphically by its sensitivity and specificity. A great deal of insight and information is available from visual perusal of such geometric presentation either in the form of the Test ROC, or even more so in the form of the QROC (Chapter 6).

The same approach can be used with the predictive values. Each test could be located by the predictive value of a positive test (PVP) and that of a negative test (PVN) (data presented in Table 7.2 for comparison with Table 6.3) as in Figure 7.1, where we once again review the results (Garth et al., 1983) of the evaluation of duplex ultrasound scanning (compare Figures 6.1 and 6.2).

Since legitimate tests have PVP exceeding P and PVN exceeding P', all legitimate tests evaluated in a population against a certain diagnosis must lie in the corner rectangle above the point (P, P'). If one

Table 7.2 Evaluation of the Duplex Ultrasound Scan for Carotid Artery
Stenosis

#	Referent[1]	$P(\%)$[2]	$PVP(\%)$	$PVN(\%)$	$\kappa(0,0)(\%)$	$\kappa(1,0)(\%)$
1	$VR > 1.5$	34.8	83.3	89.8	74.4	70.8
2	$SW > 40$	36.3	56.3	86.0	31.4	61.5
3	$VR > 1.5$ or $SW > 40$	34.8	55.7	94.6	32.0	84.4
4	$VR > 1.5$ and $SW > 40$	34.8	87.4	84.6	*80.7	55.8
5	$AS > 50\%$	41.0	72.5	80.0	53.5	51.2
6	$AS > 75\%$	41.0	84.2	69.1	73.2	24.7
7	$MV > 100$	36.3	72.0	77.2	56.0	37.2
8	> 1 criterion	36.3	57.2	97.2	32.8	*92.2
9	> 2 criteria	36.3	71.0	88.6	54.5	68.7
10	> 3 criteria	36.3	78.7	82.5	66.5	51.9
11	$+4$ criteria	36.3	83.5	70.9	74.2	19.7

SOURCE: Garth et al. (1983), pp. 823-827
NOTES: 1. Criteria:
  VR = Velocity Ratio
  SW = Spectral Width
  AS = Area Stenosis
  MV = Maximum Vinca
2. Prevalence estimates vary because of missing data.

defined a base of tests, the tests in the base would form a swarm in
that corner.

Early proponents of the Signal Detection methods apparently considered and rejected the possibility of defining the ROC in terms of
the predictive values, apparently because the points defined by the
predictive values swarmed rather than formed a smooth curve (Swets
& Pickett, 1982). We now know, however, that sensitivity and specificity form a smooth curve only for a univariate test response with
absolutely continuous response distribution and with a base of nested
referents. Otherwise the sensitivities and specificities of tests within
a family also swarm. Added to this concern was the implicit belief in
the constancy of sensitivity and specificity, suggesting that the ROC
would be "independent of prevalence." But now we know that such
constancy is a myth, and the sensitivity and specificity of tests vary
from one clinical population to another, just as do the predictive
values. Consequently, there is no longer any valid reason to discard
the possibility of using the predictive values to describe the geometric
location of a set of tests.

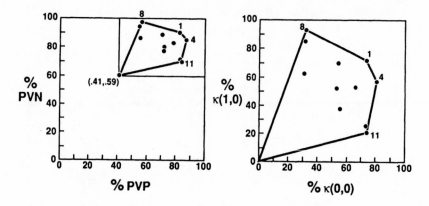

Figure 7.1 . ROC and QROC for the Duplex Ultrasound Scan
SOURCE: Garth et al., 1983.

And so, once again, we consider the family of tests defined on the base. Since all random tests are included in the base, the point (P, P') at which all random tests are located, is included in the family. The set of linear probability combinations of any two tests in the family is the set of test points on a curve connecting the two tests. Consequently, once again, the family of tests defines an area of the plane above and to the right of and including the point (P, P'). There is a familiar looking leaf-shaped configuration with its "stem" at the point (P, P'), looking very much like a miniature QROC.

In fact, that is exactly what it is. If each test is located by the quality of the predictive values, of course what results is the Test QROC (see Figure 7.1). All that happens in the transition within Figure 7.1 is that the configuration is enlarged and shifted so that the zero point of the Test QROC corresponds to the point (P, P').

Again, the choice of the optimal tests based on the quality of the sensitivity and specificity and that on the quality of the predictive values are both identified by selecting the points highest and furthest to the right in the Test QROC.

The problems of definition of a "good test" in terms of the Diagnosis QROC and the hypothetical location of the "ideal test" in terms of the Disorder QROC are identical to those when approaching the problem via sensitivity and specificity: There are no statistical differences engendered by choosing one approach versus another.

Risk Ratios, Odds Ratio, and the Test QROC

Not everyone who uses sensitivity and specificity uses the Signal Detection approach for evaluation of a medical test, nor does everyone who uses the predictive values use the Bayesian approach for evaluation of a medical test. Common alternatives in both cases are approaches similar to that used in assessing risks in epidemiological studies based on risk ratios or on the odds ratio.

There are, in fact, four different risk ratios that might be used:

$$RR1 = SE/(1 - SP),$$

$$RR2 = PVP/(1 - PVN),$$

$$RR3 = SP/(1 - SE),$$

$$RR4 = PVN/(1 - PVP).$$

The first two of these risk ratios, RR1 and RR2, are more common than are the latter two. In addition to the risk ratios, there is the odds ratio (Fleiss, 1981),that can be defined in terms of the four outcome probabilities:

$$\text{Odds Ratio} = TP \cdot TN/FP \cdot FN,$$

or in terms of sensitivity and specificity:

$$\text{Odds Ratio} = SE \cdot SP/(1 - SE)(1 - SP),$$

or in terms of the predictive values:

$$\text{Odds Ratio} = PVP \cdot PVN/(1 - PVP)(1 - PVN),$$

or in terms of the risk ratios:

$$\text{Odds Ratio} = RR1 \cdot RR3,$$

or

$$\text{Odds Ratio} = RR2 \cdot RR4.$$

All these are different ways of computing *exactly* the same quantity. Part of the appeal of the odds ratio lies in the fact that it can be computed equally well from the sensitivities and specificities easily estimated in Retrospective Sampling, or from the predictive values easily estimated in Prospective Sampling (Fleiss, 1981).

If the test is random ($\rho = 0$), then SE = Q and SP = Q'. Both RR1 and RR3 equal 1, and of course, so does the odds ratio. Similarly, if the test is random, then PVP = P and PVN = P'. Thus RR2 and RR4 equal 1, and so does the odds ratio. For legitimate tests ($\rho > 0$), SE exceeds Q and SP exceeds Q'. In such cases, RR1 and RR3 exceed 1. Completely analogously, for legitimate tests, PVP exceeds P and PVN exceeds P'. Then RR2 and RR4 exceed 1 for legitimate tests. Finally, for a legitimate test, since all the risk ratios exceed 1, the odds ratio must also exceed 1.

In general, good tests have large risk ratios and a large odds ratio; however, the theoretical upper limit of all the risk ratios and of the odds ratio is infinity. When time comes to say how large is "large enough," there is a problem. Is a risk ratio of 3.0 large? Or must it be 30? 300? 3,000? 3,000,000? Without some sense of how rapidly the risk ratios or odds ratio move up the scale from one to infinity, interpreting the magnitude of the risk ratios or the odds ratio as measures of test quality is difficult (Berkson, 1958; Feinstein, 1973, 1985; Fleiss, 1981).

In a sense, the problem here is the mirror-image of that in considerations of the sensitivity and specificity or the predictive values (Kraemer, 1985). In those cases, there was a fixed theoretical upper endpoint (1.0), but a variable random value that depended on the level of the test (for sensitivity and specificity) or on the prevalence of a positive diagnosis in the population (for the predictive values). For the risk ratios and the odds ratio, there is a fixed random value (1), but a non-finite and hence non-fixed upper limit. In dealing with sensitivity, specificity, and the predictive values, we rescaled the measures to fix both the endpoints. What we would propose to do with the risk ratios is similar.

It can easily be shown that:

$$\kappa(1, 0) = (RR2 - 1)/[RR2 + (Q'/Q)]$$

$$= (RR3 - 1)/[RR3 + (P/P')]$$

$$\kappa(0, 0) = (RR1 - 1)/[RR1 + (P'/P)]$$

$$= (RR4 - 1)/[RR4 + (Q/Q')].$$

Consequently the quality of the sensitivity, that of the predictive value of a negative test, that of RR2, and that of RR3 are essentially the same. The quality of the specificity, that of the predictive value of a positive test, that of RR1, and that of RR4 are essentially the same.

Understanding the odds ratio is a trickier matter. First of all, since, by definition, the odds ratio equals either RR1 · RR3 or RR2 · RR4, for legitimate test, the odds ratio is larger than the *largest* risk ratio. For this reason, among these measures, the odds ratio always presents the most optimistic view of the quality of a test, i.e., it tends to indicate whatever is the *best* quality of the test, for some tests sensitivity and for others specificity.

The form of the odds ratio arose in statistics as the likelihood ratio test statistic to test the null hypothesis of randomness in a 2 × 2 table. Thus by virtue of its origin, the odds ratio should be particularly sensitive to small deviations from randomness in whatever direction such deviation might occur. In presenting the most optimistic view of the best quality of a test, whatever quality that happens to be, the odds ratio does that task very well. However, the very quality that makes the odds ratio an excellent choice for detecting nonrandomness (legitimacy) creates problems in medical test evaluation. Sensitive and specific tests are used in different medical contexts. One should at least know which quality is being optimized, and the odds ratio delivers mixed information.

The exact mathematical relationship between the quality indices and the odds ratio is known (Kraemer & Bloch, 1988). When Q and P are of comparable size ($Q = P$ approximately), in which case $\kappa(1, 0)$ and $\kappa(0, 0)$ are nearly equal (for they must lie on the diagnosis line of the QROC):

$$OR - 1 = \kappa/[PP'(1 - \kappa)^2],$$

where $\kappa = \kappa(1, 0) = \kappa(0, 0)$.

In Table 7.3 are presented values of the odds ratio for various combinations of the common quality index, κ, and the prevalence, P.

What can be seen indicates that large-magnitude odds ratios are common when the prevalence is extreme, either near zero or near one. There are no uniformly accepted standards for what constitutes a "high"

Table 7.3 Values of the Odds Ratio When $Q = P$ for Various Values of $\kappa(1,0) = \kappa(0,0) = \kappa$ and Average Risk P

κ	P or P' 0.05	0.10	0.15	0.20	0.25	0.30	0.35	0.40	0.45	0.50
0.0	1.0	1.0	1.0	1.0	1.0	1.0	1.0	1.0	1.0	1.0
0.1	3.6	2.4	2.0	1.8	1.7	1.6	1.5	1.5	1.5	1.5
0.2	7.6	4.5	3.5	3.0	2.7	2.5	2.4	2.3	2.3	2.3
0.3	13.9	7.8	5.8	4.8	4.3	3.9	3.7	3.6	3.5	3.4
0.4	24.4	13.3	9.7	7.9	6.9	6.3	5.9	5.6	5.5	5.4
0.5	43.1	23.2	16.7	13.5	11.7	10.5	9.8	9.3	9.1	9.0
0.6	79.9	42.7	30.4	24.4	21.0	18.9	17.5	16.6	16.2	16.0
0.7	164.7	87.4	62.0	49.6	42.5	38.0	35.2	33.4	32.4	32.1
0.8	422.1	223.2	157.9	126.0	107.7	96.2	88.9	84.3	81.8	81.0
0.9	1,895.7	1,001.0	706.9	563.5	481.0	429.6	396.6	376.0	364.6	361.0

odds ratio, but in epidemiological contexts odds ratios or risk ratios of 3 or 4 or so are considered worth attention. One can see in Table 7.3, as measures of test quality, odds ratios of 3 or 4 may frequently correspond to medical tests with rather poor quality indices, particularly when seen in very low- or very high-risk populations.

Earlier I noted (Chapter 5) that it is particularly difficult to identify good tests in very low- or high-risk populations. At the very least, large sample sizes will be needed to identify such tests. Yet what we see here is that it is precisely in that most difficult context that the odds ratio gives the most optimistic results. To summarize, the odds ratio is a world-class optimistic statistic: it chooses the best quality of the test (and ignores its weaknesses) and gives the rosiest possible view of that quality, particularly when used in the toughest circumstances.

To fix and to illustrate the consequences, let us consider a study reported by DiMaio, Baumgarten, Greenstein, Seel, and Mahoney (1987), the evaluation of a proposed screening test for fetal Down syndrome in pregnancy based on examination of maternal serum alpha-fetoprotein levels. This study is particularly illustrative because, as with many epidemiological studies, the disorder of interest in this study was a very low-risk one: $P = .0784\%$ in the population of interest, i.e., an expected 78 cases in 100,000 screened.

The disorder here, of course, is Down's syndrome. The diagnosis is based on amniocentesis or by diagnosis at birth, each a highly reproducible diagnosis. This is important to note, for it means that the quality of the diagnosis in this study is likely to be near 100%.

The population is that of women 35 years of age or younger (and therefore not at high risk strictly because of age), 14-22 weeks pregnant, and willing to be tested. Sampling was naturalistic with a total sample size of 57,469. These were sampled in two waves: 23,115 from a sample accrued between 1981 to 1984, and 34,354 accrued later. (The samples were referred to as "retrospective" and "prospective," but these terms here do not refer to the sampling method used, but, rather, to the analytic time frame.)

The test was based on a radioimmunoassay of serum alpha-fetoprotein level. The values were entered into a calculation algorithm that compared observed level in relation to level expected on the basis of maternal weight and race, and, from this, calculated a risk level reported as 1:570 or 1:470, etc. The referent for the test selected by the authors was 1:270, i.e., those whose calculated risk levels exceeded

1:270 (the risk of a 35-year-old woman at 15-20 weeks of gestation), were considered as having a positive test.

DiMaio et al. (1987) conclude that: "The available data indicate that in our population, using a cut-off for risk at which 5 percent [$Q = 5\%$] of women under 35 are offered amniocentesis, we will detect one quarter to one third (SE = 25%-33%) of pregnancies in which the fetus has Down's syndrome ($P = .078\%$)" (p. 342). The figures in brackets are translations of the information presented into the terminology we are presently using.

We might quickly calculate the quality of the sensitivity [$\kappa(1, 0)$] as between 21% and 35% for:

$$\kappa(1, 0) = (.25 - .05)/.95 = .21, \text{ or } \kappa(1, 0) = (.33 - .05)/.95 = .35.$$

These quality indices do not seem high compared to others we have seen, particularly when the diagnosis in this case is likely to be highly reproducible. As DiMaio et al. (1987) note, however, one could change the referent and perhaps so improve the test. In their Figure 1 (p. 345) the authors give the reader the opportunity to do so, for they present a distribution of the calculated risks for the 45 women with a positive diagnosis, from which sensitivity can be calculated for various referents, and a distribution of the calculated risks for all the subjects, from which the levels of the tests could be approximated. From these pieces of information (P, Q, and SE), one can, using the methods of Chapter 5, reconstruct the necessary 2×2 tables. In Table 7.4 are presented the results for several referent values, the approximate level of each, and the risk ratios and odds ratio associated with each one. Also presented are the sensitivities and specificities and their quality indices.

Particularly striking in Table 7.4 is the variation in the magnitude of the risk ratio depending on which *form* of risk ratio is selected. If one chose to report RR4, the magnitudes would appear to be almost at the chance level (1.001-1.003). At the other extreme, RR2 values are very impressive indeed, with a maximal level of 7.07. Although this is no more statistically significant than the values of RR4, this result would certainly appear to be more convincing evidence of the quality of this test than would RR4.

This happens whenever a ratio is used in circumstances where its denominator too rapidly approaches zero. Then the magnitude of the ratio is determined in greater part by the magnitude of the denominator, inflating rapidly as the denominator nears zero. Since the

Table 7.4 Evaluation of the DiMaio et al. (1987) Test for Screening for Down Syndrome in Young Pregnant Mothers

Calculated Risk	P	Q	SE	SP	PVP	PVN	$\kappa(1,0)$	$\kappa(0,0)$	RR1	RR3	RR2	RR4	Odds Ratio
1:650	0.1%	33.7%	73.3%	66.4%	0.2%	99.97%	*59.8%	0.1%	2.18	2.49	5.42	1.001	5.42
1:450	0.1%	20.4%	64.4%	79.6%	0.2%	99.96%	55.3%	0.2%	3.16	2.24	7.07	1.002	7.08
1:350	0.1%	12.2%	37.8%	87.8%	0.2%	99.94%	29.1%	0.2%	3.09	1.41	4.35	1.002	4.36
1:300	0.1%	8.2%	33.3%	91.9%	0.3%	99.94%	27.4%	0.2%	4.09	1.38	5.62	1.003	5.64
1:250	0.1%	5.1%	22.2%	94.9%	0.3%	99.94%	18.0%	*0.3%	4.37	1.22	5.31	1.003	5.33

SOURCE: De Maio et al. (1987), p. 345, figures estimated from Figure 1.

denominators of the risk ratios and of the odds ratio in this context of medical test evaluation are all measures that we would hope would approach zero, this is exactly the context in which we would expect unstable and inflated ratios.

In Table 7.4 one can see that of sensitivity, specificity, and the predictive values, the one that is largest is PVN. Consequently the ratio with 1– PVN in the denominator will tend to be the largest: RR2. Next comes specificity, and naturally RR3 tends to be next largest, and so on. In each case, the odds ratio exceeds the *largest* risk ratio, here RR2.

We have characterized sensitivity, specificity, and the predictive values as *uncalibrated* measures of quality, in that they reflect the values of P and Q as well as the quality of the test. Risk ratios and odds ratio are uncalibrated in the same sense. How rapidly they increase in magnitude as the test quality improves is determined by the values of P and Q. To ignore this effect in evaluating a test may generate misleading results. Similar problems have long been noted in epidemiological uses of these ratios as well (e.g., Feinstein, 1985).

Of the tests we have been able to evaluate in Table 7.4, it appears that the optimally sensitive test uses a referent value of 1:650 [$\kappa(1, 0)$ = 59.8%] and the optimally specific test a referent value of 1:250 [$\kappa(0, 0) = 0.3\%$]. If judged by the magnitude of the odds ratio, the referents 1:650 and 1:250 would appear to produce tests of approximately equal quality. Yet one is the optimally sensitive and the other the optimally specific test, tests quite different in clinical performance. The odds ratio ignores this distinction.

In Figure 7.2 we see a QROC very different from those we have seen before. It is a very narrow "leaf" barely containing any area of the QROC plane.

This is, of course, a legitimate test, for with a sample size of 57,469, virtually any deviation from randomness would be statistically significant. Is this a good test? In this situation the quality of the diagnosis is likely to be very highly reproducible, setting a Diagnosis ROC or QROC closely approaching the Ideal Test Point. Thus neither the quality of the sensitivity (at best 60%), nor certainly the quality of the specificity (at best 0.3%), seems impressive. While the authors appear to believe that the results could be used to design a screening program, quantitative and objective methods would cause hesitation, a stance more in concert with the comments by Pueschel (1987) in response to this report than with the research report itself.

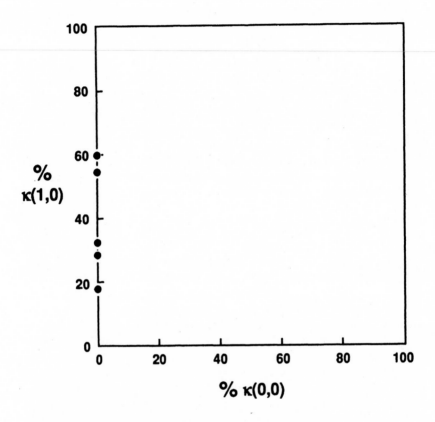

Figure 7.2. QROC of a Prenatal Test for Down's Syndrome
SOURCE: DiMaio et al., 1987.

Pueschel argues that, in this situation, false positive results cause unnecessary mental anguish and apprehension, and that the amniocentesis that would be done in response to a positive test, itself carries an estimated fetal loss between 1% and 1.5%. These effects must be taken into consideration in this situation where less than 0.1% will have Down syndrome. The only guaranteed benefit of a *true* positive would be an early warning. Abortion, here the only "preventative" or "treatment," would be morally, ethically, or legally unacceptable to many.

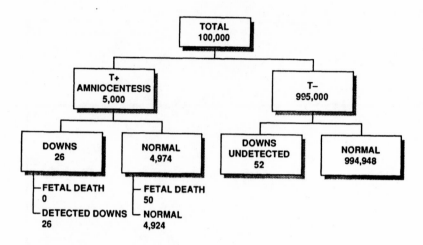

Figure 7.3. Hypothetical Results of Prenatal Screening for Down's Syndrome
SOURCE: DiMaio et al., 1987.

In Figure 7.3 we present an analysis inspired by a theoretical medical test evaluation done by Sisson, Schoomaker, and Ross (1976) to illustrate this dilemma.

Of 100,000 screened pregnancies, we would expect with a 5% level test, as recommended by DiMaio et al. (1987), to yield 5,000 positive tests. These 5,000 women would undergo amniocentesis. With the PVP as it is, we would expect to detect 26 positive results in this group. Thus there would have been 4,974 women who would have unnecessarily undergone amniocentesis, with all the anxiety and cost that entails. Worse yet, however, if the fetal loss rate associated with amniocentesis is even only 1%, we would expect to see 50 fetal deaths, virtually all of them among normal fetuses (because their numbers are so large). Among the 995,000 pregnancies with *negative* tests, there would be 52 cases of Down syndrome fetuses undetected by the test.

Now, if the test were not used, there would be in this series of 100,000 pregnancies, 78 undetected Down syndrome fetuses, and that would be sad; however, if the test were used, there would still be 52 cases undetected. There would be 26 cases in which an early warning is provided, allowing the choice of an abortion. If none chose to abort, there would still be 78 Down syndrome births, test or not. In addition, however, if the tests were used, there would be 50 iatragenic deaths, and 4,924 families put under iatragenic-induced stress. Thus one would harm, to some extent, 4,974 families, perhaps causing 50 unnecessary deaths, in order to provide a doubtful benefit to 26 families. Is the test indeed a good one?

Summary

There is no change in the process of test evaluation resulting from consideration of the predictive values. When choice of the optimal tests are made, the test that optimizes the sensitivity also optimizes the predictive value of a negative test. The test that optimizes specificity also optimizes predictive value of a positive test. Those who argue in the medical research literature about the relative merits of considering the sensitivity and specificity versus the predictive values have been arguing, in essence, about calibration issues.

We have also discussed various risk ratios and the odds ratio. Two of the risk ratios, recalibrated, prove to equal the quality of the sensitivity or the PVN; the other two, the quality of the specificity or the PVP. Thus, properly scaled, using the risk ratios to evaluate medical tests does not change the process from what it is with sensitivity and specificity and the predictive values.

The odds ratio, however, conveys mixed messages. It tends to reflect the *best* quality of the test, whatever that might be. Thus for some tests it might reflect sensitivity and for others (even for the same diagnosis in the same population) it might reflect specificity. The magnitude of the odds ratio is affected both by the prevalence and by the relation of the level to the prevalence. Odds ratio tends to increase much more rapidly for extreme values of either P or Q. Thus, particularly in those contexts, the odds ratio tends to give misleading or ambiguous information about the quality of medical tests, information that is generally over optimistic.

8

Efficiency: Choosing Clinically Optimal Tests

The Problem with Efficiency

The last of the measures briefly introduced in Chapter 5 was efficiency, defined as the probability that the test result and the diagnosis agree. The major problem with efficiency as used in medical test evaluation, both from the statistical point of view and that of the medical consumer, is its neglect. The focus of attention of those espousing Signal Detection approaches is on sensitivity/specificity; while those who espouse the Bayesian approach focus on the predictive values. While efficiency is usually defined and sometimes estimated and reported when describing the performance of medical tests, such information is neither universally presented, nor given any particular emphasis.

Efficiency, however, has not been neglected in other fields of research: psychology, education, sociology, where, under various titles (such as "percentage correct," "accuracy"), it has undergone intensive and extensive study. Its statistical properties are well known. Finally, and most important, what has been learned in those fields can be used to resolve important questions in medical test evaluation.

The Basic Model

Mathematically, the efficiency of a medical test is defined as:

$$EFF = TP + TN.$$

In terms of the parameters of the model:

$$EFF = (PQ + \rho \cdot \sigma_p \cdot \sigma_q) + (P'Q' + \rho \cdot \sigma_p \cdot \sigma_q),$$

$$= (PQ + P'Q') + 2 \cdot \rho \cdot \sigma_p \cdot \sigma_q.$$

Thus, for a random test ($\rho = 0$) the efficiency is equal to:

$$EFF = PQ + P'Q'$$

and for a legitimate test ($\rho > 0$) the efficiency must exceed the value

$$PQ + P'Q'.$$

Like sensitivity, specificity, or the predictive values, the efficiency is an uncalibrated measure with a random value that strongly depends on the prevalence (P) and the level of the test (Q). This was noted as long ago as the 1930s in the psychology research literature. Eventually Cohen (1960), among others, suggested that efficiency be simply recalibrated to facilitate quantitative interpretation as:

$$(EFF - PQ - P'Q')/(1 - PQ - P'Q')$$

This recalibrated value was called a "kappa coefficient" and, later it became known as Cohen's kappa, to differentiate it from other forms of kappa coefficients that began to proliferate (Bloch & Kraemer, 1989).

For present purposes, we will label the recalibrated measure as a quality index for efficiency $\kappa(.5, 0)$:

$$\kappa(.5, 0) = (EFF - PQ - P'Q')/(1 - PQ - P'Q').$$

Like the other quality indices, $\kappa(.5, 0)$ takes on the value zero for a random test and has an absolute maximum of 1.0 when test and diagnosis totally agree.

A little further algebra provides some insights into how this new quality index relates to the others. First of all, we note that:

$$1 - PQ - P'Q' = PQ' + P'Q.$$

Then also, since:

$$EFF = TP + TN,$$

$$EFF = P \cdot SE + P' \cdot SP'.$$

Thus:

$$EFF - P \cdot Q - P' \cdot Q' = P \cdot (SE - Q) + P' \cdot (SP' - Q)$$

$$= P \cdot Q' \cdot \kappa(1, 0) + P' \cdot Q \cdot \kappa(0, 0).$$

Thus finally:

$$\kappa(.5, 0) = [PQ' \cdot \kappa(1, 0) + P'Q \cdot \kappa(0, 0)] / (PQ' + P'Q).$$

This algebraic excursion demonstrates that the quality of the efficiency is a weighted average of the quality of the sensitivity or predictive value of a negative test [$\kappa(1, 0)$], and of the quality of the specificity or predictive value of a positive test [$\kappa(0, 0)$]. To maximize the quality of the efficiency (i.e., to optimize the efficiency) one must have *both* good quality sensitivity *and* good quality specificity. One or the other will not necessarily do, as for the optimally sensitive or the optimally specific tests. How much weight is put on the quality of the sensitivity and on that of the specificity depends on how many in the population are put at risk of each kind of error. (Hence the weights depend on P and Q.) The fundamental advantage of optimally efficient tests is that they perform well for *both* positive and negative diagnostic groups, and their results are dependable for *both* the positive and negative test results.

Once again, let us consider the various tests for diabetes previously considered in both Chapters 6 and 7, where two different approaches produced identical results (Galen & Gambino, 1975; Remein & Wilkerson,

Table 8.1 Evaluation of the Folin-Wu Method for Detection of Diabetes Done 3 Hours After the Test Meal

Referent	Q	EFF	κ(.5, 0)
80		Insufficient Sample Size	
90	94.3%	17.1%	0.8%
100	68.8%	41.6%	9.1%
110	38.2%	69.4%	25.5%
120	20.2%	84.3%	42.8%
130	12.3%	90.1%	54.0%
140*	8.5%	93.2%	*63.5%
150	6.2%	93.4%	60.9%
160	5.2%	93.1%	56.9%
170	4.3%	92.2%	49.4%
180	3.5%	91.4%	41.3%
190	3.5%	91.4%	41.3%

SOURCE: Galen and Gambino (1975) p. 107; Remein and Wilkerson (1961)
($P = 12.1$%)
NOTE: * The optimally efficient test.

1961). The disorder was diabetes based on a diagnosis from the oral glucose tolerance test. The sampling was naturalistic with 580 subjects for the blood tests and 511 for the urine tests. Four protocols were considered: the Folin-Wu method, the Somogyi-Nelson method based on blood samples, and the Clinitest and Benedict's methods, both urine tests. Various times after the test meal and various cut-off values were used to define the 136 referents considered.

For each referent for the Folin-Wu method done 3 hours after the test meal for which the sample size was sufficient, the level of the test is presented in Table 8.1, along with the efficiency and the quality index for the efficiency.

The optimally efficient test was that using a referent of 140 mg/dl, with a quality index of 63.5%. This choice differs both from the optimally sensitive test (referent 100 mg/dl) and from the optimally specific test (referent 160 mg/dl). There are times when the three optimal tests coincide, but there is no mathematical necessity that they do so, and most frequently they do not.

This process can then be repeated for all the blood and urine tests, with the results reported in Table 8.2

In each case, the optimally efficient referent for a particular test is identified by an asterisk. The overall optimally efficient test is the

Table 8.2   Identification of the Optimally Efficient Blood and Urine
Tests for Diabetes

Protocol		Referent	κ(.5, 0)
Somogyi-Nelson			
	Random	> 130	54.7%
	1	160	64.1%
	2	**140	**67.8%
	3	130	61.7%
Folin-Wu			
	Random	150	54.0%
	1	*160	*65.6%
	2	170	64.9%
	3	140	63.5%
Clinitest			
	Random	1+	38.3%
	1	2+	37.1%
	2	*2+	*47.1%
	3	2+	45.6%
Benedict			
	Random	2+	31.7%
	1	2+	39.7%
	2	*3+	*47.3%
	3	2+	45.6%

SOURCE: Galen and Gambino (1975) p. 107; Remein and Wilkerson (1961)
NOTES: *, **: The optimally efficient test for each of the protocols at different time points after the test meal, and identification of the optimal time for each test (* or **), and the overall optimal tests (**).

Somogyi-Nelson blood test, taken 2 hours after the test meal and with a referent of 140 mg/dl, with a quality index of 67.8%. If we look back now at the QROC for this test in Figure 6.5, it will be apparent that this test is on the QROC, located between the optimally sensitive test and the optimally specific tests. Of the tests on the QROC, it is the one closest to the diagnosis line.

Even though the considerations in published medical test evaluations focus on sensitivity and specificity or predictive values, when the best test is chosen, the choice frequently seems based more or less on efficiency. This is seen, for example, in the evaluation of duplex ultrasound scanning for carotid artery stenosis (Garth et al., 1983). The optimally efficient test (see Figure 6.1) is #1 (Velocity Ratio > 1.5), exactly the test selected by Garth et al. (1983). The best test selected by Galen and Gambino (1975) for diabetes we have shown not to be optimal in any sense, but one can see in Figure 6.5 that, of all the tests on the QROC, the test they selected is nearest the optimally efficient test. In cases such as these, there may be no quarrel with the choice itself. All that is troublesome is the lack of justification and documentation for the choice of one versus another of the tests. In the absence of such justification, as in the case of the Galen and Gambino (1975) choice, it is all too easy to miss the optimal choice, and for different evaluators of the same tests in the same population, perhaps even using the same data, to reach different answers.

Consideration of Medical Consequences of Errors: The Weighted Kappa Coefficient

Under what circumstances should one prefer the optimally sensitive rather than the optimally efficient, or the optimally specific test in preference to either of these? These three are frequently not the same test. Moreover, from consideration of the geometry of the QROC, there might possibly be even more than three optimal tests among which to choose. What governs the final choice?

The crucial issue underlying that choice is what difference it makes to patients whether or not the test correctly classifies them. More specifically, let R_+ be a quantification of how much difference it makes to patients with the disorder (best represented here by a positive diagnosis, $D+$) whether or not they are correctly classified by the test. Also, let R_- represent how much difference it makes to patients without the disorder (best represented here by a negative diagnosis, $D-$) whether or not they are correctly classified by the test. In defining this notation I have used a dollar sign as a reminder that these are costs, although such costs may not necessarily be measured in terms that are strictly financial. Ultimately all that will matter in the evaluations will be the relative size of R_+ and R_-, via the parameter r, where:

$$r = \$R_+/(\$R_+ + \$R_-), \qquad r' = 1 - r = \$R_-/(\$R_+ + \$R_-).$$

Which type of diagnostic error carries the greater importance will dictate the value of r. If the error of major concern is a false negative, then R_+ will predominate, and r will be near 1. At the other extreme, if the error of major concern is a false positive, then R_- will predominate, and r will be near 0. When both errors are of importance and neither predominates, then r will be near .5.

For example, suppose a woman actually free of breast cancer is to be tested for breast cancer. If the test result were a false positive, the patient might be advised to enter a hospital, undergo breast biopsy, and might, with bad luck, even undergo mastectomy, radiotherapy, or chemotherapy for no good reason. The costs, risks, and anxiety caused to the patient, as well as the short- and long-term medical consequences of undergoing unnecessary surgery, radiotherapy, or chemotherapy are to be considered in determining the value of R_-.

On the other hand, if the woman actually had breast cancer and the physician's conclusion were a false negative result, the patient might wait another year or two for detection, the malignancy would grow and spread, and her chances of successful treatment decline. Such considerations determine the value of R_+.

Which of these is larger, R_+ or R_-? Which error, the false positive or the false negative, should the patient and her physician be more concerned about? The answer may not be the same for all patients or for all physicians. The answer is certainly not the same for all disorders or in all circumstances. However, it is this clinical, not statistical, judgment that leads to the choice of which quality of the test is to be optimized.

Precisely how do these considerations affect the choice? In Table 8.3 we see listed the four outcomes of the evaluation of a medical test. In the next column, we see listed a value that represents a gain ($R_+/2$ or $R_-/2$) when the test properly classifies the patient and a loss ($-R_+/2$ or $-R_-/2$) when the test does not.

One can see that the difference between being properly classified or not for patients with the disorder is R_+ and for patients without the disorder is R_-. What is not clear is why we split the difference evenly in each case between those correctly and incorrectly classified. We could have assigned R_+ to true positives and 0 to false negatives, or $R_+/3$ to true positives and $-2 \cdot R_+/3$ to false negatives, and the definition of R_+ would still be satisfied. The simple and convenient fact is that however the split is made, the results come out the same. For convenience then, we will proceed with an even split between true and false results.

The probability of each outcome of the test appears in the next column of Table 8.3. In the following columns are the probabilities if

Table 8.3 Details of the Calculation of the Expected Benefit

| Outcome | Benefit | Probabilities of Outcomes: | | |
		Test	Random	Ideal
True Positive	$R_+/2$	$P \cdot SE$	$P \cdot Q$	1
False Negative	$-\$R_+/2$	$P \cdot SE'$	$P \cdot Q'$	0
False Positive	$-\$R_-/2$	$P' \cdot SP'$	$P' \cdot Q$	0
True Negative	$+\$R_-/2$	$P' \cdot SP$	$P' \cdot Q'$	1

$r = \$R_+/(\$R_+ + \$R_-)$
$r' = 1 - r = \$R_-/(\$R_+ + \$R_-)$

the test were a random one and with the ideal probabilities. By multiplying the benefits by their probabilities and summing over the four outcomes, we can compute the expected benefit for a test, what it would be if the test were random, and what it ideally is in this population:

$$\text{Test Benefit} = (\$R_+/2)(P \cdot SE) - (\$R_+/2)(P \cdot SE')$$
$$- (\$R_-/2)(P' \cdot SP') + (\$R_-/2)(P' \cdot SP) .$$

For a random test the same calculation gives:

$$\text{Random Benefit} = (\$R_+/2)(P \cdot Q) - (\$R_+/2)(P \cdot Q')$$
$$- (\$R_-/2)(P' \cdot Q) + (\$R_-/2)(P' \cdot Q') .$$

Finally, the ideal test gives:

$$\text{Ideal Benefit} = (\$R_+/2) \cdot P + (\$R_-/2) \cdot P' .$$

The net gain in benefit by using the test rather than a random test is:

$$\text{Net Gain} = \text{Test Benefit} - \text{Random Benefit}$$
$$= (\$R_+/2) \cdot P \cdot (SE - Q) - (\$R_+/2) \cdot P \cdot (SE' - Q')$$
$$- (\$R_-/2) \cdot P' \cdot (SP' - Q) + (\$R_-/2) \cdot P' \cdot (SP - Q')$$

which simplifies to:

$$= \$R_+ \cdot P \cdot (SE - Q) + \$R_- \cdot P' \cdot (SP - Q'),$$

and thus to:

$$\$R_+ \cdot PQ' \cdot \kappa(1, 0) + \$R_- \cdot P'Q \cdot \kappa(0, 0).$$

The Ideal Net Gain is realized when the quality indices are both equal to 1, and thus:

$$\text{Ideal Net Gain} = \$R_+ \cdot PQ' + \$R_- \cdot P'Q.$$

The gain of using the test relative to the ideal gain is:

$$\text{Relative Gain} = \frac{\$R_+ \cdot PQ' \cdot \kappa(1, 0) + \$R_- \cdot P'Q \cdot \kappa(0, 0)}{PQ'\$R_+ + P'Q\$R_-}.$$

Dividing both numerator and denominator by $\$R_+ + \$R_-$, we then have:

$$\kappa(r, 0) = \frac{PQ'r \cdot \kappa(1, 0) + P'Qr' \cdot \kappa(0, 0)}{PQ'r + P'Qr'},$$

the quality index of the test for a relative clinical cost of r. The index $\kappa(r, 0)$ is a "weighted kappa coefficient" between test and diagnosis (Fleiss, 1981) with a long history of statistical development.

To optimize the choice of test for a particular value of r, which reflects patient's, clinician's, or researcher's clinical concerns, one would choose the test to maximize the value of $\kappa(r, 0)$. Clearly, if $r = 1$, one maximizes $\kappa(1, 0)$. If $r = 0$, one maximizes $\kappa(0, 0)$. If $r = .5$, one maximizes $\kappa(.5, 0)$. These results are consistent with those obtained from the Signal Detection approach, from the Bayesian approach, as well as from using the efficiency. This observation also expands the various approaches in that, in theory, one could actually use whatever value of r corresponds to a *precise*, rather than approximate, determination of the relative costs of the two types of clinical errors and optimize that particular quality of the test.

In fact, this is an advantage more in theory than in practice, for precise determination of the relative costs and risks of the two types of errors is usually not possible (McNeil et al., 1975). In the case of a woman undergoing a test for breast cancer, for example, how does one measure the risk of suffering and early death against the risk of unnecessary anxiety, surgery, radiotherapy, or chemotherapy and the attendant consequences to the quantity as well as to the long-range quality of life? My own personal view is to attach some weight to both types of errors and to use $r = .5$. That would mean that I would prefer that the optimally efficient test be used for me. Others might disagree. No matter, if the test evaluator provided complete information in the form of $\kappa(1, 0)$ and $\kappa(0, 0)$ as well as a definition of the population and test (P and Q), the test might be tailored for the particular patient, physician, and situation.

In Chapter 7 we considered the evaluation of a screening test for Down syndrome. In the original report of the evaluation of the test (DiMaio et al., 1987), by focusing completely on avoiding false negatives, in effect the evaluators set $r = 1$. In critiquing these results, Pueschel (1987) pointed out that false positives have cost comparable to or even overwhelming that of false negatives, in effect, proposing that $r = .5$ or at least $r < 1$ might be more appropriate. Which choice of r is right: that of DiMaio et al. (1987) with $r = 1$ or Pueschel's (1987) with $r < 1$? For a woman with no objection to abortion and major difficulties with carrying or raising a Down's syndrome child, $r = 1$ may be the appropriate choice. For a woman who would not choose to abort, for whatever reason, some $r < 1$ is the appropriate choice.

Making such choices, which frequently, as here, carry moral and ethical overtones, should not be the function of the test evaluation, but, rather, the choice of the individual patient and physician based on the results reported from test evaluation. The function of the test evaluation is to present data in complete and accurate enough form so that such choices can be rationally made.

A Geometric Approach: The Test QROC

Since the location of a test point in the QROC plane is determined by $\kappa(1, 0)$ and $\kappa(0, 0)$, the qualities of the sensitivity and of the specificity of any test are easy to spot in the QROC plane. Similarly, the optimally sensitive test in a family of tests is easy to spot on the QROC: It is the test that is highest on the QROC. The optimally

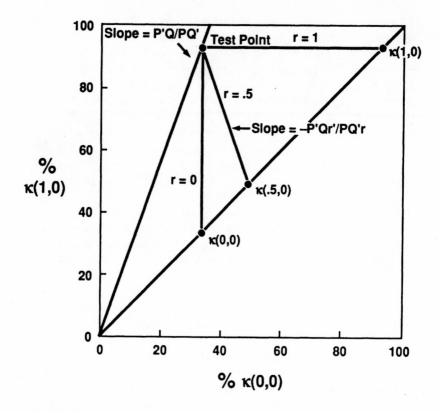

Figure 8.1. Visualization of κ(r, 0)

specific test, too, is easy to spot: it is the test furthest to the right on the QROC. Spotting the optimally efficient, or, in greater generality, the test that is optimal for any value of r set between 0 and 1 is a bit trickier.

Let's start with a general solution that is still more analytic than geometric. In the QROC of Figure 8.1 is shown a single test with level Q, and quality indices κ(1, 0) and κ(0, 0). From the geometry of the QROC plane, we know that this test (and all Q-level tests) lie on a ray (line from the origin) with slope $P'Q/PQ'$. For any value r of interest, draw a line through the test point with slope $-(P'Q/PQ') \cdot (r'/r)$ to the diagnosis line. We will call this line the *r-projection line* of the test. The r-projection line of a test intersects the diagnosis line at the point [κ(r, 0), κ(r, 0)].

For example (see Figure 8.1), if $r = 1$, we would draw a horizontal line (slope = 0) through the test point to the diagnosis line, and it would obviously intersect at κ(1, 0). If $r = 0$, we would draw a vertical line (slope = ∞) through the test point to the diagnosis, and it would obviously intersect at κ(0, 0). For $r = .5$, we would draw the line with slope $-P'Q/PQ'$. Where it intersects the diagnosis line is κ(.5, 0) units above the horizontal axis and κ(.5, 0) to the right of the vertical axis. What is more, this could be done for any value of r between 0 and 1.

That is not fully a geometric approach, however, since some calculation is involved, where strictly speaking, a geometric approach should require only a straightedge and a pencil to implement. Let us do it strictly geometrically (see Figure 8.2).

1. Draw the ray through the test (dashed lines). If the test lies on the diagnosis line, then κ(r, 0) is the same for all values of r; the test point lies at [κ(r, 0), κ(r, 0] for all values of r, and the process is finished.

2. If the test lies above the diagnosis line ($P < Q$), find the point that splits the ray in proportions r:r'. The easiest way is to draw a horizontal line from the y-axis to the diagnosis line at κ(1, 0) = r. Where this construction line intersects the ray divides the ray in the required proportion.

If the test lies below the diagnosis line ($P > Q$), find the point that splits the ray in proportions r':r. Again the easiest way is to draw a vertical line from the x-axis to the diagnosis line at κ(0, 0) = r. Where this construction line intersects the ray is the desired point.

3. Draw an arrow from the nearest off-diagnosis line corner of the QROC plane through the point just located, to the diagnosis line.

4. Draw a line parallel to the arrow above through the test point. Where this line intersects the diagnosis line is [κ(r, 0), κ(r, 0)].

This sounds like a horrendously complicated process, but a little practice makes the whole simple, because very rapidly one need not actually draw in the construction lines and arrows to complete the process. Furthermore, when time comes to evaluate tests, it will be done analytically, not geometrically. What purpose this exercise serves is to increase insight into the procedures and to educate the eye to better "read" QROCs.

A few observations: The slopes of the r-projection lines for tests at a given level, Q, are all equal. If there were many tests in the family

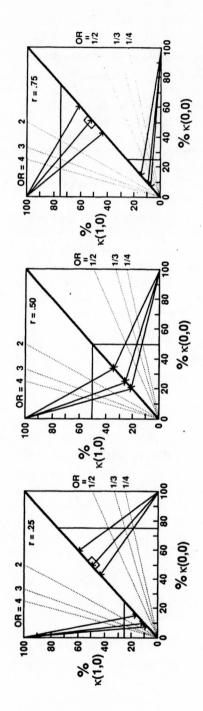

Figure 8.2. Geometric Interpretation of κ(r, 0) for r = .25, .50, and .75

with the same level, the test with the highest value of $\kappa(r, 0)$, whatever the value of r, must be the one furthest along the ray on which all the Q-level tests lie, i.e., the one on or closest to the Test QROC. If that point does not actually lie on the QROC, then a probability combination of the two tests on the QROC on either side of the Q-level ray would have both sensitivity and specificity better than the best Q-level test.

Furthermore, since each distinct test on the QROC lies on a different ray from the Random QROC, each is optimal for a different value of r. As r moves from 0 to 1, the optimal test on the QROC moves from the optimally sensitive test at the top of the QROC to the optimally specific test furthest to the right of the QROC.

In Figure 8.2 are QROC planes showing no tests, only construction lines, to locate tests optimal for r = .25, .50, and .75. Study of these figures will help to understand the following observations.

The r-projection line of the tests within a family of tests is perpendicular to the diagnosis line for tests having level Q such that:

$$P'Q/PQ' = r/r'.$$

Tests having levels Q such that $P'Q/PQ'$ lies between r/r' and 1 ($P = Q$) have an r-projection line that slants *forward* toward the Ideal Test Point. All others slant *backward* toward the Random QROC (the origin). The implication is that the tests in a family having the best chance of being optimal for values of r between 0 and 1 have levels Q with $P'Q/PQ'$ between r and 1. In particular, the tests in a family with the best chance of being optimally efficient (r = .5, r/r' = 1) are those with level near the prevalence, i.e., near the diagnosis line. In absence of limiting assumptions on the nature of the family of tests, we cannot make more precise comments about the location of optimal r-level tests (McNeil et al., 1975). As we have already seen, the shape and structure of the QROC "leaves" of real families of tests are as variable as their counterparts in nature. Somes QROC "leaves" are long and narrow, some short and broad; they may slant upward or lie flat; they may be regular or not, symmetric or not.

To see how this works for real data, let us examine once again the evaluation done by Garth et al. (1983) of duplex ultrasound scan for diagnosis of carotid artery stenosis (compare Figure 6.2 and Figure 7.1). In Figure 8.3 I have now added to the QROC the .5-projection lines for each of the tests in the family. Note how the slopes of the

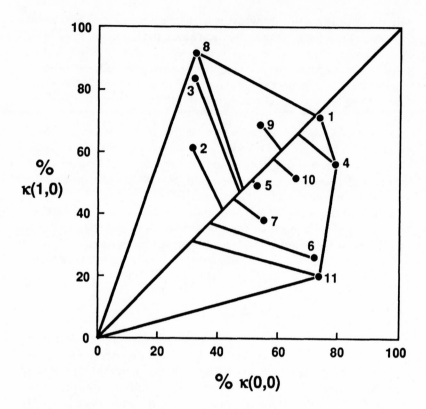

Figure 8.3. Visualization of κ(.5,0) for Duplex Ultrasound Scan, to Compare the Quality of Efficiencies of the Test
SOURCE: Garth et al., 1983.

r-projection lines from the various test points change with the levels of the various tests. They do, in fact, resemble the "veins" of a leaf.

In order of the quality of efficiency, the tests are #1, #4, #9, #10, #5, #8, #3, #7, #2, #6, and #11 (ordered by where the .5-projection lines cut the diagnosis line). Garth et al. (1983) selected Test #1 as the optimal test, and it is now geometrically clear that it is, in fact, the optimally efficient test. Test #8 remains the optimally sensitive test, and Test #4, the optimally specific test. Since there are no more tests on the QROC, and only tests on the QROC can be optimal for any value of r, this short list exhausts the possibilities for optimal tests. For all other values of r, the optimal tests would be probability combinations of either #1 and #8 or of #1 and #4.

Summary

The efficiency of a medical test, like its sensitivity or its specificity or its predictive values, is an uncalibrated measure in the sense that its magnitude depends strongly on the level of the test and its relation to prevalence. As I did in the other cases, I propose to recalibrate the efficiency so that its value is zero for a random test, and 1 if test and diagnosis always agree.

With this measure, called $\kappa(.5, 0)$, which is Cohen's kappa, we could compare all the tests in the family and identify the optimally efficient test. Generally, this is not the same test as the optimally sensitive or the optimally specific test.

When does one decide to use one and when another? To aid this decision we appealed to a concept that is not a new one in medical research: The relative clinical importance of a false positive versus a false negative result must be considered in choosing the optimal test. Here the relative clinical importance is represented by a parameter r, lying between 0 and 1, representing the relative clinical importance of false negatives over false positives. If $r = 1$, false negatives are considered of overwhelming importance; if $r = 0$ false positives are considered of overwhelming importance. Finally if $r = .5$, both are considered of roughly equal importance. These three values corre-spond to the three general situations most frequently discussed in the medical literature, that corresponding to the search for a screening test ($r = 1$), for a definitive test ($r = 0$), and for a good differential or discriminator test ($r = .5$). In what follows we focus on these three situations, but it should be noted that there is no impediment to looking at other values of r that might be of interest.

A model was proposed, based on consideration of the relative clinical importance of false positives and false negatives, that led to the definition of a set of quality indices $\kappa(r, 0)$, $0 \leq r \leq 1$, of which rescaled sensitivity [$\kappa(1, 0)$], rescaled specificity [$\kappa(0, 0)$], and rescaled efficiency [$\kappa(.5, 0)$] were special cases.

The geometric interpretation of these indices is not as simple in the general cases as it has been in the special cases when r is one or zero.

However, the geometric interpretation is clear and adds to under-standing of the methods. In particular, the geometry of the situation clarifies why the only optimal tests in a family of tests are those that lie on the QROC between the optimally sensitive and the optimally specific tests, and why the test on the QROC nearest the diagnosis line is most likely to be the optimally efficient test.

9

Taking Test Costs into Account: Costworthy Tests

Introduction

To this point in the development, every step has been foreshadowed in some form in the medical or statistical research literature on medical test evaluation. Perhaps, predictably, to this point in the development, test cost and risk have been bemoaned, but otherwise ignored. In consideration of the relative clinical cost (Chapter 8), discussion was based on how much difference it made to those with and without correct classification. However, because the costs of the test, how much time it takes, and its risks and discomforts are suffered by both those with and without correct classification, this consideration was canceled out, hence, ignored. That, to date, has been the story of much of medical test evaluation.

To a medical consumer, that situation seems deplorable. If there were two medical tests for the same disorder, both about equally accurate in a particular population (at the same point in the ROC or QROC plane), one of which was free and one of which cost \$1,000, surely the free medical test would be unequivocally preferred. If one test were essentially risk-free, and the other involved anesthetization, surgery, radiation, stress, or some other procedure that posed some, however minor, risk of medical accident, surely the risk-free test should be preferred.

Unfortunately, such is not always the case. In fact, if the costly or risky test were based on high technology (e.g., angiography or MRI) whereas the cost- and risk-free one, were based on simple clinical observation of signs and symptoms, clinicians may well simply assume that the high-technology test must be better. Their assumption would not be disputed by the results of the methods developed so far, which indicate that two such tests (for the same disorder in the same population with the same accuracy) would have all the same quality indices [$\kappa(r, 0)$] regardless of their disparate costs. That would suggest that the choice between them is arbitrary. Clearly something very important is missing from the evaluation process.

From a statistical viewpoint, what is required is mathematically simple but fraught with operational and practical difficulties. To take into explicit account a test's fixed cost and risk (hereafter T) as well as its benefit to those with or without the disorder (here, as before, R_+ and R_-), such costs, risks, and benefits must be measured on some *one* scale. Here I will denote these costs as T, R_+, R_- as if I were discussing only monetary costs, but the units of measurement are immaterial and frequently involve other than monetary considerations. (I would prefer to refer to T, R_+, R_- as "utilities," but to do so would not ease the problem and might obscure the meaning to medical clinicians and researchers.)

In the previous chapter, I began this process by considering R_+ and R_-, but as the evaluation process developed, it emerged that we did not need to have precise estimates of these benefits. All that mattered was the relative magnitude of the two via $r = R_+/(R_+ + R_-)$. This then corresponded to the three clinically recognizable situations when the cost of false negatives predominated ($r = 1$), when the cost of false positives predominated ($r = 0$), and when they were about equally of concern or where it was difficult to choose the predominant concern ($r = .5$).

Now I add consideration of what I will call the "fixed" cost or risk of the test. This cost represents that additional cost/risk that applies to any patient in taking the test regardless of whether or not he has the disorder or whether or not the test correctly classifies him. By "additional cost" I mean what extra expenditure of time, money, pain, or discomfort there is when the test is done as opposed to when it is not. Thus when a patient enters a doctor's office for an examination, that patient (or his insurance coverage) pays a certain fee. Ascertainment of the patient's gender, age, or race as well as observation of some obvious signs and symptoms carries no extra charge. Generally, weighing the patient, taking a pulse and blood pressure, and asking a few questions also carry no extra charge. However, sending the patient to the lab for blood and urine tests or scheduling an hour or two for extensive interview and other such procedures will add to the cost of the visit. When, in what follows, I refer to "free" tests, this refers to those tests that generally are either self-administered by the patient or would be done by the nurse or physician with no extra charge to the patient (or his insurance coverage).

In Table 9.1 are listed the approximate monetary costs of a number of "ordinary" tests, mostly from Moskowitz and Osband (1984). From this listing, we see what are essentially free tests, those based on self-examination, history, interview, clinical observation, and/or physical examination. The least expensive laboratory tests tend to cost less than $100. Tests requiring hospitalization, anesthetization, surgical costs, etc., or those based on new high technology (e.g., MRI) can cost up to $10,000. Note also that low-cost tests tend to be low in risk and discomfort, whereas tests that carry such risk and discomfort tend to be expensive ones. The obvious, and most important, observation is simply that there is no money-back guarantee if the test result is wrong. The patient (or his insurance coverage) pays $1,200 for cardiac catheterization, whether the results are true or false, hence a fixed cost.

That raises another problem, however. Most costs listed in Table 9.1 were obtained from a book published in 1984 by authors based at Boston University School of Medicine. To see why this matters, Stanford costs in 1990 for cardiac catheterization total approximately $5,000, not $1,200.

In 1986 at Stanford Medical Center, the exercise stress test, for example, might cost approximately $175; In 1990, it might cost approximately $350. A few miles down the peninsula in San Jose or a few miles up the peninsula in San Francisco, the cost of this test may be $150 or it may be $500.

Over time and over sites, no test cost is inexorably fixed. By the year 2000, if such tests come into routine use, the costs may decrease with increasing automation and experience. It is more likely, however, that continued inflationary trends may mean that the cost of such tests will increase.

Table 9.1   Approximate Costs of Various "Ordinary" Medical Tests

Test Name or Type	Approximate Cost (in dollars)
Blood Pressure, Pulse Rate, etc.	0.00
Height, Weight	0.00
Breast, Testicular Self-Examination	0.00
Medical History	0.00
Home Diabetes Testing	1.00
Blood Glucose Test	5.00
Hemoccult II	5.00
Home Pregnancy Test	10.00
PAP Smear	20.00
Urine/Stool Cultures	25.00
Allergy Tests	30.00
Microbiology Tests	35.00
Electrocardiogram	40.00
Dexamethasone-Suppression Test	45.00
Phenylketonuria	65.00
X-Ray	75.00
Mammography	90.00
Ultrasound	100.00
Lumbar Puncture	100.00
Exercise Tolerance Tests	140.00
Electroencephalogram	165.00
Holter Monitor	240.00
Karyotyping	250.00
Nuclear Medicine Tests (Scans)	250.00
HLA Typing	300.00
Endoscopy	400.00
Angiography	400.00
Lymphangiogram	400.00
CT Scan	500.00
Amniocentesis	600.00
NMR	1,000.00
Cardiac Catheterization	1,200.00

NOTE: Except for the approximate cost of NMR, costs are estimated from information in Moskowitz & Osband (1984). The NMR cost is the average approximate local cost for a brain NMR.

Added to such problems is the fact that, while it is easy enough to find out the approximate financial costs of tests (I simply called Stanford's billing office and asked), attempting to quantify precisely the risk or discomfort of this test can only lead to frustration. One patient might find a test procedure merely challenging, another extremely stressful. There are individual differences from patient to patient in reaction to a test procedure. Frequently the risks associated with medical tests are themselves unknown, since these do not typically appear in medical test evaluations. In any case, how does one express time loss, risk, or discomfort in terms of dollars or, for that matter, utility units?

Yet with all this, I am about to start an evaluation procedure on the premise that I can somehow come up with a precise enough measure of test cost, T, that reflects both the financial cost of the test and its risk and discomfort to a patient. As before, I will denote by R_+ and by R_- how much difference it makes to patients who respectively have or do not have the disorder whether or not the test properly classified them. The sum of R_+ and R_-, denoted R, I will call the "potential clinical benefit"; the ratio of $R_+/R = r$ will, as before, be called the "relative clinical benefit"; and the ratio of the cost of the test $T/R = t$ will be called the "relative test cost."

Statisticians are accustomed to the process of working with hypothetical values in a mathematical model that may in practice be difficult or even impossible to estimate. Frequently the process of evaluating such a model encourages insights that are otherwise impossible, but that can be verified thereafter from real observations. Frequently, also, the process itself clarifies how such hypothetical values might be well enough estimated, something that might not be obvious from the onset. Such was the case in Chapter 8 when we first considered the relative and potential clinical benefits, and here will also be the case. I hope that other researchers will hold their doubts in abeyance while we build the model in absence of full understanding of how it will be actuated, at least until the model is completely explicated. Then they can judge the outcome.

The Basic Model

Derivation of the Quality Index $\kappa(r,t)$

In Table 9.2 is presented the complete and final model for the medical test evaluation. In the first columns are listed the four possible outcomes of the test evaluation: True Positive, False Negative, False Postive, and True Negative.

Table 9.2   Details of the Calculation for Cost-Benefit Balance

			Probabilities		
Outcome	Benefit		Test	Random	Ideal
		Cost:	$T	$0	$0
True Positive	$-\$T + \$R_+/2$		$P \cdot$ SE	$P \cdot Q$	P
False Negative	$-\$T - \$R_+/2$		$P \cdot$ SE'	$P \cdot Q'$	0
False Positive	$-\$T - \$R_-/2$		$P' \cdot$ SP'	$P' \cdot Q$	0
True Negative	$-\$T + \$R_-/2$		$P' \cdot$ SP	$P' \cdot Q'$	P'

In the second column, headed Benefit, are listed the benefits to the patient of each of the outcomes, with costs listed as negative benefit. First, the fixed cost of the test, $T, is debited to everyone, for, by definition, that represents the cost/risk that pertains to everyone regardless of the outcome of the test. The values of R_+ and R_- are entered as they were before (see Table 8.3). In the third, fourth, and fifth columns, as before, appear the probabilities of each outcome for the test under evaluation (Column 3), a random decision (Column 4), and the Ideal test (Column 5).

A crucial new consideration appears in the heading of these three columns: the cost of each test. The cost of the test under evaluation is $T. A random decision should be free to the patient and poses no discomfort or risk—even a statistician could use a random number table to generate such test results and need never see the patient. The ideal test also is risk-free and cost-free, as well as perfectly reproducing the gold standard, perhaps an unachievable ideal.

We can now calculate the expected benefit of using one of these three tests (the one under evaluation, the random decision, the ideal) by multiplying each benefit by its corresponding probability and adding them up:

$$\text{Expected Benefit} = P \cdot \text{SE} \cdot (-\$T + \$R_+/2) + P \cdot \text{SE}' \cdot (-\$T - \$R_+/2)$$

$$+ P' \cdot \text{SP}' \cdot (-\$T - \$R_- /2) + P' \cdot \text{SP} \cdot (-\$T + \$R_- /2) .$$

A bit of algebraic simplification leads to:

$$\text{Expected Benefit} = -\$T + P \cdot (\$R_+/2) \cdot (2\text{SE} - 1) + P' \cdot (\$R_- /2) \cdot (2\text{SP} - 1) .$$

For a random test, $\$T = 0$ and if the test is a Q-level test, SE $= Q$ and SP $= Q'$ and hence:

Random Benefit $= 0 + P \cdot (\$R_+/2) \cdot (2Q - 1) + P' \cdot (\$R_- /2) \cdot (2Q' - 1)$.

The Expected Gain of using that real Q-level test rather than a random Q-level test is the difference between the Expected Benefit and the Random Benefit:

Expected Gain $= -\$T + P \cdot (\$R_+) \cdot (SE - Q) + P' \cdot (\$R_-) \cdot (SP - Q)$,

Again, with a little simplification,

Expected Gain $= \$R[-t + PQ'r\kappa(1, 0) + P'Qr'\kappa(0, 0)]$

where

$$t = \$T/\$R, \quad \text{the relative cost of the test,}$$

and, as before:

$$r = \$R_+/\$R \quad \text{and} \quad r' = 1 - r = \$R_-/\$R.$$

The quality indices $\kappa(1, 0)$ and $\kappa(0, 0)$, of course, are exactly the same as those defined earlier, with $\kappa(1, 0)$ representing the quality of the sensitivity or the predictive value of a negative test, $\kappa(0, 0)$ representing the quality of the specificity or the predictive value of a positive test.

The final step is to compare the Expected Gain of using the test against the Ideal Expected Gain, obtained for the ideal test [$\$T = 0$; $\kappa(1, 0) = \kappa(0, 0) = 1$], and we will call this ratio the quality index $\kappa(r, t)$:

Equation 1:

$$\kappa(r, t) = \text{Expected Gain/Ideal Gain}$$

$$= \frac{-t + PQ'r\kappa(1, 0) + P'Qr'\kappa(0, 0)}{PQ'r + P'Qr'}$$

When t is set equal to zero, the values of $\kappa(r, 0)$ are exactly what we defined then to be earlier. Thus $\kappa(r, 0)$ demonstrates the quality of the medical tests, when test cost is ignored ($t = 0$), either because the test is free ($\$T = 0$) or because the potential clinical benefit is so large that it overwhelms the test cost ($\$R \to \infty$).

What we have in $\kappa(r, t)$ is a quantitative and objective measure of the quality of a test that takes into consideration:

- the accuracy of the test, via $\kappa(1, 0)$ and $\kappa(0, 0)$;
- the relative clinical consequences of false positives and false negatives, via r;
- the fixed cost of the test, with $\$T$ measured against the potential clinical benefit $\$R$ of the test, via $t = \$T/\$R$

The Benefit Threshold of a Medical Test

There are also a few more algebraic gyrations that will simplify what follows as well as provide further insight. For example, it follows from Equation 1 above that for any r:

Equation 2:

$$\kappa(r, t) = \kappa(r, 0) - t/(PQ'r + P'Qr').$$

This indicates that the relative cost of the test (t) and its relative benefit (r) is "charged" against the accuracy of the test as reflected in $\kappa(r, 0)$. This makes good sense, for now if there are two tests for the same disorder in the same population having the same accuracy, the less costly test will unequivocally have a larger $\kappa(r, t)$, and will be preferred.

Furthermore, if we had two tests, one for cancer and one for the common cold, both equally accurate (i.e., at the same point of the ROC or QROC plane) and both costing $1,000, one test might well be recommended *for* cancer, and the other recommended *against* for the common cold. This is because $\$R$ for detection of early cancer is large, whereas $\$R$ for a self-limiting and not very serious disorder like the common cold is small. Since both here have the same cost (the same $\$T$), the relative cost for the test for cancer ($t = \$T/\$R$) is near zero, but will be much larger for the test for the common cold. Consequently, when $\kappa(r, t)$ is computed from Equation 2, $\kappa(r, t)$ for the test for cancer will be much larger than that for the test for the common cold. That too corresponds to good common sense.

From Equation 2 can also be seen that only if:

Equation 3:

$$\kappa(r, 0) > t/(P \cdot Q' \cdot r + P' \cdot Q \cdot r')$$

do the costs outweigh the benefits. Tests for which Equation 3 holds I will call "costworthy" tests. Clearly, if a test is free ($T = 0$) or if the potential clinical benefit is very great ($R \to \infty$), in both of which cases the relative test cost is zero ($t = \$T/\$R = 0$), a legitimate test is costworthy and a costworthy test is legitimate. However, the higher the cost of the test, or the lower its accuracy, or the lower its potential clinical benefit, the less costworthy is a test. In such cases, a costworthy test must be legitimate, but a legitimate test may not be costworthy.

Equation 2 can be reexpressed in several interesting and equivalent ways. For example, a test is costworthy if its accuracy is such that:

$$k(1, 0) > t/P \cdot Q' \quad \text{and} \quad k(0, 0) > t/P' \cdot Q .$$

To be costworthy, the accuracies of the test must exceed a certain threshold level. In effect, in using $\kappa(r, t)$ to judge the quality of a test, the standards for accuracy are set higher, the more costly the test.

To put this in yet a different way, for a test costing T and having accuracy characterized by $\kappa(1, 0)$ and $\kappa(0, 0)$, to be costworthy the potential clinical benefit must exceed:

Equation 4:

$$\$R > \$T/[P \cdot Q' \cdot \kappa(1, 0)] = \$T/(\rho \cdot \sigma_p \cdot \sigma_q) ,$$

or

$$\$R > \$T/[P' \cdot Q \cdot \kappa(0, 0)] = \$T/(\rho \cdot \sigma_p \cdot \sigma_q) .$$

Note that the right-hand sides in the above two equations are the same. There is only one threshold R per test. Thus costly tests will be costworthy only if the potential clinical benefit is high enough to outweigh the cost of the test and its inaccuracies.

Finally, there is one last relationship that will prove very useful:
Equation 5:

$$\kappa(r, t) = [PQ'r\kappa(1, t) + P'Qr'\kappa(0, t)]/(PQ'r + P'Qr').$$

Thus $\kappa(r, t)$ bears the same relationship to $\kappa(1, t)$ and $\kappa(0, t)$ as did $\kappa(r, 0)$ to $\kappa(1, 0)$ and $\kappa(0, 0)$. This means that we can geometrically express the costworthiness of various tests for a particular diagnosis in a certain population (thus P, \$R$ are fixed) by locating each test by $\kappa(1, t)$, and $\kappa(0, t)$ (different \$T$ for different tests) just as we earlier did by $\kappa(1, 0)$ and $\kappa(0, 0)$. This plane will be called the QCROC plane (standing for Quality and Cost ROC). The rules for locating optimal tests are the ones already developed for the QROC.

To find the optimally costworthy sensitive test, we locate the test highest on the QCROC. To find the optimally costworthy specific test, we locate the test furthest to the right on the QCROC. To find the optimally costworthy test for any value of r (usually $r = .5$), we move along the QCROC between these two optimally costworthy tests. Usually the test on the QCROC nearest the diagnosis line is the optimally costworthy efficient test. This will become clearer with examination of a real example.

Full Evaluation of a Test Family

To illustrate the use of these quality indices, $\kappa(r, t)$, let us consider the exercise stress test as presented in the CASS study (Weiner et al., 1979). Here the disorder of interest was coronary artery disease, with the diagnosis based on coronary arteriography. The population was that of patients presenting with chest pain. Sampling was naturalistic with a sample size of 2,045, and the prevalence in this population was estimated to be $P = .583$. The exercise stress test included a resting EKG. Let us estimate the cost of the exercise stress test as approximately \$175 ($\$T = \$175$). If only the resting EKG were needed, we estimate the cost as approximately \$50 ($\$T = \$50$).

I will consider four possible referents for the test among those presented by CASS. A positive test result could be attributed:

1. To those with either a positive resting EKG or a positive stress test,
2. To those with a positive stress test regardless of the EKG result,
3. To those with both a positive resting EKG and a positive stress test, or
4. To those with a positive EKG regardless of the stress test outcome.

These four tests are described in Table 9.3.

Table 9.3 Evaluation of the Resting EKG and the Exercise Stress Test
(ST) for the Diagnosis of Coronary Artery Disease

	Test #1 EKG+ or ST+	Test #2 ST+	Test #3 EKG+ and ST+	Test #4 EKG+
Test Cost = $T	$175	$175	$175	$50
Level = Q	65.1%	59.0%	19.2%	23.3%
Sensitivity	82.5%	79.1%	23.7%	27.1%
Specificity	59.2%	69.1%	87.1%	77.3%
Efficiency	72.8%	74.9%	50.2%	48.0%
PVP	73.9%	78.1%	72.0%	62.5%
PVN	70.7%	70.3%	45.0%	43.1%
$\kappa(1, 0)$	*49.8%	49.0%	5.6%	2.4%
$\kappa(.5, 0)$	42.7%	*48.3%	9.6%	3.9%
$\kappa(0, 0)$	37.3%	*47.6%	32.9%	10.0%
Threshold Benefit	$1,727	$1,494	$6,634	$4,784

SOURCE: Weiner et al. (1979)

In this table are presented the quality indices when the test costs
are taken to be zero, as I have done in earlier chapters. In this family
of tests, the optimally sensitive test is the one in which a positive
result is attributed to those with either a positive EKG or a positive
stress test (Test #1). The optimally specific and efficient test is the
exercise stress test alone (Test #2).

It should be noted, for this will later become a crucial issue, that it
is not necessarily better to use two tests rather than one (compare #2
versus #3), and that how one combines tests can make a profound
difference to the quality of the test (compare #1 versus #3). Finally, to
get concordance on two tests (as in Test #3) may produce a less
accurate result than would basing decisions on the result of a single
test, contrary to what intuition might suggest (compare #3 versus #2).

Also listed in Table 9.3 is the threshold level of potential clinical
benefit for each of the tests at which the test becomes costworthy
(Equation 4). It can be seen that much more potential clinical benefit
would have to be offered to patients to justify Tests #3 and #4, neither

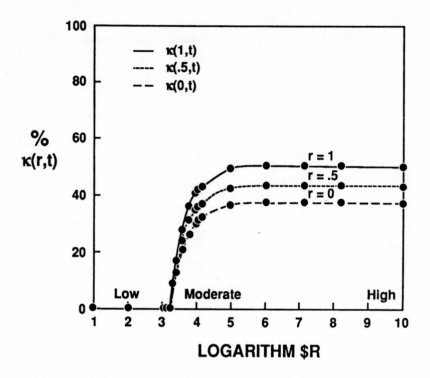

Figure 9.1. For Text #1, κ(r, t) versus $R

of which is very accurate, than to justify Tests #1 and #2 which are. This is true even though Test #4 (the resting EKG alone) costs a fraction of what Tests #1, #2, and #3 (including the exercise stress test) cost. The resting EKG used for this diagnosis in this population is simply not very accurate, and, therefore, because it has cost, it is not costworthy.

Now suppose we take test cost into consideration. Thus I propose to evaluate κ(1, t), κ(.5, t) and κ(0, t). For $T I propose to use $175 for Tests #1, #2, and #3 and $50 for test #4, but how do I propose to measure $R?

In Figure 9.1 are presented graphs of κ(r, t) for a full range of choices of $R for Test #1 (a positive test result to those who had either a positive EKG or a positive stress test.)

What is seen in Figure 9.1 is typical of any test that has cost: $T > 0. First of all, note that the scale of $R is logarithmic. The divisions correspond to $R = \$10, \$100, \$1,000$, etc. This is done because the graph of $\kappa(r, t)$ changes *very* slowly as one changes the values $R. That in turn means that the *exact* measurement of $T or of $R is *not* crucial to the results. Unless one errs by a factor of 10 or so, that is, an order of magnitude error, the error is likely to have little influence on the results.

For this reason, the fact that Moskowitz and Osband (1984) suggest that the cost of cardiac catheterization is \$1,200, while in 1990 at Stanford is appears to be closer to \$5,000, is, despite appearances, not a major discrepancy. Since over the same span of time, treatment options also may have become more numerous and more effective, $R is likely to have grown as well. Thus the value of t, crucial to these considerations, may be little changed over time.

Furthermore, since the financial cost of a test is frequently a good indicator of its risk and discomfort, I will recommend that in most cases, $T be expressed simply as the financial cost of the test, and $R as at most the order of magnitude of the clinical benefit. Thus hereafter I will be discussing only whether $R = \$10, \$10^2 = \$100, \$10^3 = \$1,000, \$10^4 = \$10,000$, etc. That begins to make the problem of applying these results more tractable, for while it may be difficult to get a precise number for $R, it is more feasible to estimate its order of magnitude.

The second observation has to do with the shape of the curve. Below a certain level (the threshold benefit, here \$1,727 from Equation 4), all the quality indices are negative. Below that level of potential clinical benefit, the costs and risks of the test outweigh the potential benefits of correct diagnosis, and the test should not be recommended.

Once past that threshold level, however, the quality index rapidly rises to a stable level. The level to which it rises is that where the test cost is discounted ($t = 0$: $T = 0$ or $R \to \infty$), which is $\kappa(r, 0)$ for $r = 0, .5, 1$.

Since it is unnecessary to measure $R very precisely, it would suffice to evaluate it at a few strategic values, say \$100, \$10,000, infinity. These values are, of course, suggested by the orders of magnitudes of test costs listed in Table 9.1.

As a result of such considerations, I propose in practice the following: Each test should be evaluated at $r = 0, .5, 1.0$ in order to evaluate its value as a definitive, a discriminative, and a screening test. This corresponds to usual clinical usage. Then I propose that it be evaluated at $R = \$100, \$10,000$, and infinity to correspond to potential clinical benefits that are "low," "moderate," or "high." Of course if more precise determinations of $R and $T are available, those should be used in preference to these rather gross approximations.

Table 9.4 Evaluation of the Costworthiness of the Tests for Coronary
Artery Disease Based on the EKG and Stress Test. Test (ST)
for the Diagnosis of Coronary Artery Disease

Potential Clinical Benefit	Test #	Sensitivity $\kappa(1, t)$	Efficiency $\kappa(.5, t)$	Specificity $\kappa(0, t)$
Low ($R = $100)	1	—	—	—
	2	—	—	—
	3	—	—	—
	4	—	—	—
Moderate ($R = $10,000)	1	41.2%	35.3%	30.9%
	2	*41.7%	*41.1%	*40.5%
	3	1.9%	3.2%	11.1%
	4	1.3%	2.1%	5.3%
High ($R→∞)	1	*49.8%	42.7%	37.3%
	2	49.0%	*48.3%	*47.6%
	3	5.6%	9.6%	32.9%
	4	2.4%	3.9%	10.0%

SOURCE: Weiner et al. (1979)
NOTE: * Optimal tests.

The practical definitions of "low," "moderate," or "high" clinical
benefit might parallel guidelines correponding to clinical usage, similar to those suggested by Galen and Gambino (1975) and others:

Low ($R = $100): The disorder is not serious, or it is self-limiting
and requires no treatment (e.g., the common cold). The test is being
done to satisfy the patient's or physician's curiosity, or to further the
physician's education or research.

High ($R → ∞): The disorder is serious, painful, and chronic or
life-threatening, and requires treatment. There is effective and safe
treatment available to the patient upon proper diagnosis (e.g., early
detection of cancer). Alternatively elimination of the possibility that
the disorder is present (AIDS is a good example) carries major health
and/or social benefits.

Whatever does not fall in these two categories, either because of
the nature of the disorder or because of the lack of availability of
treatment or because of serious doubt as to the efficacy or safety of
available treatment, will fall into the *Moderate* ($R = $10,000) category.

When these guidelines are applied to the exercise stress test described in Table 9.3, the results, presented in Table 9.4, can be derived.

If the potential clinical benefit were low, all the κ(r, t) are negative, and none of these tests should be recommended, for the risks and costs of the test outweigh the potential clinical benefit. However, coronary artery disease is a serious disorder, perhaps life-threatening and often painful. There are treatments, both medical and surgical, that may not necessarily cure the disorder, but may provide pain relief and, perhaps, enhance survival. One would think that here the potential clinical benefit is at least moderate and, perhaps, even high.

With moderate potential clinical benefit, the results indicate that the tests are costworthy. The optimal referent is to ignore the results of the EKG and to designate as positive those with a positive stress test (#2). Once more, using more information than required (the EKG result along with the stress test result) may diminish both the accuracy and the costworthiness of the test.

If the potential clinical benefit were considered High (a matter of opinion), one would recommend Test #1 (EKG+ or ST+) for screening and continue to recommend Test #2 (ST+) for discrimination and definitive results. The gain in using Test #1 rather than #2 for screening is marginal at best ($49.8% versus $49.0%), but when the potential clinical benefit is high, one must take every advantage, no matter how small.

The selection of $R = $100 as a "low" level of potential clinical benefit, of $R = $10,000 as a "moderate" level are clearly both arbitrary and crude, and others might choose to set them otherwise or to use more than three reference points on the $R curve. Because of the shape of the curves of κ(r, t) for fixed values of r and of $T, as illustrated in Figure 9.1, which test will be recommended will not change radically when values somewhat different from those proposed are used.

A Geometric Approach: The QCROC

The geometric approaches of the earlier chapters, when test costs were being discounted, can easily be generalized to the present case when the cost of each test is taken into account. Instead of locating each of a family of tests by κ(1, 0) and κ(0, 0), one would now locate them by using κ(1, t) and κ(0, t). The outer boundary will now be called the QCROC: the ROC taking both quality and cost into account.

From Equation 5, κ(r, t) is a weighted average of κ(1, t) and κ(0, t), as earlier κ(r, 0) was of κ(1, 0) and κ(0, 0), and the location of optimal tests proceeds along the same lines. The optimally costworthy sensitive test is highest on the QCROC, the optimally costworthy specific test is furthest to the right. Those optimally costworthy for other values of relative clinical benefit (r), including the optimally costworthy efficient test (r = .5), lie on the QCROC between these two points and would be located geometrically using the methods described in Chapter 8.

It would be useful now to retrace the steps taken from the initial geometric approach proposed for the classic ROC to the QROC, and finally to the QCROC.

In Figure 9.2b is the classic ROC, where each test is located by its sensitivity and specificity, and the ROC is the outer boundary defined by these tests and the points (0, 1) and (1, 0), the classic arc shape (Chapter 6). There the problem was that it was difficult from perusal of this geometric configuration to decide which test is optimal, when, and why. This was so because the random values of sensitivity and specificity shift with the level of the test and are not obviously visible in the ROC. From the ROC, however, it is clear that the only two tests that can possibly be optimal in this particular family are Tests #1 and #2, for the others fall below the ROC.

What I proposed (Chapter 6) was to rescale the sensitivity and specificity so that their values would be zero for random decision making and have a maximal value of one and to locate the tests by these rescaled values $\kappa(1, 0)$ and $\kappa(0, 0)$, as in Figure 9.2b, the Test QROC.

In doing this we mapped the two outer boundaries (outer double lines) of Figure 9.2a into the outer boundaries of Figure 9.2b (also outer double lines). The diagnosis line in Figure 9.2a (inner double line) was mapped into the diagonal line in the QROC plane (also inner double line). Then the Random ROC (open circles) was drawn together into a single point and mapped into the point (0, 0) of the QROC plane (also open circle). The lines of Q-level tests in the QROC plane, lying parallel to the diagnosis line, were each mapped into a line of Q-level tests, a ray in the QROC plane. The result of this reconfiguration was that the arc of the ROC became the leaf of the QROC; however, now the highest point on this QROC leaf corresponded to the optimally sensitive test and the right-most point to the optimally specific test.

I then proceeded (Chapter 7) to reexamine the issue by locating each test in the family by its predictive values (see Figure 9.2c), and noted that this configuration seemed to be a miniature version of the test QROC. So it was. The boundaries from $(P', 1)$ to (1, 1) and from

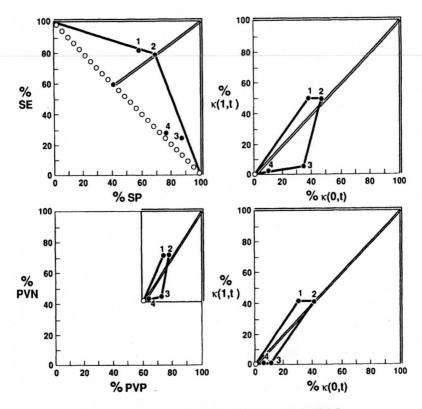

Figure 9.2 . The Evaluation of the ROC, QROC, and QCROC

(1, 1) to (1, P) (outer double lines) mapped into the two outer boundaries of the QROC (also outer double lines). The random point at (P, P′) mapped into the point (0, 0), and the configuration of tests, except for scale, remained the same.

This now clarified that the QROC identified the optimally sensitive test, which was also the one with highest predictive value of a negative test, and the optimally specific test, which was also the one with highest predictive value of a positive test. The fundamental difference between the Signal Detection and Bayesian approaches has been the calibration of the descriptors used. In addition, it was pointed out that other descriptors such as risk ratios or risk differences are similarly related to $\kappa(1, 0)$ and $\kappa(0, 0)$.

Then I looked at efficiency. Because the quality of the efficiency was a weighted average of the the qualities of the sensitivity and specificity, this test had to lie on the Test QROC between the optimally sensitive and optimally specific test. In fact, all optimal tests corresponding to different views of the clinical importance of which of the two possible errors were the most important (as reflected in the parameter r of $\kappa(r, 0)$) constituted the set of tests between the optimally sensitive ($r = 1$) and optimally specific ($r = 0$) tests and could be easily seen on the test QROC.

So far I have discounted the test cost, i.e., setting $\$T = 0$ either because the test cost is negligible (which it seldom is) or because relative to the potential clinical benefit ($\$R$), cost is negligible (which occasionally is true). If the test cost and potential clinical benefit are taken into account, a new measure of test quality emerges: $\kappa(r, t)$. I now propose to locate each test by its value of $\kappa(1, t)$ and $\kappa(0, t)$: the QCROC. In Figure 9.2d we see the QCROC when the potential clinical benefit was considered moderate ($\$R = \$10,000$). What is seen here is also a leaf, but one that tends to be shorter and narrower than the leaf of the QROC.

Any test that is free remains in the same position in the QCROC as it was in the QROC plane. Each test with cost is shifted toward the origin, a distance determined by its cost ($\$T$) and by its level ($Q$). The prevalence ($P$) and the potential clinical benefit ($\$R$) are fixed here for all the tests in the family. Hence the leaf may be shortened and narrowed. The higher the costs of the tests under consideration, the more the leaf may be diminished, and the more tests in the QROC plane may disappear from the QCROC plane (legitimate tests that are not costworthy). If the tests in the family have different costs, the general configuration will change, and the identification of the optimal tests may change as well.

In the case of the exercise stress test in the Weiner et al. (1979) study, the QCROC for low potential clinical benefit would have had no points at all. After all, if you can promise no more than $100 worth of clinical benefit as a result of testing, what justification can there be for using even an accurate test costing $175 or an inaccurate test costing $50?

When the potential clinical benefit is high, the QCROC is identical to the QROC. In this case, Test #1 is the optimally sensitive test. However, when one begins to "charge" for mistakes by taking into consideration the cost of the test, then the optimally sensitive test becomes #2, ($\$T = \$175$ and $\$R = \$10,000$). In narrowing the leaf, the small advantage of #1 relative to #2 seen in the QROC changes to a small advantage of #2 relative to #1 seen in the QCROC. Thus #1 is more legitimate, but #2 is more costworthy.

The Costs and Risks of Too Much Information

Physicians, whether clinicians or researchers, as well as patients tend to assume that the more information, the better the outcome. Surely there can't be too *much* information! The fact is, however, that as we have seen, there can be too much information. In the above example we noted that combining the results of the resting EKG and those of the stress test in the wrong way (Test #3) gave results far poorer than those obtained by ignoring the resting EKG (Test #2). To assume that there can't be too much information creates a problem, for accepting such a proposition provides rationalization for doing any and all tests on a patient, ones that are costly and risky and not at all associated with the disorder, tests that are unreliable and misleading, tests that are never actually needed or used in the clinical decision process.

It is not too drastic to say that seeking too much information can kill or maim patients. Robin (1984) presents a case history of a patient who underwent a brain biopsy (the test) in order to decide whether or not he should be treated for herpes virus rather than some other viral encephalitis (the diagnosis). As a result of the brain biopsy procedure, the patient sank into an irreversible coma. The test indicated that the patient had viral encephalitis (a negative test), but this result was ignored, and the patient was treated for herpes encephalitis (a positive diagnosis).

If, in fact, the patient was to be treated for herpes encephalitis whether or not the brain biopsy was positive, why was the test done? Whatever the patient's initial disorder, what the patient now has is an iatragenic disorder resulting from seeking unnecessary information.

One might argue that this is a single case, only one rare, although frightening, example. A more general and challenging example is that discussed by Sisson et al. (1976) in a paper subtitled: "The Hazard of Using Additional Data," an approach I have already emulated in evaluating the screening test proposed by DiMaio et al. (1987) for Down's syndrome.

The question addressed is that of the effect of using a new (let us assume a cost- and risk-free) test for detection of pancreatic cancer. In their population, 12 of 1,000 patients in fact are likely to have pancreatic cancer ($P = 1.2\%$). Undetected and untreated, all 12 would die.

The test being considered has a sensitivity of 80% (SE = .80) and a specificity of 95% (SP = .95). Those positive on the test would undergo a surgical procedure with a 10% mortality risk. The pancreas would be removed, examined, and, if cancer were found, the patients would be treated. No cost of treatment is presented, but it is proposed that the treatment is 50% successful. Let us even assume for the moment that the treatment is cost-free and risk-free. Many physicians would consider such a test a good one, offering the opportunity to save half of the otherwise doomed patients by using a no-cost/-risk test that appears to have "high" sensitivity and specificity.

The problem is that the consequences of using the test would be that more than 12 (12.5 expected) of 1,000 patients would die (compared to 12 without the test): 4.5 from detected but uncured cancer, 6 from the surgical procedure, 2 from undetected cancer. In addition, 44 patients who originally were free of cancer are likely to survive with pancreatic insufficiency, an iatrogenic disorder in this case. What this means is that the test would have benefited 4.5 of every 1,000 patients, but harmed 49.

We could have made the situation worse (and more realistic) if we had included consideration of a cost or risk for the test and a cost of treatment. Every patient would be charged for the test (988 of each 1,000 unnecessarily). Of every 1,000 patients, 59 would be charged for hospitalization, anesthetic, and surgical costs (50 unnecessarily). Finally, the 44 patients with the iatrogenic disorder of pancreatic insufficiency would bear lifetime treatment costs associated with this disorder.

This is the type of situation in which specificity must be very high ($r = 0$). Asking a patient likely to be without cancer to undergo a surgical procedure with a 10% mortality risk, which (if he survives) would leave the patient with pancreatic insufficiency, is clearly to be avoided. In the example, the specificity of the test is 95%, but in a population with an prevalence of 1.2%, it has a quality index of 15.3%:

$$Q = P \cdot SE + P' \cdot SP'$$

$$= 0.012 \cdot 0.80 + 0.988 \cdot 0.05$$

$$= 0.0590.$$

Then

$$\kappa(0, 0) = (SP - Q')/Q$$

$$= (0.95 - 0.941)/(1 - 0.941)$$

$$= 0.153.$$

The quality of specificity of this test is not high, even when no cost or risk is attributed to the test. A specificity of 95% is simply not high enough in such a low-risk population.

Informed Consent for Medical Tests

Every patient is entitled to give informed consent prior to an invasive procedure such as surgery. Many share the opinion that medical tests having cost are themselves invasive procedures, even when no surgery is involved, and should also be done only with *informed* consent of the patients. This is currently inadequately done, not because physicians are loathe to share their information on the subject, but, rather, because the information available to the physicians from medical test evaluations is not adequate to the purpose.

A case in point is demonstrated in *The Complete Book of Medical Tests* by Moskowitz and Osband (1984). For each of a range of common medical tests, the authors provide information on:

Purpose of the test
Background
How the test is done
How the results are given
Patient preparation
Risks and discomforts
Symptoms for which this test is commonly obtained
Diseases for which this test is commonly obtained
Cost

This is all, of course, very useful; however, nowhere in this book is there any information on the accuracy of any of the tests.

Some, physicians and patients alike, will protest that requiring informed consent when it is *only* a blood or urine test that *only* costs $10 or $25 is wasteful of time and money. This ignores the fact that the costs of medical testing frequently lie *not* in the test per se, but, rather, in the actions the physician will take as a result of the test. In the Sisson et al. (1976) hypothetical example above, no one died or was injured *in the testing*, but several died and were injured as a result of the actions taken as a result of inaccurate tests.

For any medical test entailing cost or risk, the patient should have access, I believe, to the following information:

1. Why is the test proposed for this particular patient? What disorder is the test designed to detect? Is the test costworthy for patients like the one for whom the test is being considered? What would happen if the patient did not take the test?

2. What is the cost and risk of the test? What does taking the test entail? How much will the patient or his insurance coverage be charged for the test? How long will the test take? Will it cause pain, discomfort? Are there any risks, aftereffects?

3. What would a positive test mean? What actions would follow a positive test? What would the benefits be to someone with the disorder? What would the risks be to someone without the disorder?

4. What would a negative test mean? What actions would follow a negative test? What would the benefits be to someone without the disorder? What would the risks be to someone with the disorder? but most important:

5. Test accuracy—How accurate is the test? How costworthy? Are there other more costworthy tests available?

In the Sisson et al. (1976) hypothetical case, a patient should have been informed that without the test 1.2% would die from undetected pancreatic cancer. With the test 1.25% would die, either of undetected pancreatic cancer, from untreatable pancreatic cancer, or from surgical risks, and that another 4.4% would suffer lifelong iatrogenic disorder resulting from a false positive test.

How many clinicians would recommend such a test to a patient if they were required to present such information to the patient? How many patients would sign such a consent form? The difficulty is that neither clinicians nor patients generally have access to such information, given the current state of medical test evaluation.

To be honest, as a patient, I would prefer *not* to have to read through an informed consent form for each and every test. However, I would like to believe that in ordering a test for me, the physician could, if asked, either answer each of the above questions or refer me to sources from which such information could be obtained. That, however, can come about only if each test were to come with a "package insert," full and complete information provided by the proponents of the test describing:

1. For which patients such a test is to be used and not used,
2. What the protocol should be;
3. What the optimal referrent would be;
4. What the costs and risks of the tests are; and
5. *Documentation* of the accuracy and cost-worthiness of the test.

Summary

A quality index for use in medical test evaluation that incorporates consideration of test accuracy, relative clinical benefit, fixed test cost, and potential clinical benefit is $\kappa(r, t)$:

$$\kappa(r, t) = \frac{-t + P \cdot Q' \cdot r \cdot \kappa(1, 0) + P' \cdot Q \cdot r' \cdot \kappa(0, 0)}{P \cdot Q' \cdot r + P' \cdot Q \cdot r'}$$

where $\kappa(1, 0)$ and $\kappa(0, 0)$ are indices reflecting the quality of the sensitivity and specificity of the test.

The parameter r represents the relative clinical importance of a false negative over a false positive outcome. Thus a test designed as a screening test would focus on $r = 1$. A test designed to yield a definitive positive result would focus on $r = 0$. A test for which false negatives and false positives are equally important, a discriminative test, would focus on $r = .5$. Any value of r between 0 and 1 can be used if more specific needs are articulated.

The fixed cost of the test is T. The relative clinical benefits, R_+ and R_-, represent how much difference it makes to patients with and without the disorder whether or not the test gives the correct result. The potential clinical benefit, $R = R_+ + R_-$, is small when the disorder is not serious or is self-limiting, and increases as the seriousness of the disorder increases, the necessity for treatment becomes more imperative, and the availability of safe and effective treatment is assured. The relative cost of the test is defined to be

$$t = \$T/\$R.$$

It was demonstrated that the quality index changes very slowly in response to shifts in the magnitudes of $\$T$ and $\$R$. As a result, one need only measure $\$T$ and $\$R$ accurately, more or less to their order of magnitude. Operationally, it was suggested that three reference benefits might be of interest: $100, $10,000, and infinity corresponding to low, moderate, and high potential clinical benefit. Again, if more exact and specific values of $\$R$ are available, they can be used in the formulation of $\kappa(r, t)$.

10

Basic Issues in Using Multiple Tests

Introduction

"Dubiously costworthy respiratory therapy, diagnostic radioisotopes, electroencephalography, and cobalt therapy involve excesses of $995 million . . . [We] can add the CT scanner for another $200 million, . . . savings from the elimination of excess clinical lab tests probably would amount to another $4.0 billion" (Menzel, 1983, pp. 12-13). Menzel estimates the grand total for what he calls "dubiously costworthy" medical tests and treatments combined as "$19.15 billion, over 10 percent of the 1979 medical-care budget in the United States. This amount is clearly no pittance" (pp. 12-13).

As a more specific instance of such excess, Menzel (1983) reports six so-called inexpensive tests ("guaiacs") for detection of intestinal cancer:

> The benefits of the first two tests are significant. However, when calculations are done for each of the last four tests to determine the costs of detecting a case of cancer (not even curing it), the costs are discovered to be $49,150, $469,534, $4,724,695, and $47,107,214 respectively. To some these calculations suggest that the routine should be reduced, say to a three-guaiac test. (p. 6)

These comments pinpoint the most serious problem of all with regard to medical tests, that resulting from the promiscuous use of multiple tests, some or even all of which may not be costworthy, and that may, in fact, not even be legitimate. In the preceding chapters I have focused first on evaluation of the quality of a single test, and then, using these principles, on selecting the optimal single test. Then, I focused on identifying the optimal single test from a family of tests. This evaluation was based on simultaneous consideration of the accuracy of the tests (sensitivity, specificity, predictive values, or efficiency), on the potential benefit of correct decisions to those with and without the disorder of interest (R, r), and on the cost, time expenditure, risk, and discomfort of the test itself (T).

In Chapters 11, 12, and 13, I will go on to develop methods to select optimal ways of combining two or more medical tests so as to maximize accuracy at minimal risk or cost to the patient. Before I do so, however, there are a few questions regarding the use of multiple medical tests that can be answered very quickly using only the principles already enunciated.

Tests in Parallel or Tests in Sequence

Suppose we had two tests, T1 and T2, respectively costing $T1 and $T2, both costs greater than zero. When, from the point of view of costworthiness, should these tests be used in parallel (ordered simultaneously), and when should they be used in sequence (first one is ordered and then perhaps the other, depending on the results of the first test)? We ignore for the moment what the most accurate combination of the two test results is. For the moment let us consider only the question of when tests should be obtained in parallel versus in sequence to get the most costworthy presentation of the tests.

The answer is unequivocal: unless one or the other test is free, tests should *always* be ordered in sequence, the order determined by the costs of the tests, with the least costly test ordered first. To demonstrate why this must be, regardless of how the tests will be combined to reach an accurate decision, consider Table 10.1 where the test results and costs are listed if the tests were ordered in parallel.

If the tests are ordered in parallel each patient pays $T1 + $T2 for the two tests. Then what do physicians do with the results? The physician must decide on the basis of the tests whether or not the result is positive or not, i.e., whether or not to treat. To do this the four

Table 10.1 Evaluation of Test Cost for Tests in Parallel Versus Tests in Sequence ($T1 < $T2) Medical Tests

Test Outcomes		Combined Test Results Based on Parallel Tests			
Test 1	Test 2	A	B	C	D
T1+	T2+	+	+	+	+
T1+	T2−	+	−	+	−
T1−	T2+	−	+	+	−
T1−	T2−	−	−	−	−

	Per Patient Test Cost
Tests in parallel:	$T1 + $T2
Tests in sequence:	
A: Use T1 alone.	$T1
B: Use T2 alone.	$T2
C: Use T1 first, T2 only if T1 is negative.	$T1 + ($T2)?
D: Use T1 first, T2 only in T1 is positive.	$T1 + ($T2)?

outcomes must be separated into two classes: positive and negative. Clearly, when both are legitimate tests for the disorder, if both come out positive, the patient is more likely to have the disorder than not. If both came out negative, the patient is more likely not to have the disorder. When the test results are concordant, the decision is easy. What happens when the tests are discordant?

Then there are the four possible alternative strategies of assigning T+ and T− on the basis of the two tests, listed as A, B, C, and D in Table 10.1. Which is ultimately preferable depends on the accuracies of the tests, but whichever is preferable, the test can be done with equal accuracy but less cost by ordering the tests in sequence. This is seen at the bottom of the table.

For example, the decision in A is clearly based only on Test #1; the decision in B is clearly based only on Test #2. To order two tests when only one actually figures in the decision clearly costs the patient unnecessary money, time, discomfort, and risk. In A, Test #1 alone should be ordered; in B, Test #2 alone should be ordered.

For situation C, for example, one need order only one test, the less costly one, and only if that one is negative, need the other be ordered. Many patients (all those with a positive first test) would not need to pay for both tests. Similarly, for situation D one need order only one test, the less costly one, and only if that one is positive, need the other be ordered. Again, not all patients need to pay for both tests to get the full quality obtainable.

If there is a whole battery of tests available, this result quickly generalizes. If there are free tests on the battery (ones that the patient is not charged for and that take little time and carry no discomfort or risk to the patient), it does not matter how or when they are ordered. If such free tests are inaccurate, they can be ignored in making any decisions about the patient. Ignoring such a test is of no matter, for the patient loses nothing in the testing.

However, when the decision is made for the patient's benefit, tests that are not free should *never* be ordered in parallel, for that only increases the cost of the testing without any increase in the quality of the test outcomes over what could be achieved by using the same tests in appropriate sequence.

Tests with costs should *always* be ordered only after all the free tests are evaluated, and then only if they are needed to supplement the free tests to achieve an accurate diagnosis. A test with risk or cost should never be ordered only to be ignored in the clinical decision process, for then the physician has ordered and charged for an unnecessary and unneeded procedure, one that subjects the patient to unnecessary cost and risk for no purpose.

Let us consider a real example of two tests to see the kinds of impact that might be expected. Melin et al. (1981) evaluated several tests for coronary artery disease using coronary arteriography to define the diagnosis. Let us focus here on the two tests' evaluation of angina ($T1 = \$0$) and the thallium test (let us say $T2 = \$1,000$). In Table 10.2 are presented the test costs and the quality of specificity, efficiency, and sensitivity when the potential clinical benefit is at the three suggested reference levels.

If the two tests were done in parallel, the per patient cost of the tests would be $1,000, the cost of the thallium test. Because the clinical evaluation of angina is free of additional cost and risk, we argue that should be done first in all cases. If the selected referent declared those with either typical angina *or* a positive thallium test positive, then the evaluation of chest pain would be done first. Only if it were negative (28.1% of total cases) would the thallium test be required. The expected cost to the patient then would be:

Table 10.2 Evaluation of the Quality and Cost of Tests for Coronary
Artery Disease Based on Clinical Assessment of Angina

		Quality of:		
Referent	Per Patient Test Cost	Sensitivity $r = 1$	Efficiency $r = .5$	Specificity $r = 0$
Potential Clinical Benefit High ($R = \infty$)				
A+	$0.00	82%	64%	52%
Th+	$1,000.00	69%	74%	80%
A+ and Th+	$719.00	64%	*76%	*94%
A+ or Th+	$281.00	*96%	61%	45%
Potential Clinical Benefit Moderate ($R = $10,000).				
A+	$0.00	*82%	*64%	*52%
Th+	$1,000.00	30%	32%	35%
A+ and Th+	$719.00	30%	35%	44%
A+ or Th+	$281.00	24%	15%	41%
Potential Clinical Benefit Low ($R = $100).				
A+	$0.00	*82%	*64%	*52%
Th+	$1,000.00	30%	32%	35%
A+ and Th+	$719.00	30%	35%	44%
A+ or Th+	$281.00	24%	15%	11%

SOURCE: Melin et al. (1981)
NOTE: (A: $T = 0$) and the Thallium Test (Th: $T = $1,000)

$$\$0 + 0.281(\$1,000) = \$281.$$

If the selected referent declared those with both typical angina and
positive thallium test positive, then the evaluation of chest pain would
again be done first, and only if it were positive (71.9% of total cases)
would the thallium test be required. The expected cost would be:

$$\$0 + 0.719(\$1,000) = \$719.$$

Which referent would be preferred in each case depends on the
quality of the tests [i.e., $\kappa(r, t)$] as listed in Table 10.2. If the potential
clinical benefit here were considered low or moderate, only clinical
evaluation of angina would be done at no extra cost to the patients,
for the cost of the thallium test would not be justified in view of its
inaccuracies.

Only if the potential clinical benefit were considered high would
the thallium test be recommended, but only following evaluation of

angina, not before it. For an optimally specific or efficient test, the thallium test would be ordered for those with a positive angina evaluation. The expected cost per patient would then be $719. For an optimally sensitive test, the thallium test would be ordered for those with a negative angina evaluation. The expected cost per patient would then be $281. Both these figures are to be compared to $1,000 per patient if the tests were done in parallel. In short, the cost saving between ordering tests in sequence and in parallel is not trivial. Cutting test costs in half or more is not atypical.

In many cases a physician will order two tests because it is more convenient to do so and in the hope and expectation that the two results will concur. If they concur, the physician may well feel more secure that the clinical decision based on the outcome of the tests is correct. Any such increased sense of security may be misplaced. We have already seen cases where the concurrence of two test results (one of which is much less accurate than the other) yields a less accurate result than would the better of the two tests alone. We have already seen cases where doing a test puts the patient at greater risk than not doing the test.

In the case of two tests, what happens when, as frequently does happen, the two results are discordant? The time to make this decision on such a course of action is *before* the tests are ordered, not *after* the patient has already incurred unnecessary test costs and risks.

Ordering tests in parallel is done, not for the benefit of the patient, but, rather, generally for the convenience of the physician. It is easier to check off a list of available tests than to devise a plan for testing appropriate to each patient. However, in all justice, with the current state of medical test evaluation, the information a clinician needs on test quality to knowledgeably devise such a plan is not readily available.

Even when such information is available, there is major pressure discouraging making the effort. With the specter of malpractice suits, there is some measure of security and comfort in having exhausted test resources for each patient even if many of the tests are unneeded and ignored. Since the hazards of unnecessary and irrelevant tests are ill-recognized, and malpractice suits are seldom based on too much or ill-selected testing, pressure is exerted in the direction of excessive testing.

Added to that is the profit motive. To maintain a quality laboratory to run a full range of medical tests, enough demand must be generated to cover personnel, equipment, and other overhead. When each medical clinic and each hospital, however small, seeks to maintain its own testing laboratory in order not to have to reimburse outside its walls for tests, this too exerts yet more pressure toward promiscuous use of tests. The resulting multiple tests per patient, and repeated testing, proliferates non-essential tests. The obvious answer to this is, of course, that not every clinic and not every hospital should seek to maintain its own laboratory. The quality of the test results might well be more accurate and less expensive, and the quality of medical care better and less costly, if all but the most routine and common medical tests were done in central, well-established laboratories with high levels of quality control.

The Quality of Combined Tests

Another mathematical myth that surfaces occasionally concerns what the sensitivity and specificity of a test are when based on combining two tests in terms of the sensitivities of the two component tests. It is perhaps worth a brief note to forestall any misunderstanding in this area.

Suppose we had two tests for the same disorder in the same population, each with known sensitivity and specificity against a clinically valid diagnosis for that disorder: SE1, SE2, SP1, and SP2. If we were to combine the two tests, what would the sensitivity and specificity of the combined test be? The correct answer is: With the information given, we don't know. However, we do have some small clues: If we were to combine the two tests by attributing a positive result to those who are positive on both tests (an "and" rule), the combined test is nested within each of the individual tests. Thus the level of the combined test is less than the level of either of the individual tests. The sensitivity of the combined test is less than the sensitivity of either of the individual tests, and the specificity of the combined test is greater than the specificity of either of the individual tests. How much less or greater depends on how the two tests relate to each another, as well as on how each relates to the diagnosis. If, on the other hand, one were to combine the two tests by attributing a positive result to patients positive on one or the other of the individual tests (an "or" rule), then each of the individual tests is nested within the combined test. Thus the level of the combined test is greater than that of each of the individual tests; the sensitivity of the combined test is greater than that of each of the individual tests; and the specificity of the combined test is less than that of each of the individual tests.

Now here's the myth: If you combine the tests by using an "and" rule then:

$$SE_{comb} = SE1 \cdot SE2$$

$$SP_{comb} = 1 - (1 - SP1)(1 - SP2) = SP1 + SP2 - SP1 \cdot SP2 .$$

If, on the other hand you combine the tests by using an "or" rule, then:

$$SE_{comb} = 1 - (1 - SE1) \cdot (1 - SE2) = SE1 + SE2 - SE1 \cdot SE2 ,$$

$$SP_{comb} = SP1 \cdot SP2 .$$

This myth is closely related to the myth of the constancy of the sensitivity and specificity of a test for a diagnosis across different clinical populations (see Chapter 6). If, in fact, the diagnosis were absolutely reproducible ($p_i = 0$ or 1 for all patients in the population) and if, in fact, those with a positive diagnosis were absolutely homogeneous (if $p_i = 1$ then $q_i = A$), and those with a negative diagnosis were also absolutely homogeneous (if $p_i = 0$ then $q_i = B$) for both tests, and if, *in addition*, the tests were independent, only then would the above equations hold true.

There are too many "ifs" in this series of statements. Most diagnoses are *not* absolutely reproducible. Patients with the disorder *are* likely to be differentiated in terms of severity, stage, or which symptoms they manifest. Patients without the disorder *are* likely to be differentiated in terms of predisposition to the disorder. Two tests for the same disorder are frequently *not* independent.

Regrettably, to evaluate the performance of a combined test, there is no alternative to performing both tests on a sample, combining their results, to see exactly how the combined test performs relative to the diagnosis. There is no easy mathematical alternative to doing such an evaluation.

When Should a Test Be Repeated?

A special case of using two tests is that when the two tests are two repeats of the same test. When is this a good idea? There are generally two motivations for using two tests instead of one. The second test may serve to correct errors that are made on the first test. The second test may add unique new and valuable information to the information gained by the use of the first test.

When the second test is, however, a repeat of exactly the same test as the first test, it cannot add unique new information. It can only serve to correct errors made in the first test. Consequently, if a legitimate test is highly reproducible, no purpose is served by using the test again, for the second test result will only reproduce the first, rightly or wrongly. As a result, it is most important to repeat a test when the information it provides is, first of all, valuable but comes from a test that itself is not highly reproducible. A test that is of questionable costworthiness should not be used even once. A test that is costworthy should possibly be repeated if it is poor in reproducibility, and not otherwise.

Should a Test Be Done Blind to Previous Test Results?

There is nothing in these statistical approaches that requires that in an evaluation study the multiple tests used for a subject need be done blind to each other. It was a requirement for valid medical test evaluation that the test(s) and diagnosis be done blind to each other.

However, if tests are not done blind to the results of preceding tests, the risk is that erroneous results on previous tests may exacerbate the risk of error on later tests. While subsequent test results may appear to confirm earlier tests, such confirmation may be artificial and wrong. One might be merely repeating the same error. For this reason, if multiple tests are to be used in a test evaluation, from a statistical point of view it is better to do each test blind to earlier results.

However, clinicians tell me that the interpretation of many tests cannot be done without knowledge of test results previously obtained, and researchers tell me that is nearly impossible to blind each and every test in a series. Since there is no absolute statistical necessity for such blinding, it seems preferable to leave it to the researcher doing the evaluation as to whether tests are done blind or not. If, however, there is not blinding, information on the order of tests and what information is or is not shared from test to test must be conveyed as part of the protocol for use of multiple tests.

Summary

Three general points have been made. First, if the choice of testing procedure is based on the benefit to the patient, multiple tests having costs should never be done in parallel. They should always be done in sequence with the least costly tests done first. The pressures to using tests in parallel are based on consideration of factors other than the benefit to the patient.

Second, one repeats a test only if the test is both costworthy and not highly reproducible. Third, what the performance of tests is, when used in combination, either in parallel or in sequence, cannot be calculated from the individual performance characteristics of each test used alone. The quality of two or more tests used in combination can only be assessed by performing the tests in combination on a sample of patients and directly assessing performance.

11

Evaluating Batteries of Medical Tests:
Optimal Sequences

Introduction

The problem now is to develop from the methods of the earlier chapters a methodology to evaluate cost-effective use of *multiple* tests. To do so I will introduce one more term: a "battery of tests." By a battery of tests I mean a family of tests (as defined in Chapter 4) that can be subdivided into smaller families, possibly overlapping, that can be done separately and at separate costs.

For example, in Chapters 6, 7, and 8, we considered a family of tests for diabetes that included the Somogyi-Nelson and Folin-Wu blood tests and the Clinitest and Benedict's urine tests, each done at 1, 2, 3, and random hours after the test meal, and each with multiple possible referents. Within this family we found that (not counting costs) the optimally efficient test was the Somogyi-Nelson procedure done 2 hours after the test meal with a referent of 140 mg/dl [$\kappa(.5, 0) = 67.8\%$]. It may or may not be true that the Folin-Wu procedure done 1 hour after the test meal with a referent of 160 mg/dl [$\kappa(.5, 0) = 65.6\%$], a test with only slightly less quality as an efficient test, combined with the Somogyi-Nelson test might improve the quality of decision making. Without doubt, however, whether quality is improved or not,

165

doing this additional test increases the cost of testing (two blood samples must be drawn, one at 1 and one at 2 hours after the test meal, and two different assay procedures be used, etc.). Is combining two such tests cost effective? If so, combining them in what way, and for whom?

The Basic Model

If a battery of tests included n test responses, some of which are measured on a continuous scale, the number of possible ways of combining the tests is infinite—and that is not hyperbole. Mathematically, this results from defining a test as a partition of the n-dimensional space of possible test responses into two subspaces, one of which is designated a positive test, the other negative. There are an infinite number of such partitions even if only one of the test responses is measured on a continuum.

For those who find visualizing n-dimensional space as problematic as I do, let us consider the case when n is only 2: the Somogyi-Nelson test 2 hours after the test meal and the Folin-Wu 1 hour after the test meal. We can locate each possible response on a graph by locating the response of the Somogyi-Nelson test (on the x-axis) and of the Folin-Wu test (on the y-axis). Then this graph is split into two parts (partitioned), with all points in one part assigned positive test results, all points in the other, negative test results. Figure 11.1a-11.1h presents eight such partitions.

In Figure 11.1a is the partition obtained by using only the Somogyi-Nelson test. In this case all patients whose test response lies to the right of the partition line have a positive test, all those to the left are negative, and the Folin-Wu test is ignored. In Figure 11.1b is the partition obtained by using only the Folin-Wu test, the positive and negative tests as indicated. In the earlier chapters we have been examining primarily partitions of this sort, moving the partition lines up and down, or right and left (as indicated by the arrows) to identify the optimal referent for each of these tests separately.

In Chapter 6, however, we began to consider tests defined by combining two tests using "and/or" rules. Here we might consider giving a positive test score to those with a positive Somogyi-Nelson *or* a positive Folin-Wu (see Figure 11.1c) or to those with a positive Somogyi-Nelson *and* a positive Folin-Wu test (see Figure 11.1d). Now we have the option of moving one of the partition lines up and down and the other right and left to find the optimal partition.

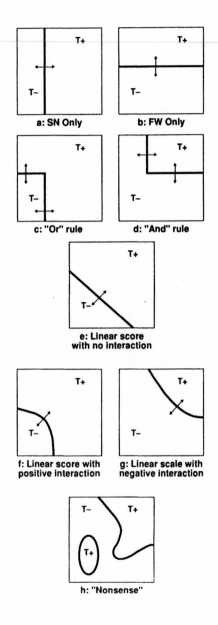

Figure 11.1. Test Partitions for Two Test Results: The Somogyi-Nelson Procedure (SN) on the *x*-axis and the Folin-Wu Procedure (FW) on the *y*-axis.

We could also consider combining the two test responses into one by taking a weighted average of the two test responses as a test score:

$$\text{Score} = w_1 \cdot \text{Somogyi-Nelson} + w_2 \cdot \text{Folin-Wu},$$

and declare the test positive if the score is high. This type of partition is described in Figure 11.1e. Now we have the option of changing the weights w_1 and w_2, which changes the tilt of the line, as well as moving the line in or out from the origin. This is a "linear score without interaction."

We could also consider a more complex score such as:

$$\text{Score} = w_1 \cdot \text{Somogyi-Nelson} + w_2 \cdot \text{Folin-Wu}$$

$$+ w_3 \cdot \text{Somogyi-Nelson} \cdot \text{Folin-Wu},$$

and declare the test positive if this score is high. Such partitions are described in Figures 11.1f and 11.1g. The one in 11.1f is obtained if w_3 is positive, the one in 11.1g is obtained if w_3 is negative. These are "linear scores with positive or negative interactions." We can change the shape of the curve by varying the weights, as well as the placement of the curve by varying the cut-off.

Depending on the shape of the curves in Figures 11.1e, 11.1f, and 11.1g, one can frequently find a rule of the types seen in Figures 11.1a, 11.1b, 11.1c, and 11.1d that carves up the space in approximately the same way. Figures 11.1a, 11.1b, 11.1c, and 11.1d are what result from sequentially structured batteries, Figures 11.1e, 11.1f, and 11.1g from scored batteries. This observation indicates why it is frequently possible to develop a sequentially structured battery with performance characteristics that approximate or better that of the same battery scored (and, of course, vice versa).

Technically, we could carve up that two-dimensional space in any way we choose, designate each subspace created as representing either a positive or negative test result (see Figure 11.1h). However we did it would constitute the definition of the referent of a test; an incredible and nonsensical test, perhaps, one almost impossible to apply in clinical situations, and probably not a very high-quality test, but a test nevertheless. In fact, when tests are structured for clinical use, fanciful partitions are almost never used, and most are structured either sequentially by using "and/or" rules or by scoring with or without interactions.

There are many old and powerful mathematical methods available for scoring tests, and these will be discussed in Chapters 12 and 13. These methods are designed to find the best set of weights. The cut-off can be optimally set by treating the resulting weighted score as a new single test response and applying the methods of the earlier chapters or, as is frequently done, set arbitrarily.

Such scoring has major drawbacks: No consideration is given to the cost of tests, to the potential clinical benefit to patients, or to the relative clinical benefit in deriving the optimal weights for the score. As a result, every test response with a non-zero weight in the score must be used for every patient. The cost of combining multiple tests into one by using a score consequently tends to be higher than the cost of using the same tests appropriately in sequence. Furthermore, scoring rules tend to select weights to optimize efficiency, even when the clinical situation demands the optimally sensitive or specific test.

To use such a score in a clinical situation, after all the tests are done (in parallel now since they are now regarded as one test) the clinician computes the score for each patient and checks whether it falls above or below the designated cut-off. Only the rare clinician, I suspect, performs such computations in clinical decision making. In fact, sequential structuring ("and," "or" rules) are what clinicians tend to do. This suspicion is fed by the fact that, as we will later see, medical test evaluations reported in the research literature designed to develop optimal scores frequently fail to give the instructions necessary to do the computation of the scores and to present the cut-off. Such an omission precludes clinical use of the score, even for clinicians motivated to do computations to obtain the score.

From the consumer's viewpoint, sequential structure is generally more cost effective (see Chapter 10), for only those tests required to decide outcome for a particular type of patient need be used. Consequently, maximal accuracy can be obtained at minimal cost.

Despite the fact that sequential rules are generally preferable to both medical consumers and to physicians, most evaluations of test batteries have been based on scoring rules. This appears to be primarily for the convenience of the medical test evaluators. There are many old, powerful, familiar, and easily available statistical methods to develop scoring rules (Multiple Discriminant Analyses, Multiple Regression Analyses, etc.). Systematic statistical methods to develop sequential rules have come upon the scene only since about 1980, are relatively unfamiliar, and can be implemented only with computer programs that are still not generally available (e.g., Breiman, Friedman, Olshen, & Stone, 1984). Furthermore, currently available programs are not yet structured to incorporate consideration of test cost, clinical benefits, etc., although, as will be soon be apparent, there is no reason why this cannot be done. It is merely a matter of time and demand.

Important for now is the realization that the methods in this chapter produce what is likely to be the most costworthy as well as easiest test battery to apply in clinical practice. It is the *evaluation*, not the application, of such a battery that is tedious and time-consuming.

In this chapter I will demonstrate how the methods of the previous chapters can be used to identify the optimal sequential structure, taking into consideration accuracy, test cost, and the potential benefit to patients at each stage of the iteration. No new methods will be introduced; the methods we have been using will be iterated to obtain the results.

Compiling the Raw Data Base

The evaluation of a battery of tests, just as does the evaluation of a single test or a family of tests, starts with a properly sampled group of patients. Sampling in this case may be naturalistic, in which case we have N_0 patients constituting a representative sample from the population of interest. Alternatively, Retrospective Sampling may be used, in which case we have N_1 patients with a positive diagnosis, and N_2 patients with a negative diagnosis, these appropriately sampled from a representative screening sample of size N_0 from the population of interest. The prevalence may be estimated by the proportion of the N_0 patients in the Naturalistic Sample with a positive diagnosis, and for Retrospective Sampling is estimated by the proportion of the patients in the *screening* sample with a positive diagnosis. *Prospective Sampling cannot be used,* for this sampling procedure can only be used when there is one and only one test of interest, not a family of tests, and certainly not a battery of tests. The estimation of the performance characteristics and quality indices must be done correctly, corresponding to the sampling method used (see Chapter 5).

Each patient must have a diagnosis and should be tested on each of the tests in the battery. It is not possible to infer what the results are of combining tests from knowledge of the separate performances of the individual tests (see Chapter 9). Thus each patient must also have n test responses. The whole then can be organized in a matrix with N_0 rows, each row corresponding to a patient, and $n + 1$ columns comprising the n test responses and the diagnosis. This matrix constitutes the "raw data base."

What of missing data? If sampling is retrospective, then there will be $N_0 - (N_1 + N_2)$ planned missing test responses. These will be a *random* subset of the total subjects by the conditions of the sampling procedure, and this necessitates use of the special estimation procedures described in Chapter 5. Otherwise, it is best if there are no missing data, but anyone with experience in clinical research knows that some missing data is almost inevitable.

No patient with a missing diagnosis can be included in analysis, for each step of the procedure unequivocally requires the diagnosis. If too many diagnoses are missing, furthermore, there may be serious question as to possible sampling biases.

On the other hand, a few missing test responses do not preclude including a patient in at least some of the analyses, and a few *randomly* missing test responses will not compromise the validity or the power of the results to be obtained. In compiling the raw data base and later the working data base the occasional missing test response is given a missing data code.

The next three steps to be described (surveying and cleaning the data set and reorganizing it to form the "working data base") are not absolute necessities to the analysis, but are very useful in avoiding human errors in processing the data, to understanding why results come out as they might, to making decisions along the way, and to speeding up the data processing.

First, for each test response in the raw data base, we compute some descriptive statistics:

The number of non-missing test responses. It occasionally happens that there are slips in the entering or processing of whatever is used as the missing data code. The number of missing responses per test response should be checked against what is known to be true. Furthermore, if there are too many missing responses for some test response, dropping that test response from the evaluation might have to be considered.

The minimum and maximum values of observed test responses. The only tests that can be evaluated in this study are those with at least 10 positive and 10 negative responses (or whatever the "rule of thumb"). When we begin to consider the possible cut-off values for each test response, no cut-off can be below the minimum or above the maximum value of the test response. Frequently the lowest and highest of the cut-offs that can be considered are well within these limits. It is wise to know for each test response what those limits are.

Furthermore, knowing explicitly the values of the minimum and maximum is a reminder of the units in which the test response is expressed (kilograms or pounds?), and of the number of significant figures entered (age = 35 or age = 35.249?).

Finally, if there are outliers in the data set, that is, either extraordinary responses or gross errors in entry, these are likely to show up as extreme values. Thus an unbelievable minimum or maximum value should stimulate some close attention to the accuracy of the data collection or entry procedures.

The mean and standard deviation of test response for those with a positive diagnosis, the mean and standard deviation of test responses for those with a negative diagnosis, and measures of the association between test response and diagnosis. The primary reason that a particular test response will be ignored in structuring the battery is that it is irrelevant to the diagnosis. The fact that the test response is included at all in the raw data base suggests that the evaluator had no prior reason to doubt the relevance of that test to the diagnosis and may well be surprised, puzzled, or dismayed to find such a test response later ignored. It is as well to have some early warning of this possibility, to give the evaluator the opportunity to ascertain whether there might be some problem in the way the test response was obtained, coded, or entered. In particular, a test response with near zero variance in both groups should be carefully scrutinized.

For example, in a study of tests for alcoholism among patients with documented liver disease (Ryback, Eckardt, Felsher, & Rawlings, 1982), there were 25 test responses considered. One of the tests that is described as one of the "liver tests traditionally evaluated" is lactic dehydrogenase (LDH). For this test response, the mean and standard deviation for those diagnosed alcoholic were:

$$223.4 \pm 81.9 \text{ mU/mL}.$$

The mean and standard deviation for those diagnosed non-alcoholic were:

$$202.1 \pm 61.8 \text{ mU/mL}.$$

From this information, one can see that there is only a small difference between the alcoholics and non-alcoholics and begin to suspect that this test, traditional though it may be, may not ultimately be included in the optimal battery.

There are many measures of association that are informative in this context, but two easy and useful ones are related to the point biserial correlation coefficient (the usual product moment or Pearson coefficient applied when one variable is binary) and to the variance ratio. These are both easily computed from the above means and standard deviations.

First, we compute a pooled within-group variance:

$$\text{Pooled Variance} = (50 \cdot 81.9^2 + 55 \cdot 61.8^2)/(50 + 55).$$

$$\text{Pooled Standard Deviation} = (\text{Pooled Variance})^{1/2}.$$

Here the sample sizes were 51 and 56, and thus the weights are one less: 50 and 55. From the above, the pooled standard deviation is 72.1. Then:

$$d = (223.4 - 202.1)/72.1 = 0.30.$$

and the correlation coefficient (a point biserial correlation coefficient):

$$r_M = d/[d^2 + 1/(PP')]^{1/2},$$

here,

$$r_M = 0.30/(0.09 + 4.0)^{1/2} = 0.15.$$

The sign indicates the direction of association (here positive) and its magnitude the strength (.15 on a scale of 0 to 1). The low magnitude of r_M suggests that LDH may not be very useful for diagnosing alcoholism within this battery. Use of this correlation measure provides a unit-free comparison between the $D+$ and $D-$ groups and facilitates easy comparison across the available test responses of the potential relative importance of those test responses to the battery results.

Table 11.1 Testing for Alcoholism Using 25 Blood Tests in a Population Having Liver Disease

Test	r_M	r_V
1. Alanine Aminotransferase (ALT)	-0.350	-0.955
2. Glucose	-0.094	-0.802
3. RBC count	-0.649	0.280
4. WBC count	0.289	0.676
5. Alkaline Phosphatase	0.220	-0.543
6. Aspartate Aminotransferase (AST)	0.060	-0.275
7. Urea Nitrogen	-0.105	0.341
8. Cholesterol	0.174	0.711
9. Albumin	-0.392	0.280
10. Calcium	-0.368	0.385
11. Carbon Dioxide	-0.289	0.208
12. Chloride	-0.254	0.337
13. Creatinine	0.000	0.280
14. Hematocrit	-0.519	0.223
15. Hemoglobin	-0.531	0.229
16. Lactic Dehydrogenase (LDH)	0.146	0.274
17. Mean Corpuscular Hemoglobin	0.514	0.159
18. Mean Corpuscular Hemoglobin Concentration	-0.384	0.946
19. Mean Corpuscular Volume	0.573	0.361
20. Phosphorus	-0.118	0.658
21. Potassium	-0.152	0.153
22. Sodium	-0.272	0.117
23. Total Bilirubin	0.317	0.344
24. Total Protein	-0.164	0.220
25. Uric Acid Concentration	-0.600	0.111

SOURCE: Ryback, Eckardt, Felsher, and Rawlings (1982)
NOTE: ($N = 107$, $P = .476$)

The values of r_M for the 25 test responses of the Ryback, Eckardt, Felsher, and Rawlings (1982) study are listed in Table 11.1.

The strongest discriminator in terms of the mean difference appears to be the red blood cell count (RBC), ($r_M \doteq -.649$), the negative sign indicating the the alcoholics in this population had lower RBCs than non-alcoholics. Uric acid concentration and other blood chemistry values (hematocrit, hemoglobin, and mean corpuscular hemoglobin, all highly clinically correlated) are also quite strong in this respect.

Another very useful indicator compares the spread of the test responses in the positive and negative diagnosis groups and equals the difference between the variances in the two groups divided by the sum of the variances in the two groups. In this case, this measure is:

$$r_V = (81.9^2 - 61.8^2)/(81.9^2 + 61.8^2) = 0.274.$$

Again, this is a unit-free measure scaled to lie between −1 and 1, where a value of 0 indicates that the two groups have equal spread (as measured by the variance), and the value approaches a magnitude of 1 (plus or minus depending on the direction) as the spreads differ. In this case, a value of +0.274 indicates that the variance of LDH is slightly greater in the $D+$ group.

The values of r_V for the Ryback, Eckardt, Felsher, and Rawlings (1982) study are also listed in Table 11.1. It can be seen that there is very strong differentiation between the alcoholic and non-alcoholic groups in alanine aminotransferase (ALT) and also in glucose level.

If neither r_M nor r_V is large, the test response is an unlikely, but not impossible, candidate for the optimal test battery. However, there is no statistical reason to remove a test response for low associations at this stage, unless the evaluator were now to question that the test responses were validly obtained. It is possible that a test response with low r_M and r_V at the initial stage of analysis may be found valuable at a later stage for a minority subgroup of the population, or when combined with other test responses. What examination of r_M and r_V accomplishes at this stage is to alert the medical researchers to possible difficulties, allowing them to anticipate possible problems with the test responses before too much time or effort is expended.

In Table 11.1 appears a "report card" on the 25 tests for alcoholism evaluated to detect alcoholism in a population having liver disease (Ryback, Eckardt, Felsher, & Rawlings, 1982).

One can see on this list several test responses that give little indication of differentiating alcoholics from non-alcoholics: carbon dioxide, LDH, potassium, total protein. There are also several that seem to have quite different means but similar variances (e.g., RBC), and several more (e.g., alanine aminotransferase) that seem to have similar means but different variances.

Intercorrelations between test responses. As noted above, the primary reason a test response is ignored in structuring the battery is that the response is poorly related to the diagnosis. A second frequently encountered and less obvious reason is that the test response is redundant to some other quite reproducible test response in the battery. As we discussed in Chapter 10, there is little gain in repeating a reproducible test. Two tests that may not be identical, but, still, yield highly correlated responses, behave like two tests that are identical but not completely reproducible. Once the result of one is obtained, the other can add little.

Having the intercorrelations among the test responses in hand before the evaluation warns of such possible redundancies and makes the omission of some tests that are otherwise highly correlated with diagnosis understandable. Robust correlation coefficients should be used: Spearman or Kendall rank correlation coefficients rather than the Pearson (or product moment) correlation coefficient. Very frequently the distributions of test responses are non-normal, have very long tails, and two test responses may be directly (monotonically) but not linearly related. In all such cases, use of the common product-moment or Pearson correlation coefficient may be misleading. Using a non-parametric or robust correlation coefficient (like the Spearman or Kendall) provides somewhat more protection against such problems.

It is not mandatory that redundant test responses be omitted. Inclusion of such tests in the process of sequential structuring of tests, as described in this chapter, merely slows the process. On the other hand, when, in later chapters, we begin to discuss scoring methods, then this so-called collinearity of test responses can cause serious problems and perhaps lead to inaccurate results. Then we would urge removal of such redundant tests, perhaps by combining them. Since there can be no advantage to inclusion of redundant tests in either case, for the sake of economy and clarity, then, while not mandatory, removing redundant test reponses is recommended.

Compiling the Working Data Base

At this point it should be verified that each test response is recorded in the proper units. If, for example, weight is measured in pounds, but the rule must ultimately be expressed in kilograms, it is at this point that pounds should be converted to kilograms. No major change results from such a rescaling, but it is easier and avoids confusion to make the conversion once and for all at this stage.

At this point, too, each test response should be expressed commensurate with its accuracy of measurement. For example, if age is determined accurate to the year (35 years), it should not appear in the data base with one decimal place (35.1 years). If the accuracy of an assay is +.1mµ/mL, the results should not appear in the data base with two or three decimal places.

The next step is to choose appropriate cut-off points for the referents. For example, for LDH we might choose to consider 200, 201, 202, etc., or we might choose 200, 210, 220, etc. The choice should reflect both the accuracy of measurement in the clinical context in which the tests are to be used and what cut points are convenient or conventional in clinical use. The size of the steps in the series of cut-off points determines the rapidity and costs of the evaluation, but at the same time determines the accuracy and completeness of the results. One might also consider rounding the test responses to the nearest cut-off point, e.g., LDH values of 200.1, 200.2, etc., might reflect the accuracy of measurement, but if the only cut-off points to be considered are 200, 201, etc., there is no need for the extra decimal place.

If there are relatively few test response patterns, identical test response patterns in the working data base might be combined so that the final version of the working data base might appear like that in Table 11.2.

These data are drawn from the CASS study of the exercise stress test for coronary artery disease (Weiner et al., 1979). There were four test responses: gender, evaluation of chest pain, resting EKG, and stress test. The working data base was published. Since there were 2,045 subjects and four test responses, the raw data base had dimensions 2,045 × 5. With the choice of three possible cut points for chest pain, and only one for the stress test, the number of distinct possible response patterns was reduced to 24. For each response pattern, there is listed the number of positive and negative diagnosis, listed as CAD+ and CAD−. The resulting working data base is thus a compact 24 × 6 matrix. (At this point, the raw data base can be stored safely away, for all the remaining work can be done with the working data base.)

Also presented in Table 11.2 are approximate test costs for each test response, and the estimate of the prevalence in this population (P = .583). Here sampling was naturalistic and I will focus on the calculation associated with such sampling. The prevalence is estimated by the proportion of the total sample (N_0 = 2,045) having a positive diagnosis (1,192/2,045 = .583).

Table 11.2 Compilation of Test Responses and Diagnosis (CAD) Results from the CASS Study

Gender	Chest Pain	Resting EKG	Stress Test	CAD+	CAD−	Risk
1	2	0	1	360	17	95.5%
1	2	0	0	68	42	61.8%
1	2	1	1	113	5	95.8%
1	2	1	0	13	2	87.7%
1	1	0	1	211	30	87.6%
1	1	0	0	84	118	41.6%
1	1	1	1	102	17	85.7%
1	1	1	0	18	14	56.3%
1	0	0	1	20	33	37.7%
1	0	0	0	24	126	16.0%
1	0	1	1	9	13	40.9%
1	0	1	0	1	25	3.8%
0	2	0	1	31	12	72.1%
0	2	0	0	8	16	33.3%
0	2	1	1	21	7	75.0%
0	2	1	0	1	2	33.3%
0	1	0	1	36	31	53.7%
0	1	0	0	18	68	20.9%
0	1	1	1	36	31	53.7%
0	1	1	0	5	15	25.0%
0	0	0	1	2	31	6.1%
0	0	0	0	7	135	4.9%
0	0	1	1	2	37	5.1%
0	0	1	0	2	26	7.1%

Additional Costs
| $0 | $0 | $50 | $175 | | | |

Total Count   1192   853

Test Responses:

Gender	Chest Pain:	Resting EKG:	Stress Test:	
Male = 1	Definite = 2	Abnormal = 1	Positive = 1	$N_0 = 2,045$
Female = 0	Probable = 1	Normal = 0	Negative = 0	$P = .583$
	Nonischemic = 0			

SOURCE: Weiner et al. (1979)

Selection of the Optimal First Test
and Reiteration

For each test response (n of them), and for each selected cut-off value for each test, we will compile the 2×2 table of diagnosis versus test results. We would make sure, in doing this, that there are at least 10 each with a positive and negative diagnosis and 10 each with a positive and negative test. We would make sure also, that the test is legitimate. If the correlation between test response and diagnosis is positive ($r_M > 0$), high test responses should lead to a positive test; if the correlation is negative ($r_M < 0$), low test responses should lead to a positive test.

The potential clinical benefit ($\$R$) and the relative clinical benefit (r) must be specified, for the results are different depending on what the level of clinical benefit is relative to the test costs and for screening, discriminative, or definitive test. In fact, a complete test evaluation should probably be repeated for different levels of clinical benefit (at least $\$R = \$100$, $\$10,000$, ∞) and for all three clinical purposes (at least $r = 0$, .5, 1). Done on a computer, doing all nine (or more) combinations at the same time costs little extra effort, time, or money, than doing only one. To do so allows the test evaluator to present the most comprehensive information to allow patients and their physicians to make rational choices about medical tests. For clarity of presentation, however, for the moment, let us focus on finding the optimally efficient sequence ($r = .5$) for moderate clinical benefit ($\$R = \$10,000$).

For *each* test response, and for *each* possible cut-off, we compile the familiar 2×2 table of test versus diagnosis results, compute whatever measures of test performance we might be interested in (the ROC perhaps), compute the quality indices with test costs ignored [$\kappa(r, 0)$, and the QROC perhaps], and, finally, for the selected values of r and $\$R$, the quality index $\kappa(r, t)$. Which computation formulae are used, of course, is determined by the sampling method: naturalistic or retrospective. Here $r = .5$ and $\$R = \$10,000$, and $\$T$ is the listed cost of the test in Table 11.2. The test maximizing $\kappa(r, t)$ is identified as the optimal first test. In this case it is the evaluation of chest pain, where those with probable or definite ischemia are given a positive test result, and those classified nonischemic are given a negative test result.

The entire sample is then split into two subsamples on the basis of the first test: here those with nonischemic pain versus those with probable or definite ischemia. The process of test evaluation is then repeated separately in each subsample with all the remaining tests.

Repeating the process with these two subgroups splits the sample into four (2^2) subgroups, within each of which the process is repeated. And so on, in theory at least, to 8 (2^3), 16 (2^4) . . . subgroups. A flowchart showing the eventual outcome for the CASS data in Table 11.2 appears in Figure 11.2.

When the process stops, the total population will have been split into subgroups that differ from each other in prevalence. In Figure 11.3, for example, we stopped with seven subgroups with prevalences ranging from 5% (women with nonischemic chest pain) to 92% (men with probable or definite ischemia and a positive stress test).

Why did we choose to continue testing in some subgroups and not in others? Why did we stop when we did? Finally, when the process is completed, how do we decide which of the resulting subgroups will be given a positive battery result and which a negative one? As a result of this process, what is recommended to the clinician for future medical testing? A number of questions yet remain to be addressed.

Increasing the Yield

By these successive splits and reevaluations, we are implementing a process that is frequently termed "increasing the yield" of a test procedure.

If what we are seeking is the optimally specific battery of tests, what is of concern are false positives. To avoid false positives, i.e., to increase the yield of true positives, we follow up on each *positive* test, that is, we seek the optimally specific single test for the subgroup who were positive on the preceding test. Those on the preceding test who are negative are automatically assigned a negative battery outcome.

For example, in Figure 11.3 is a flowchart for the same set of CASS data in which the optimally cost-effective specific test is sought ($r = 0$), for moderate clinical benefit ($R = \$10,000$). As can be seen, following

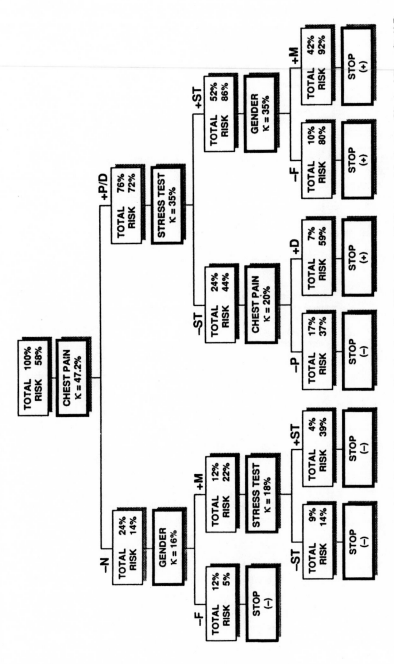

Figure 11.2. Evaluation of the CASS Battery for the Optimally Efficient (*r* − .5) Battery, Moderate Clinical Benefit ($*R* = $10,000)

SOURCE: Weiner et al., 1979.

181

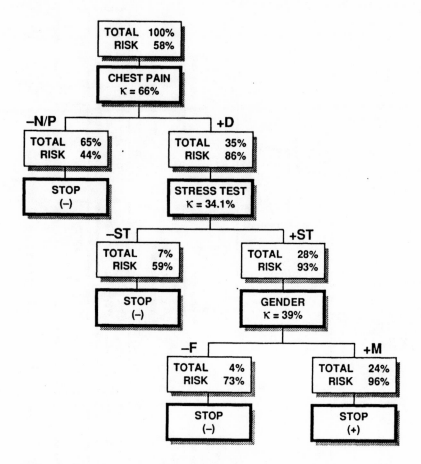

Figure 11.3. Evaluation of the CASS Battery for the Optimally Efficient (*r* = 0) Battery, Moderate Clinical Benefit ($R = $10,000)
SOURCE: Weiner et al., 1979.

every negative test result is the word STOP(–), i.e., patients with this outcome have a negative battery outcome.

Similarly, if what we are seeking is the optimally sensitive battery, what is of concern is a false negative. To avoid false negatives, i.e., to increase the yield of true negatives, we follow up on each *negative* test, that is, we seek the optimally sensitive test for the subgroup who were

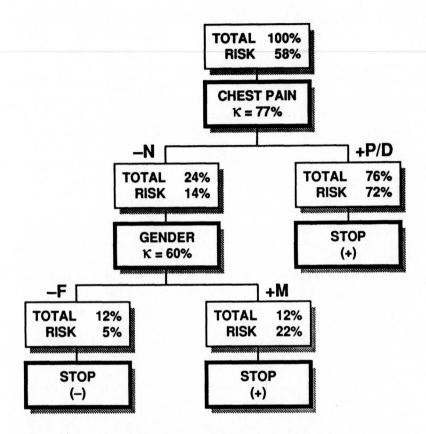

Figure 11.4. Evaluation of the CASS Battery for the Optimally Sensitive ($r = 1$) Battery, Any Clinical Benefit (any $\$R > 0$)
SOURCE: Weiner et al., 1979.

negative on the preceding test. Those on the preceding test who were positive are automatically assigned a positive battery outcome.

In Figure 11.4 is presented an example of this evaluation. Here the optimally costworthy sensitive test is sought ($r = 1$) when potential clinical benefit is moderate ($\$R = \$10,000$). (In fact, in this case, when $r = 1$, whatever the potential clinical benefit, the results come out the same.) Every time the optimal test has a positive test result, the word STOP(+) appears, indicating that testing stops with a positive battery outcome.

The most difficult situation is that of seeking the optimally cost-worthy efficient test (r = .5), for here we are equally concerned with false positives and false negatives. Thus both initial test results must be followed up, and the optimally efficient test for each subgroup identified. The situation dealt with in Figure 11.2, then is the most complex case there is: when the optimally efficient test is sought. In the search for the optimally sensitive and optimally specific batteries, one need follow up on only one arm of each subdivision. In the search for the optimally efficient battery, both arms of each subdivision should be followed up. Eventually those subgroups with risks exceeding P (here 58.2%) stop with a positive result (STOP+) and those below with a negative one (STOP–).

However, in Figure 11.2 as well as in Figure 11.3 and 11.4, it is clear that some further stopping rule was used. If there were no such further stopping-rule, the end result must always be that we use all tests in the battery, even those that are irrelevant or redundant, or non-costworthy.

Sometimes the process will stop of its own accord. For example, if at some step there are fewer than 10 patients with a positive or negative diagnosis, no further evaluation can take place. One way of stopping is to run out of subjects for analysis.

If, of course, all the test responses in the battery have already been used in some arm, then the process will stop. Another way of stopping is to run out of test responses.

However, it is clearly not desirable to include tests that are illegitimate or non-costworthy, for such tests add costs but not accuracy. There must be some way of stopping the process by running out of *good quality* tests. If all the tests were of negligible cost ($\$T$ = 0), or if the potential benefit were high ($\$R$ = ∞), in both of which cases t = 0 in the computation of the quality index, then one might consider performing a 2 × 2 Chi-Square test at each split and to stop if the optimal single test at any split were not of statistically significant quality. In this way there is some protection against including illegitimate tests in the battery.

When the tests have cost ($\$T$ > 0) and the clinical benefit is low or moderate ($\$R$ finite), ascertaining that the optimal single test is legitimate does not suffice, for legitimate tests may not be costworthy. Such a test may still have quality below zero, as would a test costing $\$175$ when the potential clinical benefit was $\$100$. What is needed is some check that the quality index [$\kappa(r, t)$] of the optimal single test is significantly above zero.

Testing the Quality Index
Using a Statistical Jackknife

The problem is that when, as in the first step of Figure 11.2, the quality index of the single test is found to 47.2%, this represents an estimate having some margin of estimation error. How large this error is, as was seen in Chapter 5, depends on the size of the sample, the prevalence, P, and of the level of the test, Q, as well as which sampling method was used. When, as in the first test of the CASS battery, this estimate is based on 2,045 subjects, 1,192 with a positive diagnosis and 853 with a negative diagnosis, 1,552 with a positive test and 495 with a negative test, we are reasonably sure that the sample estimate, 47.2%, is reasonably close to its population value and is (at the very least) above 0%. If we had obtained the same estimate with, say 41 subjects, 24 with a positive diagnosis and 17 with a negative diagnosis, 31 with a positive test and 10 with a negative test, we would have obtained the same estimate, but could not have been as confident of the accuracy of the estimate.

What I propose to do is to obtain an interval estimate of the quality index—one that indicates the margin of error, and to stop the evaluation procedure when that interval includes the value zero. To do this I will use a "statistical jackknife" estimation procedure.

The statistical jackknife, like its namesake, is a sturdy, all-purpose instrument, not necessarily what one would choose to use if there were more powerful or specialized instruments available. To date, no more powerful or specialized instruments have been identified for kappa coefficents (Bloch & Kraemer, 1989), and present indications are that the jackknife works quite well in this situation. The jackknife estimation is done as follows: We begin with the basic estimate of the parameter of interest, the quality index, κ_0 [equal to $\kappa(r, t)$ for whatever values of r, t are of interest and computed from formulas appropriate to the sampling method]. We have now appended the subscript 0 to indicate that this estimate is based on the full sample, no subjects omitted. Then we proceed to drop one subject at a time, and to compute the estimate of the quality index on the remaining subjects. When subject i is omitted, the estimate so obtained is labeled κ_i, a so-called pseudo-value. Thus we generate N pseudo-values. The mean of these pseudo-values is $\bar{\kappa}$ and their standard deviation is SD. The jackknife estimate of the true quality index is $J(\kappa)$ given by:

$$J(\kappa) = N_0 \cdot \kappa_0 - (N_0 - 1) \cdot \overline{\kappa}$$

and the estimate of its standard error is:

$$\text{Standard Error} = (N_0 - 1) \cdot \text{SD}/(N_0)^{1/2}.$$

For Naturalistic Sampling, the problem of obtaining the pseudo-estimates is simplified by the fact that the same value is obtained no matter which True Positive result we drop, and the same is true for the False Negatives, the False Positives, and the True Negatives. There are only four distinct pseudo-values occurring with the same frequency as do the four outcomes. For Retrospective Sampling, there are six possible outcomes, $D+$ and no test; $D-$ and no test from the screening sample; and then True Positive, False Negative, False Positive, True Negative. Thus there are only six distinct pseudo-values occurring with the same frequency as do the six outcomes.

In Table 11.3 is presented the jackknife procedure in detail for Naturalistic sampling for the Wiener et al. (1979) results as applied to the first test on the search for the optimally efficient test:

The four different pseudo-values are 0.4714, 0.4724, 0.4722, and 0.4710 compared to the original value of 0.4715. How close the pseudo-values are to the original value is here explained by the large sample size. When sample sizes are small, there may be remarkable differences among the pseudo-values. Here the jackknife estimator is 0.4717 with a standard error of .0004 (47.17% ± .04%).

For interval estimation it is suggested that we use the critical value of the standard normal distribution. Thus for a 95% confidence interval (95% of intervals so obtained would be expected to cover the true value) we would use $z = 1.96$ and for the 99% level, $z = 2.58$. The interval would be:

$$J(\kappa) \pm z \cdot \text{Standard Error}.$$

In Table 11.3, therefore, we find that the 95% confidence interval for $\kappa(.5, 175/10{,}000)$ is 47.0% to 47.3%, verifying our subjective impression that with the sample sizes involved, the "raw" value of 47.15% must be quite near the true population value.

If the lower bound of such an interval falls below zero, this indicates that the observed quality index is not significantly above zero:

Table 11.3 Using the Jackknife Procedure to Obtain a Confidence Interval Estimate for the Quality Indices

		Omit:			
Outcome:	Total	TP	TN	FP	TN
TP	1,125	1,124	1,125	1,125	1,125
FN	67	67	66	67	67
FP	427	427	427	426	427
FN	426	426	426	426	425
N_0	2,045	2,044	2,044	2,044	2,044
k	$k_0 = 0.4715$	0.4714	0.4724	0.4722	0.4710 $\bar{k} = .4717$
					$SD = .0004$

$$J = .4717$$
Standard Error = .0004
95% Confidence Interval: .4717 ± 1.96 · .0004
47.0% to 47.3%

at the 5% significance level if the confidence level is 95%, at the 1% significance level if the confidence level is 99%. Thus if the lower bound of such an interval falls below zero, we would stop the evaluation at the last split.

Completing the Search for the Optimal Battery Structure

Let us now return to Figure 11.2. After the best first test is found (P/D: probable or definite angina) in the CASS results, and is verified as a test of significant quality (using the jackknife to verify that $\kappa = 47.2\%$ is significantly above zero), we follow up on both subgroups (because we are seeking the optimally efficient battery). Among those with probable or definite angina, the best single test is the exercise stress test with a quality index of 35.3% (significant at the .001 level). Among those with nonischemic chest pain, the best single test is gender with a quality index of 15.9% (significant at the 0.05 level).

Now there are four subgroups, comprising 11.8%, 12.3%, 24.1%, and 51.8% of the total group with prevalences respectively 5.4%, 21.5%, 43.7%, 85.8%. In each of these subgroups we seek the best single test once again.

For females with nonischemic chest pain, the process stops, for there are no further tests in the battery with significant quality indices. The sample size remains adequate and two more test responses, the resting EKG and the stress test, remain in the battery. This subgroup comprises 11.8% of the total group and has a prevalence of 5.4%. To identify this relatively low-prevalence group, only tests with low cost were used.

For the other groups, however, the process goes on. Among men with nonischemic chest pain, the stress test is found to have significant quality and only after it is used does the process stop. Among those with probable or definite chest pain, the stress test is identified as the best next test. This is followed by some further subdivision of type of chest pain (probable versus definite) and an even further subdivision by gender.

When the process finally stops entirely, the resting EKG result is ignored. There are seven subgroups with prevalences ranging from 5.4% (females with nonischemic chest pain) to 91.9% (males with probable or definite angina and a positive stress test).

Which results are positive and which negative battery outcomes? If this had been a search for the optimally sensitive or specific test, the choice would have been easy. For the optimally sensitive battery outcome, only those negative on all tests used are negative; for the optimally specific battery outcome, only those positive on all tests used are positive. Here for the optimally efficient battery outcome, we capitalize on what was learned from consideration of the Test QROC and the Test QCROC and propose that every subgroup with a prevalence above the prevalence for the whole group (here 58.3%) is declared positive, and every subgroup with a prevalence at or below the prevalence for the whole group is declared negative. Examination of the results in Figure 11.2, then, show that all patients with definite angina and those with both probable angina and a positive exercise stress test are positive.

The Final Recommendation for Battery Structure

In summarizing the battery results for clinical application, the test formulation is stated in the simplest way possible, with no tests listed that are not needed to obtain the final battery result. Although gender was used at certain points in Figure 11.2, as things turn out, test battery results remain the same regardless of gender. In the recommendations to clinicians, therefore, no mention is made of gender.

The next point is vital: Regardless of the order in which tests enter the statistical evaluation, the recommended order of clinical testing is from the least to the most costly test. Each successive test in the sequence is done only if needed to define the outcome. As a result, the only group in the CASS population requiring use of the exercise stress test are those with probable angina. Those with definite angina have a positive battery outcome regardless of how the exercise stress test might come out, and those with nonischemic chest pain are negative regardless of how the exercise stress test might come out. Consequently, only 40.8% of the total group will require the exercise stress test, and the average per patient cost of the battery then is:

$$0.408 \cdot \$175 + 0.592 \cdot \$0 = \$71.57$$

instead of \$175 if the tests had been done in parallel or combined into one test.

Table 11.4 summarizes the recommendations based on the CASS data for the optimally sensitive ($r = 1$), efficient ($r = .5$), and specific ($r = 0$) tests, for low ($\$R = \$100$), moderate($\$R = \$10,000$) and high ($\$R = \infty$) potential clinical benefit. This constitutes the contents of the "package insert" for the use of the exercise stress test for the CASS population using the CASS test protocol. The materials reported in all the earlier tables and figures are what might be reported in the scientific literature documenting that "package insert."

Then for screening purposes a positive test would be given to all males and to females with probable or definite angina. This would constitute 88.2% of the population (those reporting with chest pain). The PVN on this test is 94.1%, and the test battery result is essentially cost free.

For specific diagnosis, when the potential clinical benefit is low, a positive test result should be given to those who are male and have definite angina. This would constitute 30.3% of the total, would have a PVP of 89.4% and would be essentially cost free.

For specific diagnosis, when the potential clinical benefit is moderate to high, a positive test result should be given to those who are male with definite angina and with a positive stress test. This constitutes 24.2% of the total, has a PVP of 95.5%, and, since the exercise

Table 11.4 Full Evaluation of the CASS Test Battery

Optimally	Potential Clinical Benefit	Definition of T+	Level Q	PVP	PVN	Additional Cost Per Person
Sensitive	All	M, F&P/D	88.2%		94.1%	$0.00
Efficient	Low	D				
		M&P	64.2%	78.5%	78.2%	$0.00
	Moderate or High	D				
		P&ST+	59.2%	82.4%	77.2%	$71.57
Specific	Low	M&D	30.3%	89.4%		$0.00
	Moderate or High	M&D&ST+	24.2%	95.5%		$53.06

NOTES: M = Male; F = Female
P = Probable; D = Definite Angina; P/D = Probable or Definite Angina
ST+ = Positive Exercise Stress Test

stress test need be used only for males with definite angina, the average per patient cost of the test is $53.06.

For an optimally efficient diagnosis, when the potential clinical benefit is low, a positive test result should be given to all those who have definite angina, and to those males who have probable angina. This identifies 64.2% of the population as positive, with a PVP of 64.2% and a PVN of 78.5%, and is essentially cost free. For an optimally efficient diagnosis when the potential clinical benefit is moderate or high, all with definite angina and those with probable angina who have a positive stress test are positive, with a PVP of 82.4% and a PVN of 77.2%. Here, since the exercise stress test need be given only to those with probable angina, the per patient cost is $71.57.

There are several points of interest from these recommendations relative both to the question posed by the CASS study, and generally to the use of this procedure to evaluate batteries of tests:

The resting EKG is never used. Perhaps this is because the resting EKG is better used for diagnoses other than coronary artery disease in this population or for coronary artery disease, but only in other populations. Perhaps this is because when the results of the resting EKG were already incorporated into defining the exercise stress test result, all the pertinent information was used and the test became redundant. Perhaps the criteria used by the CASS study to classify the resting

EKG were not well chosen, or were not uniformly or reliably applied. We will never know.

For the purpose of this demonstration, however, the fact that the resting EKG is never used is important to clarify that the suggested battery evaluation procedure does, in fact, have the capacity to exclude tests, and the exclusions may not be trivial ones.

The exercise stress test is never recommended when the potential clinical benefit is low. Common sense would dictate that when the potential clinical benefit is only of the order of $100, one would not use a test costing $175, even if it were completely accurate.

What is important to notice, however, is that evaluating sequential structure of tests produces alternatives in such a case by using tests of negligible cost that may closely approach the quality of the high-cost tests. Here, for example, the optimally specific test for low potential clinical benefit has a PVP of 89.4%, not too far below that when the potential clinical benefit is high: PVP of 95.5%. To achieve this 6% increase in PVP, we required the use of the exercise stress test for males with definite angina. That increased the average battery cost from $0 to an average of $53.06 per patient.

In fact, the optimally sensitive test is the same, and of negligible cost, regardless of the potential clinical benefit. The exercise stress test is *not* recommended for use for screening in this population.

This result is interesting because it so often tends to recur in the cases considered. Optimally sensitive tests or batteries (screening tests) seldom seem to involve additional cost. Such tests seem to depend primarily on self-examination (self-examination for breast or testicular cancer), self-report (reported signs and symptoms), patient interview (health history), or simple clinical observations and measurements (weight, blood pressure). If this result is as common as it appears to be in the various situations considered here, it would seem that the cost of screening tests could be substantially reduced with an *increase* in their accuracy!

The exercise stress test is never recommended across the board. For the optimally efficient procedure, it is recommended only for those (men and women) with probable angina. For the optimally specific procedure, it is recommended only for men with definite angina.

In general, the cost of using a sequentially structured battery is kept low in several ways. Tests that are not costworthy or are redundant are excluded (resting EKG). Costly tests are used only for that subgroup of patients for whom that test is needed to get the optimal result (stress test). However, it must be remembered that in some situations a test run in sequence may cost more (in terms of patient and clinician time as well as in terms of risk to the patient of the delay incurred) than the same test run in parallel. Such increased costs should be included into consideration in "costing out" the tests in the evaluation.

These are important points, for many discussions of the value of tests do not distinguish between a test that is of limited value in that it is of little use for all patients, from a test that is of limited value in that it is of great use, but only to a minority of patients. Structuring optimal batteries using these procedures excludes tests that are of the first type, while it seeks to identify the appropriate minority group for tests that are of the second type. The upshot is that accuracy of testing is increased, while its cost is decreased.

Generally, efficient tests are the most costly, with specific tests running second, and sensitive tests frequently having very low or no cost. Because both sensitive and specific tests figure into the structuring of the efficient battery, it is not surprising that efficient batteries should be the most costly.

The optimally sensitive battery has a high PVN, often at the cost of a relatively low PVP, and tends to overidentify (Q > P). The optimally specific battery has a high PVP, often at the cost of a relatively low PVN, and tends to underidentify $(Q < P)$. The optimally efficient battery has relatively high PVP and PVN, is relatively equally balanced, and tends to identify about as many patients as positive as there are positive diagnoses in the population $(Q \approx P)$.

This pattern merits close consideration, for it is not unusual that a test designed as a screening test is criticized because it has low specificity, or a test designed to obtain a definitive positive result is criticized because it has low sensitivity. It should be part of the "packaging" instructions for each test for what clinical use the particular formulation of the test is designed. Again it must be emphasized that there may be multiple formulations of tests based on the same set of test responses, each suited for a different clinical use. The clinician who uses the test must then use it consistent with the instructions for its use to get the best possible results. If the user requires that *both* predictive values be high or that the test be *both* highly sensitive and specific, then the optimally efficient test should be used.

An Alternative Strategy?

In illustrating this evaluation of the optimal structuring of a battery of tests, the CASS data were used for several reasons. This data base is, first of all, based on a large sample size (N_0 = 2,045). Many evaluations of test batteries are based on samples of size 100 or fewer, and such evaluations will run out of subjects for evaluation far before they will run out of "good" test responses.

Second, the working data set could be completely presented in a very concise form, so that each step of the procedure could be closely followed.

Third, some of the test responses in the battery were of negligible cost (gender, chest pain) and some had cost (resting EKG, stress test). One (chest pain) had a variable cut-off point. This permitted illustration of the various features of the sequencing procedure, important for purposes here.

However, one might well wonder in the case of the CASS data, why we went to so much bother. Here there were only 24 distinct test response patterns in the working data set, with a reasonable number of patients in each response group in all but a few cases (see Table 11.2). Could we not simply compute the prevalence of CAD for the patients for each pattern group and use that as a test score for that group? Then the methods of the previous chapters would apply with no iteration. Clearly this would entail less work, and the results might be much clearer.

The first and most important point to notice is that what I am now suggesting as a strategy is feasible only because the working data set was very compressed from the raw data set. For example, the criterion for a positive exercise stress test was set at 1 mm depression when in fact it could have been entered into the data set accurate to 0.5 mm and possible cut-offs set at .5, 1.0, 1.5, 2.0, 2.5, 3.0, ... It may well be that different cut-off points might have produced a better quality test or battery of tests. By restricting consideration to only the single cut-off, such a finding was precluded.

Furthermore, free test responses such as the age, smoking status, or obesity of the patient were not included, when such an inclusion might well have increased the accuracy of the battery while reducing its cost. Of course, if test responses such as age or obesity, or multiple cut-off points for the exercise stress test, had been included, the number of possible test response patterns might well have increased from 24 to beyond 2,045, and the number of observed test response patterns might equal the number of patients in the sample. Then the strategy we are now considering would not have been feasible.

Yet it is a fair question to ask what the result would have been *in this case* and how it would have compared with the recommendations summarized in Table 11.4. The best of all the methods to score the battery to be discussed in the next chapter can do no better than to recreate the risk structure described in Table 11.2. The results are summarized in Table 11.5.

The optimal cut-offs for the three tests, based on the risk score, are presented in Table 11.5. The cost of this battery will be $175, for to find exactly what risk group each patient belongs to requires that *all* test responses be obtained. We can compare these results of optimally sequenced battery developed above.

First of all, the entire scored battery is discarded for low potential clinical benefit, for the cost of $175 overwhelms the potential clinical benefit of $100. There is, however, quite a good battery obtainable for free from the sequential structure in these cases. When the potential clinical benefit is moderate to high, the accuracies of the two batteries are quite comparable, differing frequently by a fraction of a percentage point. However, the sequential structured battery costs from one-half to one-third as much as the scored battery.

Summary

To summarize the steps of evaluation of a battery of tests and to add a few additional comments about the process:

1. *Sampling*: The basis of a sound objective and quantitative evaluation of a test or test battery must be a representative sample from the population in which the test or battery of tests is to be used. To evaluate the battery, sampling may be Naturalistic or Retrospective, but not Prospective.

The sample size necessary to evaluate a single test must be large enough to yield at least minimally accurate estimates of the characteristics of the population. For a single test, the rule of thumb we have been using is that there must be at least 10 with and 10 without a positive diagnosis, and 10 with and 10 without a positive test result. Evaluating a battery of tests involves successive reiteration of the process of evaluating a single

Table 11.5 Comparison of the Optimally Scored Battery with the
Optimally Sequenced Battery

	Clinical Benefit	Risk Level	Optimally Scored Battery		Additional Cost	Optimally Sequenced Battery*		Additional Cost
			PVP	PVN		PVP	PVN	
Sensitive	Low	None	—	—	—	—	94.1%	$0.00
	Moderate	≥ .20	—	91.1%	$175	—	94.1%	$0.00
	High	≥ .04	—	95.2%	$175	—	94.1%	$0.00
Efficient	Low	None	—	—	—	78.5%	78.2%	$0.00
	Moderate	≥ .53	82.9%	77.9%	$175	82.4%	77.2%	$71.57
	High	≥ .53	82.9%	77.9%	$175	82.4%	77.2%	$71.57
Specific	Low	None	—	—	—	89.4%	—	$0.00
	Moderate	≥ .88	95.6%	—	$175	95.5%	—	$53.06
	High	≥ .88	95.6%	—	$175	95.5%	—	$53.06

NOTE: *See Table 11.4

test. The above requirement applies to each successive step of the procedure. If one intends to consider evaluating using two tests per patient, there are at least two separate test evaluations, each of which involves minimally 20 patients, i.e., a total of 40. In general, if one intends to use all n tests per subject, evaluation minimally must involve $10 \cdot 2^n$ patients. Thus with four tests as in the CASS battery, one cannot adequately proceed without at least 160 subjects, and with 25 tests as considered in the Rybeck, Eckardt, Felsher, and Rawlings (1982) study, the minimal number of subjects is around 336 million! (The actual number in the 1982 study was 106.)

Of course, the intent in evaluating a 25-test battery is *not* to use all 25 tests, but, rather, to eliminate some (perhaps many) from consideration. Nevertheless, what this discussion suggests is that: (1) the necessary sample size for battery evaluation must be much larger than it is for the consideration of any single test response in the battery, and (2) the necessary sample size generally increases as the number of test responses in the battery increase.

2. *Test inclusion and exclusion*: The choice of which test responses to include in and exclude from consideration for the battery is completely a medical one. However, the statistical repercussions of such decisions must be kept in mind as these decisions are made.

The more numerous the test responses considered in the battery, the larger the sample size necessary for adequate evaluation, the more time consuming and costly the process of evaluation, and the more likely is the occurrence of some sampling error that might limit the generalizability of the results. As a result, if something like "Religious Preference" were to be one test response in the battery, there should be good medical reason to think that this response is relevant to the diagnosis of the disorder (Tay-Sachs disease?). Otherwise one is wasting time, effort, and money and inviting errors in the results.

On the other hand, one should not omit a test response that is relevant, as were perhaps age, smoking, and obesity in the CASS study considered here. Particularly when these responses are of negligible cost, using such responses, one might be able to generate a much more accurate result for less cost.

3. *Compilation of the data base*: Each of the patients in the sample must have a diagnosis and ideally have each of the n test responses in the test battery. Missing data, as always, may cause serious problems. A few randomly missing test responses may be tolerated, but if several tests are missing for the same subject, one might consider omitting that subject. Either proceeding with that subject in the analysis or proceeding without that subject raises the possibility of sampling bias in the results. Neither is ideal.

A test response that is missing for more than a few subjects might better be omitted from the battery, lest its inclusion produce biased results. If it is a highly relevant test response, such an omission decreases the potential value of the battery. Neither including nor excluding such a test response is an attractive option.

We have suggested that the first step of analysis be that of obtaining some descriptive statistics: the minimum and maximum value of each test response, the mean and standard deviation of test responses for those with and without a positive diagnosis, some measures of association between test response and diagnosis, and intercorrelations between test responses.

These serve several purposes. They remind the investigator to check the scaling and accuracy of entry of these test responses. They provide some operational guidelines to the choice of possible cut-off values for each test response. They provide a last check that no test response that is irrelevant to the diagnosis has been inadvertently included in the list. They provide some clues as to possible redundancies among the test responses. Because test responses are omitted either because of irrelevance or redundancy, such background information helps to understand the outcome of the battery evaluation.

Suggestions for the compilation of a working data base were provided primarily to speed up and facilitate the battery evaluation process and to minimize data-processing errors.

4. *Finding the best first test*: The methods developed in the previous chapters provide the method of identifying the best first test for each potential clinical benefit and for each clinical use. The outcome on the best first test splits the group into two subgroups in each of which one considers using another test to increase the yield.

5. *Increasing the yield*: The term "increasing the yield" is frequently encountered in the medical research literature, with no precise definition. What is precisely meant here is that if the optimally sensitive battery is sought, a positive test is automatically considered a positive battery result. We follow up a negative test result to minimize the number of false negatives. A subject is given a negative result if she or he is negative on all tests given in the battery.

If the optimally specific battery is sought, a negative test is automatically considered a negative battery result. We follow up a positive test result to minimize the number of false positives. A subject is given a positive result who has all positive results on tests given in the battery.

If the optimally efficient battery is sought, both negative and positive test results require follow-up to minimize the number of false results: positive or negative. At the end of the procedure, all subgroups with prevalence above the prevalence of the total group are given a positive result, and all others are negative.

Because $r = 0, .5$, and 1 are the three values of relative clinical benefit that are salient to clinical decision making, we have focused on these. If, however, some other value of r were of interest, the process of evaluation would, in principle, be that of evaluating for the optimally efficient test, using $\kappa(r, t)$ at each step rather than $\kappa(.5, t)$. When the process stops, however, one further step remains to determine the cut-off. The prevalence of each of the groups so identified is used as a "score" for all members of that group. The optimal cut-off for that value of r is determined by maximizing $\kappa(r, t)$ on the basis of that score.

6. *Stopping rules*: After the identification of the best first test, two sub-groups are formed. Whichever subgroups require follow-up tests to increase the yield are then evaluated in order to identify the best single test for that subgroup. This partitions the total group into further subgroups and the evaluation process is iterated.

Iteration stops when one of the three events occur:

a. There is an insufficient sample size for further test evaluation. This usually occurs because there are fewer than 10 with or 10 without a positive diagnosis in that subgroup.

b. There are no more tests available for use in the battery.

c. There are no more tests of significant quality in the battery. A jackknife procedure was suggested to identify which tests were of significant quality.

7. *Battery recommendations*: At the end of the evaluation procedure, the recommendations are summarized for clinical use. Any tests that are not necessary to the final outcome (e.g., a test defining two subgroups, both of which are above prevalence in the evaluation of the optimally efficient battery) are eliminated. The tests are then presented in order of cost, not in the order of statistical identification, to minimize test cost in clinical or research applications. Finally, information on the final cost of implementing the battery should be presented in addition to information on accuracy.

12

Evaluating Batteries of Medical Tests: Optimal Scores

Introduction

Let us begin over again with a battery of medical tests containing n test responses, some of which may be measured on a continuum. In the previous chapter we discussed a procedure of evaluation that resulted in an optimal sequence of tests to reach a decision based on such a battery. Now what we would like to discuss is an evaluation procedure that results in an optimal scoring system that can be applied to the test responses in the battery to reduce the results in the battery to a single overall battery score. Then the clinical use of the battery would be defined by reporting the weights that should be applied, and the referent (cut-off value) that would be used to separate those who would be given a positive battery result from those who would be given a negative battery result.

What is here meant by a "risk score" is a weighted sum of the test responses and products of test responses of the following sort:

$$\text{Risk Score} = w_0 + w_1 x_1 + w_2 x_2 + \ldots + w_n x_n$$

$$+ w_{1\,2} x_1 x_2 + w_{1\,3} x_1 x_3 + \ldots$$

$$+ w_{1\,2\,3} x_1 x_2 x_3 + w_{1\,2\,4} x_1 x_2 x_4 + \ldots$$

(When we compute such a score for a subject i, we will append a subscript i to risk score and to the test responses used: x_{1i}, x_{2i}, etc. The weights are the same for all subjects in the population.)

The first term, w_0, is called the "intercept" or the "constant." The weights w_1, w_2, . . . are called "regression weights," or "regression coefficients," or sometimes "slopes." Single test responses, x_1, x_2, x_3, . . . are often called "main effects." Terms entered into the risk score obtained by multiplying the single test scores together are called "interaction effects" or "interactions." Those that involve a product of two test responses, e.g., x_1x_2 or x_1x_3, are called "first-order interactions"; those that involve a product of three test responses, e.g., $x_1x_2x_3$, are called "second-order interactions" and so on. Thus a risk score based on n test responses may contain interactions up to order $n - 1$.

In Figures 11.1e, 11.1f, and 11.1g, we described, for two dimensions (i.e., two test responses), what such scores can do. Inclusion only of main effects produces flat divisions (lines or planes) in the space containing all possible test responses, while inclusion of first-order and higher-order interactions permits the divisions between positive and negative test responses to have curvature. The higher the order of the interactions included, the more complex and flexible the form of the divisions between positive and negative test responses will be. A completely nonsensical subdivision such as that in Figure 11.1h will never result, but only because scores such as the one above cannot produce "holes" in the space they are dividing. Very funny-looking "wiggles" can be produced with inclusion of higher-order interactions.

The risk score is designed to order the patients in the population in such a way that those with high scores are more likely to have a positive diagnosis than those with low scores. Whether or not w_0 is included in the risk score is irrelevant, for, intercept in or out, the risk score will order patients in the same way. Similarly, multiplication of all the weights by a constant or the transformation of the resulting risk score using a monotonic transformation (logarithms, exponentials, etc.) does not change the quality of any risk score, for the resulting values will still order patients in the same way. This serves as an early warning that it is possible to generate weights that look very different from one another or to generate risk scores that look very dissimilar only to find that when their performance is compared (via the ROC, QROC, or QCROC) the results look very nearly the same. As a result, inconsistencies among test evaluations based on different models or approaches will tend to dissolve.

This is perhaps the best time also to note that a large weight attached to a test response carries no connotation of "cause." It is neither true that such a test response must reflect a cause of the disorder, nor that such a test response must reflect a direct outcome of the disorder. All a heavy weight means is that the information contained in that test response is useful in distinguishing between those with a positive or a negative diagnosis. Since the diagnosis is assumed to be a clinically valid indicator of the presence of the disorder, the test response should then also be useful in identifying those with and without the disorder. Certainly factors that cause the disorder or factors that are caused by the disorder should have heavy weights, but having a heavy weight does not necessarily indicate either causality or consequence.

Main effects and interactions are called "factors," "independent variables," "covariates," or "predictor variables." The diagnosis (usually coded 1 for a positive and 0 for a negative diagnosis) is called the "dependent variable," or the "outcome variable," or the "predictand."

The fact that there are so many different labels assigned to the same entities signals that these methods have a long history of development and of application in a variety of different research contexts. The discussion to follow will not provide complete and thorough introductions to each of the methods. There are many excellent books and papers on these subjects. Here the intention is only to show how these methods fit within the context of the evaluation of medical tests, to provide some guidelines as to how they might be applied, and to show some examples of how they have been applied in that context.

In developing a risk score based on a battery of tests, evaluators may include as many or as few of the factors as they choose. To include them all, they would need 2^n weights. This is rarely done. Most frequently only the intercept and the main effects are included, in which case a total of $n + 1$ weights are necessary. If interactions are included at all, evaluators rarely choose to go beyond first-order interactions. However, even if they so choose to limit consideration, there are a still total of $(n^2 + n + 2)/2$ weights somehow to be obtained to define the risk score. This number increases rapidly with the number of test responses to be included. For 2 test responses, the number of weights is only 4; for 5 test responses, the number is 16; for 10 responses, it is 56. The number of factors to be included is a crucial issue in these methods.

The weights to be used can be ad hoc, that is, simply arbitrarily assigned by the test evaluator. For example, Ryback, Eckardt, Felsher, and Rawlings (1982) note that the referent ratio, AST to ALT > 1 is "commonly applied for diagnosis of alcoholic liver disease" (p. 2264). In effect, those who use this rule use a risk score of AST − ALT with a cut-off of 0. Here AST refers to aspartate aminotransferase and ALT to alanine aminotransferase. In this risk score the weights are +1 assigned to AST and −1 to ALT. Since the battery of tests considered in that report included 25 test responses, this particular risk score also assigned a weight of 0 to all the 23 other test responses, as well as to all first- and higher-order interactions. That is one proposal for a risk score.

Frequently a test evaluator scores the single tests in the battery on some scale that is comparable from test to test and assigns an equal weight to each of the test responses. For example, when Garth et al. (1983) reported on the use of duplex ultrasound scan for diagnosis of carotid artery disease (discussed in Chapters 6, 7, and 8) they scored each of the four test responses (criteria) as 1 or 0 according to whether the observed quantitative test response exceeded a specified cut-off and assigned each an equal weight. The battery score then was the number of criteria observed for a patient, with possible referents of 1, 2, 3, or 4. These four tests appeared in Figure 6.1 as Tests #8, #9, #10, and #11. In fact, #8 proved to be the optimally sensitive test in that study. It is not unusual (see Chapter 11) that the optimally sensitive battery might be one that gives a positive result to a patient with any one positive criterion (true with Test #8 above), and the optimally specific battery gives a positive result to a patient with all criteria positive (not true with Test #11 above), but there are no guarantees.

In other cases, when the single test responses are measured on the same scale, the sum or average over the tests might be used as a risk score. Once again, this assigns an equal weight to each test response, zero to all the interactions.

More commonly, zero weights are assigned to the higher-order interactions, and weights for the main effects and lower-order interactions are *not* assigned, but, rather, are estimated from a sample of patients for whom diagnosis and test results are available, in order to "optimize" the weights.

As noted earlier, the prime advantage of approaching the evaluation of a battery of medical tests using the strategy of developing a risk score rather than developing an optimal sequence (see Chapter 11), is that there are many powerful methods, well-developed and familiar, easily accessible in most computer statistical packages (e.g., SAS, SPSS, or BMDP) to do this task. In return for familiarity and convenience, however, as earlier noted, costworthiness may be lost. Any test response that has a non-zero weight either as a main effect or in some interaction must be obtained for *each* patient in order to compute the risk score for that patient. This means that the cost of obtaining the risk score is the total cost of all tests in the battery with non-zero weights in the risk score.

When weights are estimated rather than assigned, nowhere in estimating the weights are the costs and benefits considered. As a result, very costly tests only marginally better than some free tests will be preferred. Tests needed only for subsets of patients will be included for all patients.

Finally, the procedures for estimating the weights are based on obtaining the best agreement between diagnosis and test results: i.e., efficiency. To achieve efficiency in a battery, both sensitive and specific tests must be included. For this reason efficient batteries tend to be the most costly, even when sequential structuring is used. Since the weights for a risk score are chosen to optimize efficiency, non-zero weights will be attached to sensitive tests when specificity is at issue and to specific tests when sensitivity is at issue. The risk score obtained should be quite good for all purposes, as efficient tests are likely to be, but may be more costly than is actually necessary and not optimally constructed for either sensitivity or specificity separately.

In Table 11.5 we considered using the estimated risks for the 24 groups in the reduced data set of the CASS study as a test response, and evaluated these tests in comparison to the optimal sequence. Whichever of the approaches to estimating the weights for an optimal risk score is used, even if *all* main effects and *all* the interactions were included, the risk score for each group could do no better than to predict that group's risk perfectly. Consequently, what we saw there was the performance of the very best of all scoring systems. In view of the above arguments, it was predictable that it did not outshine the sequential battery, particularly for optimally sensitive and specific results or when the potential clinical benefit was low to moderate.

All this means that when one elects to use one of the methods of estimating weights to implement a scoring approach, one de facto chooses to focus on optimal efficiency ($r = .5$) and to regard the clinical benefit as high ($\$R = \infty$), or the costs of the tests as negligible ($\$T = 0$). When time comes to evaluate the costworthiness of the resulting battery, as was seen in Table 11.4, we may end up rejecting the entire battery as uncostworthy, because of the uncostworthiness of some of the component tests.

The Basic Model

There are many different mathematical approaches to estimate weights for an optimal risk score. In general, one begins with a mathematical model, i.e., a proposal for how p_i relates to the test responses via a risk score:

$$p_i = f(w'x_i) + e_i .$$

In the above, p_i is once again patient i's probability of a positive diagnosis on the gold standard. (It is not the patient's probability, subjective or objective, of having the disorder of interest.) The function $f(\cdot)$ is a specification of the form of the model, and there are many different ways of defining f. I will use the shorthand vector notation x_i to represent patient i's list of test responses. This list is to include not only the main effects, but also any interactions that one chooses to include. I will use the notation w to represent the list of weights to be assigned or to be estimated. There must be as many entries on the list of w as there are on the list of x_i. Thus the shorthand notation for the formulation of the risk score above is that for subject i:

$$\text{Risk Score}_i = w'x_i .$$

Finally, e_i represents error. This error includes, first of all, any misspecification of the model. The model should be chosen to be reasonable within the context of its use and is never a perfect representation of nature. If the model used required that data have qualities not shared by the test responses, one might expect a large error. This error also reflects an inadequate choice of x_i. If test responses vital to determining the diagnosis are omitted (age, smoking status, or obesity as in the Weiner et al., 1979, study) this will produce inflated errors. Finally, this error will also reflect a poor choice of weights, whether assigned or estimated. If important interactions are assigned zero weights (omitted from consideration), or if the estimation procedures are poor (too small a sample, poor measurement of x_i, redundancy, or collinearity), that will also inflate error.

Generally, one obtains a sample (naturalistic or retrospective, *not* prospective), and the weights are estimated as follows. First of all, we ignore the error and use only the model to compute the likelihood of obtaining the observed set of results:

$$\text{Likelihood} = \prod f(w'x_i)^{D_i} \cdot [1 - f(w'x_i)]^{(1 - D_i)} ,$$

where D_i is 1 or 0 according to whether subject i has a positive or negative diagnosis, and the symbol $\prod$ represents the product over all subjects on whom both diagnosis and test are done. The weights included in w not assigned by the evaluator are then generated to maximize this likelihood, hence "maximum likelihood estimators."

Such maximum likelihood estimators are known mathematically to have desirable properties. They are consistent estimators of the "true" weights. As the sample size gets very large (i.e., asymptotically), the values of the estimators stabilize at certain theoretical values characteristic of the population and the model. Again, for very large sample size, the distribution of such estimators is known to be approximately normal (Gaussian) with a variance that can be mathematically obtained from further consideration of the likelihood function.

These are, however, large-sample properties that may not assure good estimates when the sample sizes are too small. A recurrent question is: what does "too small" mean? Here the quality of the estimators of w depend on how large the sample size is relative to the number of weights being estimated. However, the accuracy of the estimators of weights and their associated sampling results (standard errors and tests) also depend on the distribution of test responses, on the intercorrelations between test responses in the battery (redundancy or collinearity), and on the number of positive and negative diagnoses (prevalence).

For a test response with very little variability in the sample, the sample size necessary for accurate estimation of its associated weight is much larger than for one with greater variability. For example, when "race" is one factor (say white versus nonwhite), accurate estimation of the weight associated with "race" in a population in which 99% are white, would require a much larger sample size than in a population in which 50% are white. This is why, in Chapter 11, I suggested special attention to test responses with small variance in both diagnostic groups.

When multiple test responses highly correlated with others (collinearity) are simultaneously included in the estimation procedure, the accuracy of the estimation of *all* the weights suffers. For example, in a population of premature infants, simultaneous inclusion of gestational age, birth weight, birth length, birth head circumference, and duration of initial hospitalization in the same list of test responses would necessitate very large sample size for accurate estimation of the associated weights, for these are highly intercorrelated factors in this population. This is why, in Chapter 11, I suggested examining intercorrelations before beginning the process.

Finally, if positive and negative diagnoses are not *both* well represented in the sample on which the estimation is to be based, the weights will necessarily be less accurate. For a population in which the prevalence is 10% or 90%, a far larger sample size is required than for a population in which the prevalence is 50%.

No simple rule of thumb can take all these complex factors simultaneously into consideration. However, with that caveat, I would propose that there be minimally 10 subjects in *each* of the positive and negative diagnostic groups for each weight (other than the intercept) to be estimated. Thus, if there were two tests in the battery, and only main effects were to be included, there are three weights to be estimated: the intercept and two others. In this case there must be at least 20 subjects with a positive and 20 with a negative diagnosis. If the first order interaction weight were to be estimated, there are four weights to be estimated, the intercept plus three more, and there must be at least 30 subjects in each diagnostic group.

As with all rules of thumb, some statisticians will argue that this rule of thumb is too loose. On the other hand, some have recommended "rules of thumb" that are much looser. Solberg (1978), for example, says: "As a rule, the number of cases in samples from each group should preferably be at least three times the number of variables" (p. 219), and Lachenbruch and Goldstein (1979) concur. This, however, means that with one test response, one need have only three subjects with a positive and three subjects with a negative diagnosis. With two test responses with no interaction, one need have only six with and without a positive diagnosis.

Ryback, Eckardt, Felsher, and Rawlings (1982), in evaluating a battery of blood tests to determine the etiology of liver disease used 25 tests in a sample of 107 subjects, with 51 and 56 in the two diagnostic groups. With this sample size, by my rule of thumb, one should not seek to estimate more than about five weights (no more than 16 by Solberg's).

Yet, Ryback, Eckardt, Felsher, and Rawlings (1982) appear to have estimated at least 25 weights. When they then reported the "procedure classified correctly 100% of the nonalcoholic liver disease patients and 100% of the alcoholic liver disease patients" (p. 2262), one might suspect this is statistical artifact. In fact Ryback, Eckardt, Felsher, and Rawling (1982) confirmed that suspicion when they presented a small cross-validation on 18 subjects, 12 of whom were alcoholic. In this group they found, not 100% sensitivity and specificity, but, rather, a sensitivity and specificity of 83%. In general, estimating too many weights on too few subjects yields overly optimistic results in the sample on which the weights are developed. When subjected to validation in different or larger samples from the same population, such rules frequently turn out to be quite poor.

On the other hand, in the same paper, Ryback, Eckardt, Felsher, and Rawling (1982) report the results of another procedure using only nine tests with a "correct classification of 96% alcoholic liver disease and 82% nonalcoholic liver disease" (p. 2262). Here they are estimating far fewer weights with the same sample size of 107, but the results are more persuasive. In Table 11.1 are the nine best tests reported by Ryback, Eckardt, Felsher, and Rawling (1982) listed in their order of selection, followed by the remaining tests. It can be seen that there is a sizeable difference in either the means (r_M) or the variances (r_V) of the two diagnostic groups in at least the first five test responses, which supports the inference that at least these can be used to distinguish the diagnostic groups.

Most of the known mathematical procedures to estimate the weights for an optimal risk score can be implemented in several ways. One could, for example, enter all the factors and estimate all the weights simultaneously (an "all-in" procedure). The sample size to implement this approach will, of necessity, be very large. Such an approach used for medical test evaluation will exacerbate the problems of test cost common to these scoring procedures. Even tests that are irrelevant and redundant will be assigned non-zero weights simply because of estimation error. The cost of testing will then further increase without an increase in accuracy. Furthermore, with this procedure any collinearity problems will take their maximal toll on the adequacy of the results.

Another approach is to add test responses stepwise. One adds tests one at a time, at each step selecting the best of the remaining tests and assessing whether the weight assigned to that test differs significantly from zero. The procedure is iterated until no further test exists in the battery that significantly increases the accuracy of the prediction. Then the process stops. Thus the stopping rule is defined by the level of significance used for each test. Since the power of detecting each additional effect as significant decreases, if the sample size is small to begin with, the process usually stops short of my rule-of-thumb level.

This is, in principle, very similar to the iterative process suggested for evaluation of the optimal sequence of tests in a battery. Such an approach provides some, but not complete, protection against inclusion of tests that are irrelevant or redundant or against the inclusion of more tests than can be justified with the sample sizes involved. How to define the "stopping rule" is, however, a tricky issue.

Another alternative is the "hierarchical" procedure, in which the test responses are entered in an order specified by the test evaluator, and entry stops when no significant further information is added by the next specified test. Then the hierarchical and the stepwise procedures can be combined, in which certain of the test responses are "forced in first," and the remaining test responses are entered stepwise, again with the procedure stopping when no further significant test response remains.

A major difficulty with wholly or partially hierarchical alternatives lies in the fact that if the order of test responses to be entered is poorly chosen, the power available for structuring the risk score may be wasted in entering poorly chosen test responses. Little will be available to identify costworthy and valuable test responses later in the hierarchical list, or, only later yet, available for stepwise entry.

From this general discussion, it is clear that there are many choices to be made in seeking a optimal risk score. The form of the model, $f(\cdot)$, can be specified in, quite literally, an infinite number of ways. How many test responses to include, which interactions to include, and whether to assign or to estimate weights are all decisions the evaluators must make, for these should be based on clinical, not statistical, considerations. Even the computation of the estimates from a data set require some decisions—whether to do an all-in procedure, a stepwise procedure, an hierarchical procedure, or some combination of these, must also be decided by the evaluator. Finally, if stepwise procedures are used, how to define the stopping rule is not a settled issue.

The least of these problems is the infinite number of ways to specify the form of the model. There are, in fact, only relatively few such models well-enough developed mathematically and used frequently and widely enough so that computation procedures are readily available. The two most common are Multiple Discriminant Analysis and Multiple Logistic Regression Analysis; somewhat more rarely used are Multiple Linear Regression Analysis, Loglinear Models, and Quadratic Discrimination Analysis.

Which test responses to include and to exclude is truly an important decision. If an important test response is excluded, the quality of the resulting test will be impaired. If, on the other hand, unimportant test responses are included, the sample size may need to be larger if an all-in or hierarchical procedure including such test responses is contemplated, and the cost of the resulting battery may be unnecessarily increased. Stepwise procedures, on the other hand, will simply ignore unimportant or redundant test responses.

Evaluators seldom choose to include more than first-order interactions and frequently choose to ignore even those, focusing on the main effects. I have yet to see a real situation where second- or higher-order interactions played any major role in defining an optimal battery risk score, even when such interactions might be statistically significant, but ignoring first-order interactions may create more of a problem.

Whether to do the computation all-in, hierarchical, or stepwise is a major issue. The all-in procedure usually requires the largest sample sizes, and will yield a risk score generating a test that will be far less costworthy than those from the hierarchical or stepwise procedures. In this procedure every test in the battery would have to be used for each future patient in order to generate the battery risk score, and this will include useless tests, irrelevant tests, redundant tests, and noncostworthy tests. As a medical consumer I would have major doubts about this procedure.

The hierarchical procedure is frequently used to force the free tests in first in an effort to reduce the eventual cost of the battery. The difficulty, as noted above, is that if a costly test is indeed very costworthy, this procedure may obscure that fact, in that power is focused in entering the first free test responses. Such a procedure may produce a less costly test, but a less accurate one as well. That may be false economy.

Before we can deal with such issues, however, let us examine the more common mathematical models and the kinds of results they produce.

Multiple Linear Discrimination

Multiple Linear Discrimination is one of the classical problems of statistics, recognized at least since 1936 (R. Fisher, 1936) and under development and in use ever since (e.g., Solberg, 1978; Lachenbruch & Goldstein, 1979).

In its classical form, applied to this problem of test battery evaluation, the model is stated as follows:

In the subpopulation of those with the disorder (NB: the disorder, not the diagnosis), the test responses have a multivariate normal distribution. In the subpopulation of those free of the disorder, the test responses also have a multivariate normal distribution with different means, but with the same variances and inter-test response correlations in both groups. In the population of interest, a certain proportion π have the disorder.

If we randomly sampled from the population of interest and observed the test responses, the probability that a patient with test response x_i has the disorder is a function that depends only on a linear combination of the test responses. Because of the underlying assumption of multivariate normal distributions, the optimal discriminator is always a linear risk score *without* interactions.

As always, we cannot directly observe the disorder. We can only observe a diagnosis of the disorder. However, at the risk of incurring some additional error in the model, we can approximate p_i by that same function that defines the probability that a patient with test response x_i has the disorder, which depends only on a linear risk score without interactions.

There are clearly some difficulties with such a model in this context. The basic assumption of the model is that responses in the general population are a mixture from two normal distributions having equal variances and correlations. This would mean that in a sample from such a population there will be very few tied test responses. Test responses that are dichotomous (male versus female) or three-point scales (definite/probable angina/nonischemic chest pain), for example, will not fit such a definition.

Furthermore, the distribution of each test response in the population should have relatively short and symmetric tails. This is because normal distributions have relatively short tails, and the equal variance assumption would connote symmetry. Frequently in real life, the distribution of test responses on a continuum tends to have a much longer tail in one direction than in the other.

Finally, by the assumption of the clinical validity of the diagnosis, patients with the disorder have higher values of p_i than those without the disorder, but this does not necessarily mean that the probability of disorder and p_i are approximately equal. The concept of diagnostic error is completely discounted in the use of this model.

Thus, for all sorts of theoretical reasons, we might hesitate to use this form of model for the CASS study reported by Weiner et al. (1979) with the data reported in Table 11.1. Here three of the test responses (gender, resting EKG result, and stress test result) were binary variables, and the fourth is a three-point scale.

For other theoretical reasons, we might hesitate to use this form of model for the Ryback, Eckardt, Felsher, and Rawlings (1982) evaluation (see Table 11.1). There are several test responses in which the variances in the two diagnostic groups are very different (e.g., alanine aminotransferase, glucose, mean corpuscular hemoglobin concentration). Indeed that is why Ryback, Eckardt, Felsher, and Rawlings (1982) chose *not* to use the classical Multiple Discriminant Analysis, opting instead to use a relatively lesser-known procedure called Quadratic Discriminant Analysis (Ryback, Rawling, & Rosenthal, 1982).

However, the Quadratic Discriminant Analysis, while it allows unequal variances and correlations in the two groups, continues to require normal distributions. Yet, Ryback, Eckardt, Felsher, and Rawlings (1982) report that total bilirubin, measured in mg/dl (a positive number) has means of 5.72 and 2.06, with standard deviations of respectively 6.34 and 4.37. When all measured values are positive, but the standard deviation exceeds the mean, the data cannot be normally distributed. In short, the assumptions of the Quadratic Discriminant Analysis are also not likely to fit this situation well.

Nevertheless, such models are frequently applied whether they fit population characteristics well or not. One example of the application of the classical Multiple Discriminant Analysis is that reported by L. Fisher et al. (1981) using male patients from the CASS study, a portion of the same sample used in the CASS study reported by Weiner et al. (1979), where of the 35 test responses, 21 are binary.

The L. Fisher et al. (1981) study and the Weiner et al. (1979) study are based on the same sample, the same diagnosis, and the same test. In absence of statistical errors, their results should be consistent with each other. There are, however, differences in the way these two papers formulated their research questions that make comparisons both problematic and instructive.

1. Weiner et al. (1979) use the entire sample ($N = 2,045$) with gender and type of chest pain available as test responses. L. Fisher et al. (1981) use only the male subsample with no history of myocardial infarction

or previous cardiac surgery, and further subdivide that group into three separate subpopulations on the basis of type of chest pain (nonspecific chest pain $N = 267$; probable angina $N = 584$; definite angina $N = 500$). Thus, the populations are not exactly the same.

2. Weiner et al. (1979) do not define the specific intended clinical use of the test. In Table 11.4 it was found that for optimal sensitivity, whatever the potential clinical benefit, the exercise stress test was *not* used. The exercise stress test, further, was *not* recommended for any use when the potential clinical benefit was low. The exercise stress test was recommended for those with probable angina for optimal efficiency and for those males with definite angina for optimal specificity when the potential clinical benefit was moderate to high. Since these results indicate the differential usefulness of the exercise stress test for subgroups based on gender and type of chest pain, the focus on the subgroups as defined by L. Fisher et al. (1981) is an attractive modification.

In contrast, L. Fisher et al. (1981) state their goal as that of seeking the optimally sensitive test: "Our emphasis was on detecting low-risk patient subsets" (p. 988), which is consistent with graphs presented showing the complement of PVN, which is (scaling aside) equivalent to sensitivity. To be consistent with the Weiner et al. (1979) results, the conclusion should be that the exercise stress test is of no value for this purpose. But that was *not* the L. Fisher et al. (1981) conclusion.

3. Beyond gender and type of chest pain, Weiner et al. (1979) did not include any clinical information, and included only the binary responses on the resting EKG and the exercise stress test as test responses. On the other hand, L. Fisher et al. (1981) included 9 further clinical variables, and 24 further exercise test variables. Expansion of the list of test responses to be included, of course, changes the test. Inclusion of either clinical variables or further exercise test variables could indeed add value to the resulting test for any of its purposes.

4. L. Fisher et al. (1981) elect to use scoring based on weights estimated by use of Multiple Discriminant Analysis. This procedure was first applied stepwise to clinical variables only to produce the "Clinical Risk Index." Then the clinical variables selected were forced in first, and the exercise stress test variables entered stepwise thereafter to produce the Clinical + Exercise Risk Index. This procedure, too, differentiated the approach taken from that by Weiner et al. (1979), which was basically descriptive, from the reanalysis here presented in Table 11.4.

A few comments first on the estimation of weights done here: It should be noted that the weights estimated are optimal for efficiency, not for the sensitivity the authors specified as their goal. The statistical tests reported assessed whether there was incremental value in adding the variables from the exercise stress test to the clinical variables for *efficiency*, not *sensitivity*. Since test cost is not considered, the conclusion of statistical significance was also limited to the case of high potential clinical benefit. The finding that in all groups, this incremental value *was* statistically significant is thus not different from the results for *efficiency* in Table 11.4, although obviously different from the results there for *sensitivity*.

Further, the authors note that only one patient of the 267 with nonspecific chest pain had a positive response for the binary variable indicating that the exercise tests were stopped for occurrence of supraventricular arrhythmia. Thus the variance of this test response was near zero in both the diagnostic groups. Had the evaluators compiled their raw data base as suggested in Chapter 11, they would have been warned in advance that this test response was problematic and could have been omitted. Unfortunately, this variable was not omitted and was identified as statistically significant, which then raises questions about the validity of all the results in the nonspecific chest pain group.

However, these are statistical quibbles, for, whatever the process of selecting the weights, for each of the three populations (non-specific chest pain, probable angina, definite angina) we end with two battery scores to be evaluated: The Clinical Risk Index based only on clinical information ($\$T = 0$) and the Clinical + Exercise Risk Index (as before $\$T = \$175$). From the information presented, we can compute the ROC, QROC, or QCROC for each of the scores in each of the populations, identify the optimal cut-point for each index, and the optimal overall for sensitivity, efficiency, and specificity. All these results appear in Figure 12.1 for a diagnosis of CAD.

The stated focus of the L. Fisher et al. (1981) study was on optimal sensitivity, with test cost discounted ($t = 0$). From the QROCs in Figure 12.1, we see that the optimally sensitive test is based on the Clinical + Exercise Risk Index for all three populations. L. Fisher et al. (1981), on the other hand, conclude: "that exercise testing as carried out in this study is of limited diagnostic value in men with definite angina. . . . However, exercise testing does have a diagnostic role in the evaluation of men with probable angina pectoris. . . . In men with nonspecific chest pain, exercise testing is of limited diagnostic value" (p. 994).

214

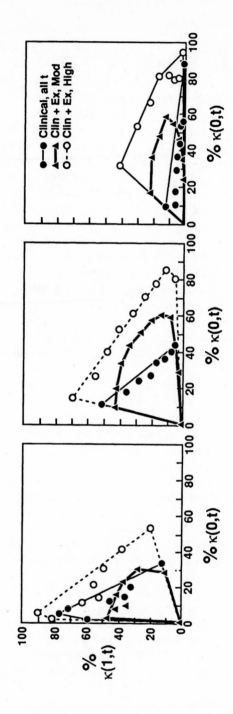

Figure 12.1. QROC Results for the L. Fisher et al. (1981) Evaluation of the CASS Data

Their conclusion was based on examination of graphs for each of the populations, of the complement of the predictive value of a negative test $(1 - PVN)$ versus the complement of level $(1 - Q)$ for various cut-offs of each of the proposed risk indices. For any population and any continuous test response positively correlated with diagnosis, such a graph of PVN must necessarily increase as $1 - Q$ increases, to "top off" at the prevalence P of that population, the random level of $1 - PVN$. How rapid that increase is depends on the heterogeneity of test responses in that population. With a relatively homogeneous low-risk population, one is likely to see a "floor" with only a small total increase, since P is small. With a relatively homogeneous high-risk population, one is likely to see a "ceiling" at the relatively higher level of P. It is only in a middle-risk, heterogenous population that one is likely to see a more or less linear pattern of $1 - PVN$ versus $1 - Q$. That is what L. Fisher et al. (1981) saw with the two risk indices proposed, each of which, by virtue of how it was developed, is likely to be positively correlated with the diagnosis in the sample.

Because of these patterns, the separation between curves related to the different test responses can never be as impressive in a low-risk (non-specific chest pain, MVCAD: $P = 6\%$ and CAD: $P = 20\%$) or in a high-risk (definite angina CAD: $P = 87\%$) as in a moderate-risk population (probable angina, MVCAD: $P = 44\%$, CAD: $P = 66\%$; definite angina MVCAD: 64%). When subjectively judging separation between such uncalibrated curves, one is likely to reach the same conclusions L. Fisher et al. (1981) did. Because of calibration reasons, there will seldom be as clear and consistent differentiation between such curves in either a low- or a high-risk population as in a moderate-risk population. On the other hand, if PVP were recalibrated, the results would be those obtained in the QROC (see Figure 12.1, High Benefit).

In the Weiner et al. (1979) results, whether exercise ST depression exceeded 1 mV during exercise or recovery (ST positive) mattered, and the resting EKG did not. No other variables from exercise testing were offered. In the L. Fisher et al. (1981) results ST depression continued to matter, and the resting EKG continued not to. However, further information from the exercise stress test in the form of assessment of the occurrence of pain *during* the test and the pressure-rate product were now added and appeared to matter for the definite and probable angina groups. In sum, the L. Fisher et al. results indicate that more information from the exercise stress test than was used in the Weiner et al. (1979) study appears to be essential to obtain full value from the testing procedure.

Logistic Regression Analysis

The logistic regression model is a rather simpler model that demands far less of the test responses on which it is used:

$$\ln[p_i/(1 - p_i)] = w_0 + w'x_i ,$$

where "ln" represents a natural logarithm, and $p_i/(1 - p_i)$ is the "odds" that patient i has a positive diagnosis (here not disorder, but diagnosis).

Unlike Multiple Discriminant Analysis, there are no assumptions about the nature or distribution of the test responses. Binary variables (gender, or positive/negative on the stress test), three-point scales (chest pain), interval scales with skewed or long-tailed distributions, are all candidates for test responses in this model.

With Multiple Discriminant Analysis, the interpretation of the weights is difficult. Here how the weights function in the model is very clear. If patients A and B have exactly the same test responses with the single exception that A has the jth test response one unit higher than does B, then the odds ratio of A's probability of a positive diagnosis to that of B is given by the weight:

$$p(\text{A}) \cdot p'(\text{B})/p'(\text{A}) \cdot p(\text{B}) = \exp(w_j) ,$$

where $\exp(\cdot)$ represents the number e (= 2.718 . . .) raised to the indicated power. If the weight attached to test jth response is 0, the odds ratio is 1. If the weight is positive, the odds ratio is greater than 1, which indicates that greater risk is associated with larger responses. If the weight is negative, the odds ratio is less than 1, which indicates that greater risk is associated with smaller responses on that test.

Let us review once again the CASS study as reported by Weiner et al. (1979). In Table 12.1 are presented the weights estimated using various different specifications for a Logistic Regression Model.

Model 1, for example, used only the clinical data: gender and chest pain and their interaction. Figure 12.2 shows the QROC for a risk score

Table 12.1 Weight Derived from Application of Various Multiple Logistic Models to the Weiner et al. (1979) Data

	Model 1	2	3	4	5	6
Constant	−2.34	−3.32	−2.67	−2.64	−2.64	−2.74
Gender (G)	1.30**	1.54**	1.07**	1.02**	1.09**	1.22**
Chest Pain (P)	1.61**	1.44**	1.15**	1.01**	1.06**	1.17**
Resting EKG (E)	—	0.10	—	−0.03	−0.32	0.35
Stress Test (S)	—	1.83**	0.81*	0.91**	0.75	1.01*
Two Way Interactions						
G×P	0.08		0.04	0.11	0.03	−0.11
G×E				0.00	−0.23	−1.36
G×S			0.65	0.70*	0.73	0.38
P×E				0.41	0.72	−0.07
P×S			0.52	0.48*	0.62	0.36
E×S				−0.35	0.39	−0.63
Three Way Interactions						
G×P×E					0.27	1.56
G×P×S			0.06		−0.01	0.35
G×E×S					−0.08	1.62
P×E×S					−0.73	0.39
Four Way Interaction						
G×E×P×S						−1.87

NOTES: $*p < .05$; $**p < .01$

based on this particular model. The quality indices for the optimally sensitive, efficient, and specific tests are respectively 77%, 54%, 74%.

Model 2 is the form of Logistic Regression Model most commonly used, including all the tests, but using only the main effects. The QROC for this risk score appears in Figure 12.2 as well, with single arrows indicating the optimally sensitive [$\kappa(1, 0) = 91\%$], optimally efficient [$\kappa(.5, 0) = 60\%$] and optimally specific [$\kappa(0, 0) = 89\%$] results.

It is important to note that this QROC is virtually that which would have resulted had I used Multiple Discriminant Analysis on these data. Despite the pronounced differences in the mathematical formation of the two mathematical models, the differences in the computation procedures for the estimates, the differences in the weights obtained, and in the optimal referents that would be chosen, the result of using a Multiple Discriminant Analysis to obtain an optimal score and a Multiple Logistic Analysis with main effects only, quite typically yields

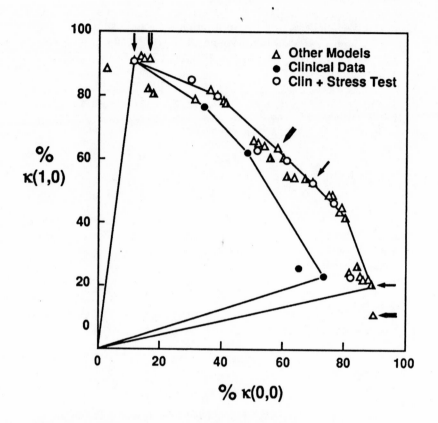

Figure 12.2. QROC for the CASS Battery as Evaluated by Weiner et al. (1979) Based on Multiple Logistic Modeling

QROCs and classification results that are very similar (e.g., Bull & Donner, 1987; Efron, 1975, 1978; O'Gorman & Woolson, 1991).

The results of using these two quite different models may yield very similar results, but using only the clinical data and using clinical data plus the stress test in the same form of model (Model 1 versus 2 above) clearly yield quite different results. There is a substantial improvement in using the results of the stress test in addition to those of the clinical evaluation. This begins to suggest that it is not the model per se, but what factors are chosen to be included in the model that spell the difference in the quality of the results.

Models 3, 4, 5, and 6 use the Multiple Logistic Regression approach used in various other different ways. Model 3 uses only the stress test in addition to the clinical data, ignoring the resting EKG. Model 4 uses all the tests but only interactions up to order 1. Model 5 uses all the tests but only interactions up to order 2. Model 6 uses all the tests and all the interactions. The test points defining the QROCs for these models appear in Figure 12.2 as well, but to avoid confusion, their QROCs are not drawn. What is apparent is that the QROCs for all these various forms are barely different from that of Model 2. The overall optimally sensitive, efficient, and specific tests are indicated by double arrows, but their qualities are hardly different from what would have been obtained on the basis of Model 2 (single arrows). The optimally sensitive test has $\kappa(1, 0) = 91.2\%$ versus 90.9%. The optimally efficient test has $\kappa(.5, 0) = 60.4\%$ rather than 60.2%. The optimally specific test has $\kappa(0, 0) = 89.8\%$ rather than 89.3%. This is well within the sampling error of estimation of the quality indices. What is more, most patients would be classified the same, regardless of which of Models 2-6 were used to generate the risk scores.

The results in Table 12.1 should be examined carefully. It should be noted that the estimates of the weights vary depending on which model is used. For example, in Model 5 the weight for the stress test result was estimated as .746 [associated odds ratio of exp(.746) = 2.1], whereas in Model 2, it was 1.829 (associated odds ratio of 6.2). In Models 2, 3, 4, and 6, the weight was found to be significantly greater than zero ($p < .05$), but in Model 5, it was non-significant. What is to be made of these seeming discrepancies?

The weight associated with a test response is model-specific. It indicates the value of that test response *within that model* in predicting the diagnosis. If one changes the model, the weights change. This causes a problem when the odds ratio computed from a model that does not necessarily perfectly fit the population is interpreted as if it did. Then what is likely to appear in an abstract or in newspaper results is that having a positive stress test increases the odds by a factor of 6.2 (or is it 2.1 or somewhere in between as indicated by the other models in Table 12.1?). Models *approximate* the population, and the magnitude of the individual weights based on model-fitting should not be taken too seriously. What matters is the prediction as a whole.

Whether a weight is found statistically significant or not depends on the sample size, on its distribution of the associated test response in the population, and on what other test responses are included in the model. All this is over and above consideration of whether or not the population value of the weight is zero. As in all significance tests, a statistically significant result indicates a nonzero weight, but a non-statistically significant result may be only a result of lack of power. Frequently such lack of power reflects the choices made by the evaluator and not the importance of the factor. The results seen in Table 12.1 and Figure 12.2 typify what one might expect to see in general. As long as it is remembered that the aim of model-fitting here is to generate a risk score to which an appropriate referent can be applied, with the weights only a means to that end, one can avoid overinterpreting the weights and their significance or lack thereof, and focus properly on the risk score and its value in classifying patients.

Let us consider another example of the applications of Multiple Logistic Regression that stimulates further insights into the process of optimal scoring. Pozen et al. (1980) evaluated a battery of tests available to the physician to diagnose acute ischemic heart disease in a population of patients seen in the emergency room with suspected ischemic heart disease. Sampling was naturalistic, with a sample size of 925 for the development of the score. There were 105 test responses in the original battery, including characterizations of clinical presentation, history, socio-demography, physical findings, and electrocardiograms. It appears that the only test response with associated nonnegligible cost was the EKG (at about $25). Stepwise logistic regression analysis yielded nine predictors, listed in Table 12.2 with their respective weights. (In the Pozen et al., 1980, presentation, presence of a condition was coded 1 and absence 2. In Table 12.2 we have presented the weights when using a coding of 1 for presence of a condition and 0 as absence. This doesn't substantively change results, but eases the following discussion.)

If no conditions are present, all the test responses are zero, and the risk score is simply the intercept, -5.29. To get an estimate of such a patient's risk p_i from this model, we compute:

$$\exp(-5.29)/[1 + \exp(-5.29)] = 0.0050,$$

or 0.5%. At the other extreme, for a patient with all conditions present, the risk score is obtained by summing all the weights, and the estimated risk from this model for such patients is 99.9%. In Table 12.2, we present the estimated risk from the model for patients having each condition in isolation. These estimated risks are individually low, but range from 0.8% for TWave (1) to 2.7% for angina.

Table 12.2 Weights in the Risk Score and Estimated Prevalences from
the Multiple Logistic Model for Patients with Each Sign or
Symptom Alone

	Weight	*Estimated Average Risk*
Constant	−5.29	0.5%
MI	3.73	2.3%
TWave(2)	3.68	2.5%
Dyspnea	4.19	1.5%
ST(1)	3.61	2.6%
Chest Pain Location	3.71	2.4%
Chest Pain Improvement	4.33	1.3%
Angina	3.57	2.7%
ST(1)	3.88	2.0%
TWave(1)	4.84	0.8%

SOURCE: Pozen et al. (1980)

With the model we can estimate the risk for a patient having any combination of conditions by adding the weights associated with the conditions present to the intercept. In Table 12.3 we present the range of estimated prevalences from the model associated with one condition, with two conditions, with three conditions, and so on.

It is important to notice how much overlap there is between the ranges of estimated risks for different total number of conditions present. It is quite possible that a patient with six conditions may have a lower risk than one with five conditions, or a patient with five conditions lower than one with four. This arises simply because not all conditions are *equally* important in identifying those with a positive diagnosis.

Granted that the estimated risks from the model apply to the population only if the model fits exactly (and it probably does not), but the same point can be made with any reasonable model, and, given a large enough sample size, directly with the population. Generally a subject's risk does not merely depend on the *number* of conditions or symptoms present, but, rather, varies depending on *which* specific ones are present. For this reason, counting up the number of positive tests or adding the responses on various tests to generate a risk score is not usually the best of ideas in terms of accuracy and certainly not in terms of test cost.

Table 12.3 Range of Estimated Prevalence for Patients with Different
Total Number of Signs and Symptoms

Number of Signs	Combinations Possible	Range of Estimated Prevalence	
		min	max
0	1	0.5%	0.5%
1	9	0.8%	2.7%
2	36	2.0%	13.1%
3	84	5.8%	43.0%
4	126	20.3%	78.6%
5	126	54.7%	94.6%
6	84	85.4%	98.6%
7	36	96.7%	99.5%
8	9	99.4%	99.8%
9	1	99.9%	99.9%

SOURCE: Pozen et al. (1980)

Some Practical Considerations
in Choosing and Using Models

The range of choices in using mathematical models to develop optimal scores for a battery of tests is daunting. There are numerous mathematical forms (Multiple Discriminant, Multiple Logistic, and many more). Within each, the evaluators choose to include only main effects or two-way interactions or go on to higher-way interactions. The evaluators choose which test responses to include and which to exclude. They choose how to scale the test responses, coding them 0 for "normal" and 1 for "abnormal," or on three-, four- or five-point scales, or on a continuum (e.g., age). The evaluators choose to assign weights or to estimate them. If they choose to estimate them, they choose to do an all-in procedure, a stepwise procedure, a hierarchical procedure, or a combination of the last two. Some of these choices have major impact; others do not.

Choice of the form of the mathematical model, provided the model is mathematically well-developed and the estimation procedures well-programmed, does not, surprisingly enough, seem to make much difference. In describing the Multiple Discriminant Analysis approach, I tried to convey my personal reluctance to use a model that makes assumptions about the data that are not well satisfied (see also Harrell

& Lee, 1985; Hosmer, Hosmer, & Fisher, 1983; Press & Wilson, 1978). In fact, given a choice, I never use a Multiple Discriminant Analysis in the context of medical test evaluation. If, however, I were challenged to *demonstrate empirically* that the results of using the models that I prefer (with main effects only) produce noticeably better results, I would fail the challenge. (I have tried it.) Generally, as was shown above for the CASS data (Weiner et al., 1979), the difference in the results (i.e., the QROC and the classification of the patients) would be negligible.

The Linear and the Loglinear Models have not been discussed here because they seem to be rarely used in this context. The Loglinear Model is based on the assumption that:

$$\ln(p_i) \doteq w_0 + w'x_i + e_i \, ,$$

and the Linear Model on the assumption that:

$$p_i = w_0 + w'x_i + e_i \, ,$$

clearly both quite different from either the Multiple Discriminant or the Multiple Logistic Models. In these models, the weights (as in the Multiple Logistic Model) have meaning. If patient A and B had exactly the same test responses except that patient A had the jth test response one unit higher than patient B, the risk ratio between them would be related to w_j in the Loglinear Model by:

$$p(A)/p(B) = \exp(w_j) \, .$$

and the risk difference between them would be related to w_j in the Linear model by:

$$p(A) - p(B) = w_j \, .$$

Consequently the weights for the Loglinear Model are related to risk ratios and the weights in the Linear Model are related to risk differences, as the weights for the Multiple Logistic Model are to the odds ratios. Thus, if one used a Loglinear or Linear Model to develop the optimal weights, the magnitudes of the weights might differ from each other as well as from those of the Multiple Logistic Model, or from those of the Multiple Discriminant Model. Nevertheless, applied correctly using the same factors, the results of using these four approaches frequently produce very similar results, both in terms of the QROC and in the classification that each patient would receive.

In short, there may be mathematical or computational reasons for preferring one model rather than another, but what the models would accomplish in terms of medical test evaluation would be similar *as long as the same factors are included*. My own preference is Multiple Logistic Regression, but I will not try to convince others with different preferences to change.

There seldom seems to be much gain in *including the higher-order interactions*. If there is clinical reason to suspect that interactions might be important, or if the sample size is large enough to be more thorough, first order interactions might well be included. What is seen in Figure 12.2 is typical. Higher-order interactions may make some difference to the QROC and to the classification procedures, but usually the difference is of negligible clinical importance. Excluding high-order interactions is what medical test evaluators have typically been doing in any case.

Which test responses to include and which to exclude is the single most important decision that is made. In Figure 12.2 we saw two QROCs, one including and the other excluding the exercise stress test results. The difference was substantial. Omission of important test responses can make a major difference. The most frequent and troublesome omissions in medical test evaluations are the obvious, simple-minded test responses such as gender, age, information from family or medical history, clinical observations from interview or physical examinations. These are omitted in favor of high-tech, frequently invasive, risky, and costly test responses that are clearly of greater interest to the medical test evaluators.

The results shown in Figure 12.2 indicate that the battery of tests from the CASS study as reported by Weiner et al. (1979) including gender, evaluation of chest pain, and the exercise stress test (the resting EKG makes no major contribution), yields a good test. Yet the CASS study as reported by L. Fisher et al. (1981) reported that in all cases, *age* was the single best predictor of diagnosis. How much better would the QROC have been in Figure 12.2 had age been included as one of the test results?

In evaluating new and particularly costly and invasive tests, such simple but relevant test responses such as gender, age, and observation of clinical signs and symptoms should be included. Otherwise both the quality and the cost of the resulting batteries will be compromised. If, in fact, knowledge only of the age and gender of the patient indeed gives as accurate a test result as does an MRI, both medical ethics and economics require that such a result be reported.

When there is a choice of *how to scale the responses on a test*, one should choose a reasonably precise scale. Age, measured on a continuum, should not be dichotomized (Age < 35 versus Age ≥ 35), or rounded to the nearest decade (20s, 30s, ...) but entered precisely to the year (26, 35, 87, etc.) as it is usually collected. The power of the scoring procedures is attenuated when the test responses entered are entered with less precision than is usual in clinical practice. In fact, if an alternative scaling is poorly chosen (e.g., if 35 years is the wrong dichotomization point) the value of the test response may be completely lost.

I have no hesitation in unequivocally recommending that if it is decided to include an effect, that *the weight be estimated, not assigned*. When a weight is assigned, the resulting risk score may generate a very good test, but if the score had been estimated, the test might have been even better. However, the major worry is not that one might not achieve the best possible results, but, rather, that with assigned weights, one might not even achieve good results because of a bad guess as to the weight. However, given a choice, I would recommend that the weights be estimated on one sample from the population (often called a "test sample"), and the evaluation of the performance (i.e., the ROC, QROC, QCROC) of the resulting score be evaluated on a separate sample from the same population (the "validation sample").

With assignment of weights, test results that are irrelevant might be included. Then the battery result would not only be less accurate in classifying subjects, but if that particular irrelevant test had cost, one would be charging more for a less accurate result.

This is particularly true in counting up positive tests or adding up test responses. If all the tests are not equally accurate, or when some tests are redundant, assigning tests equal weights may be a very poor strategy. For example, in Figure 6.2 was the QROC for a family of tests for carotid artery stenosis that included a nested family of tests based on counting the number of positive tests (#8, #9, #10, #11). Of these #8 (one or more positive tests) proved the optimally sensitive. However, the others were far inferior in efficiency or specificity to tests involving only one or two of the four test responses in the battery.

From the Pozen et al. (1980) study, with results presented in Table 12.2, we see why the strategy of counting up positive tests or adding up test responses is likely to prove inferior. Among patients having four positive tests, for example, some are at estimated risk of 20% and some at 79%—a truly wide range. If one characterized subjects only by the number of positive tests, patients with such very different risks will be classified the same. Only if the test responses are independent and equally important in predicting diagnosis will the strategy of counting positive tests or of using the average or sum of test responses provide accurate results. Moreover, since to get the count of positive tests or to get the sum of all the test responses, one needs to do all the tests in the battery, this strategy, too, leads generally to overly costly batteries.

Finally, should one do *an all-in, a stepwise procedure, a hierarchical procedure, or some combination?*

My recommendation (with reservations) would be for a stepwise procedure. Stepwise procedures have a well-deserved bad reputation among statisticians. Such procedures are frequently the basis for the most flagrant "fishing expeditions" or for doing post hoc hypothesis testing. It is not unusual to find peer-reviewed published research reports with small sample size (e.g., $N = 20$) and a very large number of variables (e.g., $n = 200$), in which every variable is correlated with every other, the strongest are picked out as independent variables, a hypothesis is formed on that basis, and then tested using stepwise methods on the same data set that generated the hypothesis. Such results produce meaningless statistical artifacts unlikely to be confirmed in future research or in clinical practice.

Why is what is proposed here any different? In this presentation an exploratory mode pervades. Statistical tests are not used to make inferences about the truth of hypotheses, but, rather, to provide reasonable stopping rules. The reason that rules of thumb for sample sizes are presented is to forestall misuse of the methods. The value of what results depends on the QROC or QCROC, which are descriptive, not tests of hypotheses. Ultimately, however, the best protection is use of external validation of the results, i.e., evaluating the optimal sequence selected or the optimal score developed on a separate sample from the population. Use of stepwise procedures is a weakness of what is proposed here, one that future research may better resolve.

With the stepwise structuring used both in developing optimal sequences and in developing optimal scores, the chance of including an irrelevant test at each stage is greater than the significance level used (generally $p < .05$). How much greater it is depends on the number of test responses, and, in the scoring approach, on how many interactions are included. The larger this number, the greater the chance of including an irrelevant test. This error rate can be controlled by setting a more stringent significance level to define the stopping rule than is usual (e.g., using Bonferroni adjustment and thus $p < .005$ instead of $p < .05$).

However, at the same time, the chance of excluding an important test result depends on the sample size, the intercorrelations between tests, the distribution of test responses etc., in short, all the factors that affect the power. Setting a more stringent significance level than usual exacerbates this problem.

At this time there is no non-controversial solution to such problems. In practice, of the options available, careful use of the stepwise procedures seems to best balance out the various types of problems, but users should remain cautious.

Summary

The overall weakness of all these scoring methods remains the lack of attention to the costs and benefits involved in using the various tests in the battery. When these methods are used, one is de facto seeking the optimally efficient test when the potential clinical benefit is high. The optimal battery that results should also have satisfactory quality of sensitivity and specificity for high potential clinical benefit, but may not be the most costworthy such tests. When the potential clinical benefit is low to moderate, the resulting battery may not be costworthy at all.

What can be said in favor of this approach is twofold: (1) They are much easier to do than are the optimal sequencing methods described in Chapter 11, for these are long-known, well-established, readily applicable methods; and (2) The accuracy of the results obtained (i.e., cost issues aside) is likely to be comparable to that of optimal sequencing and may be even a little better.

If there is one overall message from all that was considered here, it is that, to the greatest extent possible, test evaluations should be guided by data, not by arbitrary decisions of the test evaluators. These worries include decisions as to rescaling test responses crudely (Don't!); to assigning weights (Don't!); and to arbitrary choice of referents (Don't!). Where there are unavoidable choices that must be made, such as the choice of mathematical model or the exclusion of higher-order interactions, nature is kind. There do not seem to be major penalties to making one reasonable decision rather than another. On the other hand, omission of test responses that are simple and obvious (Don't!) may carry major negative repercussions both in terms of the accuracy and cost of resulting medical test batteries.

13

Evaluating Batteries of Prognostic Tests with Variable Follow-Up Times

Introduction

To this point, the evaluation of all tests was based on choosing one gold standard diagnosis at a time, some one particular fixed diagnostic procedure of the clinically valid diagnostic procedures that might be available. When evaluating *prognostic* tests with the methods thus far developed, there must be a *fixed* follow-up time. Thus one study might propose to evaluate whether or not the event of clinical interest occurs within a 1-year follow-up, another within a 5-year follow-up, and yet another within a 10-year follow-up. The risk of an event depends on the duration of the follow-up period. Patient i's risk of an event within the first year of follow-up is less than his risk within 2 years, and that risk, in turn, is less than his risk within 10 years.

As long as the follow-up period is fixed, it is reasonable to describe a subject's risk as we did in Chapter 2 as p_i, but to consider a variable follow-up period, we must be more precise and denote a subject's risk in a specified follow-up period, which I denote FU, as

$$p_i(\text{FU}).$$

Since the longer the period of follow-up, the greater the risk of having an event, p_i(FU) is a nondecreasing function of FU.

Similarly, with a constant follow-up, we denoted the prevalence in the population simply as P, where

$$P = \text{Mean}(p_i)$$

Now prevalence also depends on the follow-up time. Thus the prevalence in a follow-up time of FU is:

$$P(\text{FU}) = \text{Mean}[p_i(\text{FU})],$$

where the mean is taken over the subjects in the population of interest.

What quantitative results would be obtained in a medical test evaluation (or from the evaluation of a battery of tests) strongly depends on which fixed follow-up time was chosen. The sensitivity, the specificity, the predictive values, their quality indices, and therefore the ROC, QROC, and QCROC will all change with the follow-up time selected. Consequently, the optimal test may also change depending on what follow-up time is used.

This may come as bad news to those who prefer to believe that, despite all argument and evidence to the contrary (see Chapter 6), sensitivity and specificity, at least, are properties of the test, unrelated to the choice of diagnosis and population. The fact that it is not merely the definition of the diagnosis for a prognostic test (what event is to be noted, and how identified, etc.), but also the span of time over which one will note such events that changes the results may seem a last very low blow!

Perhaps it will soften the blow a bit to point out the advantages that such a situation may offer. Relatively few disorders appear to have a univariate etiology, that is, one and only one factor that causes the disease or determines its course. Smoking may be associated with lung cancer, but some smokers never get cancer. Obesity may be associated with heart disease, but there are obese people who live long lives and die with healthy hearts, and other lifelong thin people who die from heart attacks. In such cases, there might well be other risk factors (genetic predisposition?) that might predict occurrence. Whether a prognostic medical test is good or not may depend on whether it can detect some complex or other of the multitude of factors that predict the occurrence of the disease or its course.

How rapidly a patient succumbs to lung cancer or heart disease may depend on which particular complex of risk factors he has. One test may be better at detecting the complex of factors associated with an early event; another the complex of factors associated with a late event. Since the most appropriate preventive measures or treatments may be different for the two complexes of factors, would it not be an advantage to have two tests, one sensitive to early events, one sensitive to late events?

Whether such speculation provides some comfort or not, the incontrovertible fact is that the quality of a test or battery of tests used for prognosis *does* depend on the follow-up time selected. Yet this fact is not the prime impetus to examine more closely the problem of variable follow-up time. A more pressing one is generated by real-life experiences.

What really happens in an evaluation of a prognostic test? Let us say we recruit the first patient into the study on January 1, 1990, planning to recruit 100 patients. To do this may take five years. So, on January 1, 1995, we recruit the 100th patient and test him. At that moment we have 100 patients, one with a 5-year follow-up, one with a zero-year follow-up, and 98 with follow-up times ranging between those two extremes. If the prescribed fixed follow-up time is five years, we will have to go on until January 1, 2000, at which time we have follow-up times ranging from 5 to 10 years. To use the *fixed* follow-up time procedure, we throw out all the information available on occurrence of events after a 5-year period and proceed. What a waste of hard-earned information!

In fact, that is not the worst of the story. During the 10 years of the study, some patients will drop out by moving away, dying from causes unrelated to the events of interest (competing risks), or will simple refuse further participation in the study. For such a patient we will know, for example, that at 3.5 years of follow-up, when the patient dropped out, he was event-free, but there will be no later information. That is a "censored observation," i.e., we know that the event time of such a patient is greater than 3.5 years, but whether the event occurs at 3.6 years or 36 years, or never, we will never know. At the end of the 10-year study, we will have a pile of censored observations, in addition to event times occurring from 0 to 10 years, and follow-up times (either censored or event times) also ranging from 0 to 10 years. If we are using a fixed follow-up time of 5 years, dropouts occurring after 5 years are of no concern. Usually we are not lucky enough to avoid all earlier dropouts, which may bias the sample.

There are several approaches seen in the medical literature to deal with this situation likely to produce *invalid* results. In the following discussion, we will, first of all, present the basic model, and then we will deal with these questionable approaches to medical test evaluations. We will invest effort to describe under what circumstances these approaches are appropriate, and why these circumstances seldom prevail. Because these methods are much easier to apply than those we will proceed to recommend, these are very seductive to the test evaluator. Test evaluators must be aware of the chance they take in succumbing to this seduction and decide whether it is worthwhile.

The Basic Model

Let us begin with patient i, whose risk of the event in question during a follow-up period of duration FU is $p_i(FU)$, a non-decreasing function of FU. With a variable follow-up time, statistical methods tend to focus not on the prevalence function $p_i(FU)$, but on its complement:

$$s_i(FU) = 1 - p_i(FU),$$

which is called the "survival function" for patient i.

We will here introduce another function, called the "hazard function," that will prove both useful and informative in this context, but initially may seem awkward. We will define patients i's "crude hazard" at follow-up time FU, during a subsequent short period of time of length dt, as the probability per unit time that he will survive that additional subsequent period, given that he survives to time FU:

$$[s_i(FU) - s_i(FU + dt)]/[s_i(FU) \cdot dt] .$$

If we take the limit of this crude hazard as the length of the time span dt approaches zero, we get the hazard function, $h_i(FU)$, which mathematically equals:

$$h_i(i) = -d[\ln s_i(FU)]/dFU,$$

where $d(\cdot)/dFU$ represents the derivative of the subsequent function with respect to FU.

In an intuitive sense, the hazard function is greater at those times when the danger of the event to those still event-free is greater, and less when the danger of the event is less. Some illustrations:

Since the period during which the danger of dying from the complications of a surgical procedure is greatest during the first hours and days after the surgery, the hazard function of a surgery-related death is greatest for short follow-up times after the surgery and then decreases as the follow-up periods lengthen, i.e., "a decreasing hazard function."

Over the course of a lifetime, there are many disorders that are associated with increasing age, such as coronary artery disease, arthritis, etc. The hazard function for such disorders over a lifetime of follow-up is likely to be low and flat until perhaps the age of 40-50 or so, and gradually increases thereafter. In contrast, the hazard of death due to respiratory distress syndrome in children is highest just after birth and decreases with longer follow-ups.

Finally, the hazard of death due to complications of childbirth is zero prior to child-bearing years and zero after menopause and highest in the interim period, an arc-shaped function.

Unlike the prevalence function that increases as a function of follow-up time and the survival function that decreases, the hazard function can take on any shape, and its shape may provide clues as to the etiology of the events that occur at different points of the follow-up period.

For the moment, let us focus on one and only one test in a population with level Q. For the purposes of test evaluation, the diagnosis must be blind to the test result. Here that means that the results of the test are not given to the patient or to anyone making decisions about treating that patient subsequent to testing. Thus the course of events to follow the test, in particular those related to whatever event defines a positive diagnosis, must be unaffected by the test result. The course must be what it would have been in absence of the test. Blindness here is essential, for without such blindness, what later happens may be as much or more the result of patient and physician reaction and response to the results of testing, as it is the natural course of events.

Then in the population of interest, we can consider the average survival function over all patients:

$$S_0(\text{FU}) = \text{Mean}[s_i(\text{FU})] = P'(\text{FU}) = 1 - P(\text{FU}) .$$

We can also consider the average survival function over all patients with a positive test:

$$S_+(\text{FU}) = \text{Mean}[s_i(i), i \text{ with } T+] .$$

What this survival function describes at each value of FU is the probability that a patient with a positive test will not have a positive diagnosis at that time. That is the complement of the predictive value of a positive test for a fixed diagnosis at FU, i.e.,:

$$PVP(FU) = 1 - S_+(FU).$$

Similarly, we can consider the average survival function over all patients with a negative test:

$$S_-(FU) = \text{Mean}(s_i(i), i \text{ with } T-),$$

and what this represents is the predictive values of a negative test for a fixed diagnosis at FU, i.e.,:

$$PVN(FU) = S_-(FU).$$

Then by the definition of $\kappa_{FU}(1, 0)$, and $\kappa_{FU}(0, 0)$, we have:

$$\kappa_{FU}(1, 0) = [S_-(FU) - S_0(FU)]/[1 - S_0(FU)]$$

$$= Q[S_-(FU) - S_+(FU)]/P(FU);$$

$$\kappa_{FU}(0, 0) = [S_0(FU) - S_+(FU)]/S_0(FU)$$

$$= Q'[S_-(FU) - S_+(FU)]/P'(FU).$$

It can be seen that what $\kappa_{FU}(1, 0)$ does is to compare the survival curve for those with a negative test against the total population survival curve. What $\kappa_{FU}(0, 0)$ does is to compare the survival curves for those with a positive test against the total population survival curve.

With the two values above, $\kappa_{FU}(1, 0)$ and $\kappa_{FU}(0, 0)$ for each value of FU, with $P(FU) = 1 - S_0(FU)$ and the level of the test Q, one can now go on to compute $\kappa_{FU}(r, t)$, for whatever values of r and t are of interest and all values of FU using the formulas in Chapter 9. Once we can estimate the survival curves, all the other computations easily follow. I will return to the practical issue of *how* to estimate survival curves with variable follow-up times. For the moment, this sets the stage for evaluation of several questionable approaches to the problem.

Ignoring the Problem of Variable Follow-Up: A Possibly Invalid Approach

The first method that unfortunately enjoys wide usage is simply to ignore the problem of variable follow-up time. The evaluator reports the mean or median (and perhaps the spread) of follow-up times and proceeds with an analysis, like those discussed in the previous chapters, under the pretense that the follow-up is fixed at the mean or median for all the patients in the sample.

For example, Mogensen and Christensen (1984) "studied whether microalbuminuria (urinary albumin excretion rates of 15 to 150 µg per minute) would predict the development of increased proteinuria in Type I diabetes" (p. 89). The follow-up time in this study ranged from 7 to 14 years with a reported mean of 10.4 ± 3 years. All the estimates and tests presented took no account of the fact that some patients in the study with a negative diagnosis and a follow-up of 7 years might have had a positive diagnosis if followed for 14 years, and others with a positive diagnosis at 14 years might have had a negative diagnosis if followed for a time period shorter than 14 years.

This approach would be valid if the hazard function were zero between 7 and 14 years, that is, if the survival function and the prevalence functions were flat between these years, or equivalently if no events occur in the population between 7 and 14 years. Ignoring the problem of variable follow-up time is valid only if the evaluators can present documentation that no events could or did occur between the minimal follow-up time and the maximal follow-up time. Seldom can such documentation be produced. Without such documentation the results should be considered questionable.

Counting Time and Not Patients: Another Possibly Invalid Procedure

A second, very common, tactic is to count time, not patients, as the unit of analysis. In Chapter 5 we discussed the problem of definition of the unit of analysis, and there suggested that for reasons both logical and statistical, the unit of analysis should always be the patient. When one uses years or even months of follow-up, person-years or person-months, in effect one is assuming that 10 successive years of follow-up in a single patient is equivalent to 10 single years of follow-up in 10 different patients, or 1 month of follow-up in 120 different patients.

The circumstance in which this approach is valid requires three assumptions:

1. For each patient in the population, the survival function takes on the mathematical form:

$$s_i(\text{FU}) = \exp(-\text{FU} \cdot E_i) ,$$

where E_i is the "event rate" or "incidence rate" for subject i. This is the so-called constant hazard function, for the hazard function equals E_i for all values of FU. For such a hazard function, the expected time to event for subject i is $1/E_i$, the reciprocal of the event rate.

2. It is assumed that patients with the disorder (i.e., highly susceptible to the event) at the time of testing all have the same survival function, and those without the disorder (low susceptibility) also all have the same survival function. Thus those with the disorder at the time of testing:

$$s_i(\text{FU}) = \exp(-\text{FU} \cdot E_+) ,$$

and among those without the disorder at the time of testing:

$$s_i(\text{FU}) = \exp(-\text{FU} \cdot E_-) ,$$

where E_+ and E_- are two fixed constants, the event rates of those with and without the disorder at the time of testing. This, in effect, assumes a homogeneity among those with the disorder and a homogeneity among those without the disorder at the time of testing.

3. Finally, it is assumed that the diagnosis unambiguously identifies those with and without the disorder at the time of testing, i.e., that the two homogeneous subgroups are correctly identified by the diagnosis.

These are three very tough assumptions. If, in fact, the hazard function is *not* constant, or the population does *not* comprise two homogeneous groups, or the ascertainment of the occurrence or non-occurrence of the events is *not* accurate or complete, such difficulties may lead to invalid conclusions if this approach were used.

However, if these assumptions were correct, to estimate E_+, one merely divides the number of events observed by total time units of follow-up in the positive diagnosis group; and to estimate E_-, one divides the number of events observed by total time units of follow-up in the negative diagnosis group. The reciprocals of these estimates $(1/E_+$ and $1/E_-)$ estimate the expected time to event in the positive and negative test groups.

To take one example: Let us consider the study reported by Stampfer et al. (1985). This is not intended to be a prognostic test evaluation, but the question asked can be phrased as a testing question: Can the patient's report of post-menopausal non-use of estrogen therapy be used to identify those at high risk of coronary events? (The suggestion in this study is that use of estrogen therapy might protect against such events.)

Sampling was naturalistic and done in 1976 and 1978. In 1976, 23,698 women were sampled with a potential 4-year follow-up; in 1978 an additional 8,709 women were sampled with a potential 2-year follow-up, a total sample size of 32,317 postmenopausal women, and 105,786 person-years of follow-up.

While 32,317 is already a very respectable sample size, one can appreciate the value of the illusion of increased sample size in reporting 105,786 person-years. When the event defining $D+$ is itself a rare event (as was the case in this study), and sufficient subjects cannot be recruited (as was *not* the case in this study), such an illusion can be comforting. Thus one might have 10 subjects, but 100 person-years: 10 might seem wholly inadequate, but 100 more reasonable.

In the Stampfer et al. (1988) study a positive diagnosis $(D+)$ was given to those who had a nonfatal myocardial infarction and to those with confirmed coronary death. There were a grand total of only 90 events among the 32,317 women. This illustrates when the approach of counting time rather than patients is most attractive. The event of interest here is very rare. A positive test is not. We are told that in the 4-year cohort, 53% used hormones at some time ($Q = .47$) and that 35% were current users ($Q = .65$). The combination of a rare event and a high level test will make comparisons of survival curves problematic.

To understand why, let us accept for the moment the assumption of constant hazard functions in both the test positive and negative groups. For those in the sample who entered the study at 50-55 years of age (the largest age group) from the information given, we estimate that the event rate for current users of hormones was $8/15,239.2 = .000524$ events per person-year (a mean time to event of 1,905 years). For those who are not current users, the event rate was $55/49,004.2 = .001122$ events per person-year (a mean time to event of 891 years).

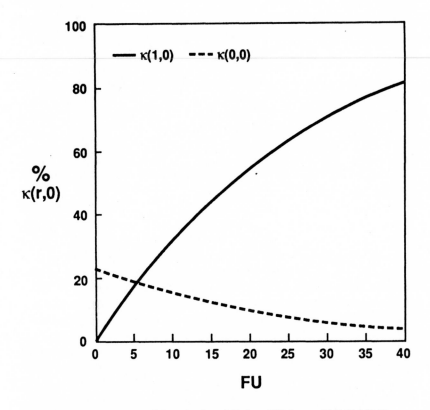

Figure 13.1. Exponential Survival and Related Values of $k(1,0), k(0.0)$

The ludicrous estimates of expected time to event means, of course, that most post-menopausal women free of coronary heart disease at the time of entry to this study between 50-55 years of age are likely to live or to die of causes *other* than coronary heart disease. As the authors point out, the total number of deaths observed in the cohort was 379, but there were only 25 deaths among the 90 with D+ in the study. The discrepancy is largely due to "the large proportion of deaths among participants with cancer at base line, who were not likely to have received estrogens" (Stampfer et al., p. 1047).

In Figure 13.1 are presented graphs of $\kappa_{FU}(1, 0)$ and of $\kappa_{FU}(0, 0)$ for two groups, each with an assumed hazard rate (the positive and negative test groups), with expected times to event of 19.05 and 8.91

years, i.e., proportional to those of current users versus non-users in the Stampfer et al. (1988) study, and with a level of test $Q = .47$, again comparable to that in the Stampfer et al. (1988) study.

What is seen there is typical of all situations where the assumptions made here are true. The graph of $\kappa_{FU}(1, 0)$ decreases from a value near zero FU of approximately:

$$Q'(E_+ - E_-)/(Q \cdot E_+ + Q' \cdot E_-)$$

(here about 35%) to zero. The graph of $\kappa_{FU}(0, 0)$ increases from a value of 0 near zero FU to 1, as FU increases. The two curves cross when the follow-up is such that:

$$P(FU) = Q,$$

here at about 8 years. If there is only a very short follow-up time, i.e., a follow-up time such that $P(FU)$ is much less than Q, one sees only a very tiny portion of these curves, that portion very near zero follow-up time (FU = 0). (To make the result comparable to that of the Stampfer et al. (1988) study, consider FU = .04 years in Figure 13.1.) Then $\kappa_{FU}(1, 0)$ is approximately equal to its value at zero (above) and $\kappa_{FU}(0, 0)$ is approximately equal to zero. Inevitably, if there is any association at all between test and diagnosis, one finds a relatively highly sensitive test, one with high predictive value of a negative test, but with little evidence of better than random specificity.

This well illustrates the difficulty in trying to evaluate a prognostic test in a population in which the event is rare. There need to be very large samples, such as Stampfer et al. (1988) had, and follow-up times long enough so that $P(FU)$ approaches levels comparable to Q, as Stampfer et al. (1988) could not, in order to have any chance of identifying either specific or efficient tests.

However, the analysis in the Stampfer et al. (1988) study was not based on examination of survival curves, but, rather, on comparisons of event or incidence rates: "The primary analysis was based on incidence rates. The relative risk was defined as the incidence rate in women who had used hormones (estimated as the number of end points divided by the rate among women who had never used them)" (p. 1045). In the context of medical test evaluation such an approach could only demonstrate that the "test" was legitimate.

Use of the constant hazards model is an approach frequently seen in epidemiological studies, as the Stampfer et al. (1988) study was intended to be. In such epidemiological studies the emphasis is on the detection of association (corresponding to establishing the legitimacy of a medical test) more so than on assessing the strength of association (as in estimating sensitivity, specificity, predictive values, and their quality indices). Detection of association is a statistical task likely to be more robust to deviations from the assumption of the constant hazard model than is the quantification of association. For this reason, one should not depend on the proven quality of this approach in epidemiological contexts to guarantee the quality of this approach in the context of medical test evaluation. In particular, the unit of analysis in medical test evaluations, I would still propose, should be persons, not person-years or person-months, unless, of course, the test evaluators could convincingly demonstrate that the hazard function is constant.

Tailoring the Data to Fit the Solution: An Invalid and Inefficient Approach

When a fixed follow-up time is proposed, as noted earlier, what frequently happens is that by the time the fixed follow-up time is achieved for the last-entered patient, one has a far longer follow-up time for the first-entered patient. To use the methods described for fixed diagnoses, one discards all information available after the prescribed fixed follow-up period. The results obtained would be valid, but at a waste of considerable valuable information.

When such discards are done with a fixed a priori follow-up time, there is no question of validity, only of efficiency or power. However, validity, as well as efficiency, comes under question under one of two circumstances: if there are a substantial number of censored observations (drop-outs) before the a priori fixed follow-up time, or if the fixed follow-up time is selected post hoc.

To illustrate the problems we will consider a small part of a study we will shortly consider in more detail, of using high-resolution examination of chromosomes in bone marrow specimens as an independent prognostic test for survival (the event was death) in adults with de novo acute nonlymphocytic leukemia (Yunis, Brunning, Howe, & Lobell, 1984).

Sampling, in this study, was naturalistic, and there was no fixed a priori follow-up time. A positive diagnosis (D+) was given to those who died. Of the 105 patients in the sample, the earliest death was at 0.5 months, the earliest censored observation was at 1.5 months. The latest death was observed at 38 months, the latest censored observation at 46 months.

The subgroup with a single chromosomal defect is chosen here for study because it constitutes the single largest subgroup, and because it is heterogeneous enough to serve as a good methodological illustration.

In this subgroup, the 21 observations were: 1, 1, 1.5+, 2+, 3, 4.5, 5+, 9+, 9.5+, 11, 12, 12, 21, 23.5, 26+, 26.5, 29+, 29.5, 38, 44+, 45+ months. Here, the earliest death was at 1 month, the earliest censored observation at 1.5 months, listed as 1.5+, meaning that death occurred sometime after 1.5 months.

Suppose we decided post hoc to use a fixed follow-up time of 3 months. Then one would have three deaths at or prior to that time (at 1, 1, 3 months) and 16 patients who survived 3 months. Then there are two patients whom we must consider dropouts (listed as 1.5+, 2+), for we do not know whether or not these survived 3 months. It is these two dropouts that begin to define the problem. As soon as there are spontaneous dropouts in a medical test evaluation, there is the possibility of sampling bias. The more dropouts there are, the more seriously one must take that possibility.

In Table 13.1, we consider various other choices for a post hoc fixed follow-up period. If one selects a short post hoc follow-up period, the number of events will be small, frequently too small for adequate analysis. If one selects a long follow-up period, the number of survivals will be small, frequently too small for adequate analysis. By then, also, the number of dropouts will be large, large enough to raise the possibility of sampling bias. The estimates of P(FU) and S(FU) have little precision when the follow-up period is either too short or too long. In the middle range, P(FU) and S(FU) may be quite precise estimates of some risk function and survival function, but they may be biased relative to the population from which the original sample was drawn.

A post hoc selection of a fixed follow-up time is a procedure not to be recommended. It is not clear how often this procedure is used in the medical research literature, for whether the choice of follow-up period was "a priori" or "post hoc" may not be reported. However,

Table 13.1 Count of Events and Survivals in the Yunis et al. Study (1984), in the Subgroup with a Single Miscellaneous Chromosomal Defect

Fixed FU (months)	Events ≤ FU	Survivals >FU	Dropouts
1	2	19	0
2	2	18	1
3	3	16	2
4	3	16	2
5	4	15	2
6	4	14	3
7	4	14	3
8	4	14	3
9	4	14	3
10	4	12	5
15	7	9	5
20	7	9	5
25	9	7	5
30	11	3	7
35	11	3	7
40	12	2	7
Total	12		9

SOURCE: Yunis et al. (1984)

what we are about to propose is more difficult, and the method described here, that of tailoring the data to fit an easier solution, will then seem more tractable and therefore more attractive. Its introduction may appear to be a straw man now, but it is best to warn of its shortcomings before its use seems too attractive an alternative.

Estimating Survival Curves with Variable Follow-Up Times: The Kaplan-Meier Method

If there is one and only one test, sampling may be naturalistic or prospective (not retrospective since we are here evaluating a prognostic test). If sampling is naturalistic we have an estimate of the level of the test, Q, from the entire sample; if sampling is prospective, we have an estimate of the level of the test from the screening sample.

I propose to evaluate a single test like this: I will divide the sample into two subgroups, that with a positive test and that with a negative test. For each of these subgroups (and for the total group if sampling is naturalistic), we will estimate the survival curve, using a method called the Kaplan-Meier method (Kaplan & Meier, 1980), that utilizes both event times and censored data (see, e.g., Lee, 1980). The survival curve estimated for the group with a positive test is $1 - PVP(FU)$; the survival curve estimated for the group with a negative test is $PVN(FU)$. Using the methods described for Prospective Sampling in Chapter 5 one may also estimate the prevalence, the sensitivity, and specificity at each follow-up time using Bayes' estimates (see Chapter 5), as well as efficiency and the quality indices.

What we need to begin this process is the Kaplan-Meier method. Again, this is a procedure well and completely defined in the research literature and in long and wide enough use to be included in standard statistical packages. We will not discuss the justification for this method. For that, the reader should consult more extensive and specialized presentations (e.g., Lee, 1980). There is, however, much to be gained by running through the computation procedure at least once, to see how the event times, as well as the censored times, are utilized in the computation.

To illustrate the computation, let us use the same data from the Yunis et al. (1984) study.

In Table 13.2 the follow-up times for the subgroup with single chromosomal defect, including times of events and censored times (indicated by the +) are listed, as they were in the Yunis et al. (1984) paper, in rank order from earliest to latest (Column 1). In Column 2 the follow-up times are ranked from 1 up to the total number of follow-up times, in this case 21. In the next column, the rank listed in Column 2 is copied over only if it corresponds to an event time, not a censored time. In the next column, we compute the quantity:

$$(n - r)/(n - r + 1)$$

where:

n = total number of patients (here 21)

r = number in Column 3.

Table 13.2 Example of the Kaplan-Meier Computation of a Survival Curve, Using the Data from Yunis et al. (1984), from the Subgroup with a Single Miscellaneous Chromosomal Defect

1 FU(mos)	2 Rank FU(m)	3 Rank Events (r)	4 (n−r)/(n−r+1)	5 S(FU)	6 P(FU)
1	1	1	0.952	0.952	0.048
1	2	2	0.950	0.905	0.095
1.5+	3				
2+	4				
3	5	5	0.941	0.852	0.148
4.5	6	6	0.938	0.798	0.202
5+	7				
9+	8				
9.5+	9				
11	10	10	0.917	0.732	0.268
12	11	11	0.909	0.665	0.335
12	12	12	0.900	0.599	0.401
21	13	13	0.889	0.532	0.468
23.5	14	14	0.875	0.466	0.534
26+	15				
26.5	16	16	0.833	0.388	0.612
29+	17				
29.5	18	18	0.750	0.291	0.709
38	19	19	0.667	0.194	0.806
44+	20				
45+	21				

SOURCE: Yunis et al. (1984)

Finally, the estimate of survival probability is computed in Column 5 as the product of the number in the same line of Column 4 and the survival probability estimate in Column 5 of the previous line. Since at time 0, $S(FU) = 1$, by definition, the first entry in Column 5, corresponding to FU = 1 month is $1 \cdot 0.952 = 0.952$. The next entry is then $0.952 \cdot 0.950 = 0.905$, etc. In Column 6 are the estimated prevalences $P(FU) = 1 - S(FU)$.

There are several points to note. Both event times and censored times influence the computation. Note that the ranks that are used in the computation include the ranks both of the event times and of the censored times. No information is ignored. The validity of the resulting estimates do not depend on any assumptions as to the shape of

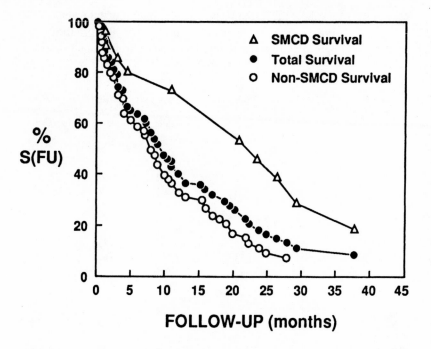

Figure 13.2. Survival curves in the total group [S_0(FU)] and in those with a positive [S_+(FU), non-SMCD] and negative [$S-$(FU)], SMCD test result.
SOURCE: Yunis et al., 1984.
NOTE: SMCD = single miscellaneous chromosomal defect.

the survival curve. Whether or not the constant hazards model holds, for example, the estimation procedure remains a valid one.

There is one assumption, however, with impact on the validity of the results, and that is a commonsense one. There must not be any selective censoring on the basis of characteristics of the subject having to do with either the test or with the diagnosis. Clearly, if we censored primarily those at high risk or those with a positive test result, the results might well yield a biased representation of the survival curve.

The usual method of presenting a survival curve is graphic, usually a graph of S(FU) versus FU. In Figure 13.2, the highest curve depicts the results obtained in Table 13.2.

Technically estimated S(FU) is a step-function with a step down each time an event occurs. The size of each step depends on the number of events seen at that time and on the total sample size. The number of steps is consequently equal to the number of *different* times at which events are observed. The larger the number of events, and the more spread out they are, the better the definition of the shape of the survival curve. Finally, how much of the survival curve is estimated depends on the range of the observed events. Here the estimation stops at 38 months, the last observed death in this group.

This suggests that there are three factors in obtaining a precise estimate of a population survival curve: the total number of patients, the total number of observed events, and the range of event times. When the total numbers of both patients and of events are large, and the follow-up times are long enough to see the later occurring events, the steps will be closer together and smaller in "rise," and the curve begins then to look more curve-like and will not be cut short as it is in this case at 38 months when the last death was observed.

If we propose to give the patients listed in Table 13.2 a negative test result, the upper curve in Figure 13.2 is PVN(FU) for this test. Now the Kaplan-Meier method can be repeated for the 84 patients with a positive test result, and, since this is a naturalistic sample, for the total group as well. This is the sort of computation that is tedious and subject to error when done by hand, and easily done on a computer. Computer software is readily available in most statistical software packages to perform the computations, and many of these give as output, graphs of the survival curves as well as the numerical results.

The lowest survival curve then in Figure 13.2 is that of the 84 subjects who were not in the "Single miscellaneous chromosomal defect" (non-SMCD) group, which, because this is the group to whom we propose to give a positive test result, is $1 - $ PVP(FU), and the overall survival curve, $1 - P(FU)$. Since this was a naturalistic sample, one could estimate $P(FU)$ by applying the Kaplan-Meier method to the entire sample of 105 patients. If this had been done with prospective sampling, we could use the indirect estimate:

$$S_0(FU) = Q \cdot S_+(FU) + Q' \cdot S_-(FU) \, .$$

Before we go on with the evaluation of the test, it is worth noting that there is a great deal of additional valuable information in the survival curve. For example, it is easy to estimate the median (or the 25th or 75th percentiles, or any other percentiles) of event times from the graph. One need only draw a horizontal line at 50% (or 25% or 75%) and see at what follow-up time this line intersects each of the survival curves. Here, for example, the median survival time (or event time) is about 22 months for those with a single miscellaneous chromosomal defect, about 8 months for those in other categories, and about 10 months for the group as a whole. Yunis et al. (1984) present median survival times for various of the test subgroups using precisely this method.

In Figure 13.2, one can also visualize the qualities of the test at each value of FU. For each follow-up time, the distance from the middle survival curve to the upper survival curve, relative to the distance from the middle survival curve to the upper border is $\kappa_{FU}(1, 0)$, reflecting the quality of the sensitivity. Similarly, the distance from the middle survival curve to the lower one relative to the distance to the lower border is $\kappa_{FU}(0, 0)$, reflecting the quality of the specificity. Visually one begins to appreciate that the test here considered must be quite sensitive [$\kappa_{FU}(1, 0)$], but not very specific [$\kappa_{FU}(0, 0)$]. As Yunis et al. (1984) point out, the group with single miscellaneous chromosomal defect is a clinically heterogeneous one.

In Figure 13.3 are presented the sensitivities, specificities, and efficiencies evaluated at each month of the follow-up time and in Figure 13.4 are presented the quality indices evaluated at each month of the follow-up time. The irregularities reflect the effects of estimation error of these parameters, but it is very clear the sensitivity, specificity, and efficiency change with the follow-up.

As the length of follow-up increases, the quality of the sensitivity tends to decrease, the quality of the specificity to increase, the quality of the efficiency first increases, peaks, and then decreases. In the illustration, the test under evaluation ($T+$: non-SMCD) has a level of 80% ($Q = .80$). The 80th percentile of the survival times in the total sample is 24 months (see Figure 13.2). For follow-up times less than this percentile, the quality of the sensitivity is greater than that of specificity; for follow-up times greater than this percentile, the quality of the sensitivity is less than that of the specificity. The quality of the efficiency is always intermediate to these two.

Is this test a legitimate test? It certainly appears to be, since all the quality indices are above zero. As a more rigorous demonstration, one would use a test for the equality of survival curves that can be applied to the two curves from the subgroups with positive and negative test results (see, e.g., Lee, 1980).

Is the test a good test? (See Chapter 6.). Here, because there is no way to obtain test-retest data on a prognosis, and no standard of excellence (the best-known prognostic test for this outcome in this

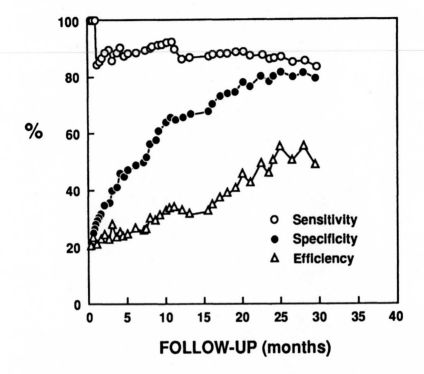

Figure 13.3. Curves of Sensitivity, Specificity, and Efficience of Test Based on Observation of a Single Miscellaneous Chromosomal Defect
SOURCE: Yunis et al., 1984.

population) was presented, we must be content to choose the best test within the specified family of tests or the best test sequence or score within the battery of tests. Ultimately the clinical value of a prognostic test will depend on whether one can prevent or delay the events that define $D+$ by accurate identification of those at risk using $T+$.

Some General Observations on the Choice of Follow-Up Time and Its Impact on Test Evaluation

In both the constant risk model applied to the Stampfer et al. (1988) data, and in the consideration of the Yunis et al. (1984) data, the

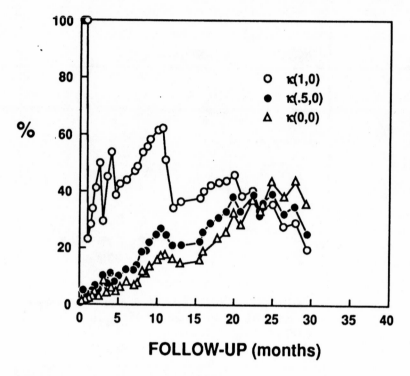

Figure 13.4. Curves of κ(r, 0), r = 0, .5, 1, of Test Based on Observation of a Single Miscellaneous Chromosomal Defect
SOURCE: Yunis et al., 1984.

dependence of the quality of the test on the duration of follow-up is apparent. To gain some insight into this phenomenon, consider the following:

When we consider *one* test versus *one* diagnosis, the only distinction between test and diagnosis is the relative value placed on them by the evaluators. The clinical validity of the diagnosis is assumed, and the value of the test is evaluated by how well it corresponds to the diagnosis. If next month or next year another evaluator were to propose to use what is now the test as the gold standard, and the value of what is now the diagnosis as a test, labels would change, but statistical properties would not.

If we switched the roles of test and diagnosis, the following inversion of labels would occur:

Test versus Diagnosis		Diagnosis versus Test
Prevalence	becomes	Level of Test
Level of Test		Prevalence
Sensitivity		PVP
Specificity		PVN
PVP		Sensitivity
PVN		Specificity
Efficiency		Efficiency
$\kappa_{FU}(1, 0)$		$\kappa_{FU}(0, 0)$
$\kappa_{FU}(0, 0)$		$\kappa_{FU}(1, 0)$
$\kappa_{FU}(.5, 0)$		$\kappa_{FU}(.5, 0)$
$\kappa_{FU}(r, 0)$		$\kappa_{FU}(r', 0)$

With a fixed diagnosis, we kept the diagnosis fixed and varied the test, often by changing the cut point in a nested family of tests. In the evaluation of a fixed single prognostic test against a diagnosis that depends on a variable follow-up, we are doing the mirror-image process. We are holding the test constant and changing the cut point in a nested family of diagnoses. However, because of the mirror-image relationship of test versus diagnosis and diagnosis versus test, from the knowledge of what happens as the cut point of a test in a nested family is varied, when the diagnosis is held constant, we can easily infer what happens as the cut point of a diagnosis in a nested family is varied, when the test is held constant.

Briefly put, what was seen in Figure 13.1 and 13.4 depicts what generally happens. For a short follow-up time, the quality of the sensitivity will be high and that of the specificity low. For a long follow-up time, the quality of the sensitivity will be low and that of the specificity high. The dividing point between a short and long follow-up time is that time, FU, at which $P(FU) = Q$, the level of the fixed test. When $P(FU) = Q$, all three qualities are equal. These are, of course, comments on the true quality indices. When estimates are based on a sample, one would expect to see such trends, but with an overlay of perturbations due to sampling and estimation error.

What this suggests is that a fixed follow-up that is too short yields limited information. When there are many tests to be evaluated, a family of tests or a battery of tests, one would speculate that the best choice of fixed follow-up time in this situation where the levels of tests vary would be at least at the median survival time of the population. Too short a fixed follow-up time will yield a sensitive test, but not an efficient or a specific one; too long a fixed follow-up time will yield a specific test, but not an efficient or sensitive one. A long follow-up time, however, allows the test evaluators to investigate the test performance for any shorter follow-up time. Thus technically there cannot be "too long" a follow-up time provided information is collected as to the timing of the events.

Evaluating a Family of Prognostic Tests with a Variable Follow-Up Time

In the Yunis et al. (1984) paper, patients were classified into one of 17 categories depending on cytologic characteristics. A test can be defined by giving a positive test result to any one or to any combination of the 17 categories there specified. A bit of counting gives the dismaying result that in this family there are more than 65,000 different possible combinations! Of course, many of these individual combinations cannot be evaluated because of inadequate sample size. For example, while theoretically there are 17 tests based on a single category (e.g., single miscellaneous chromosomal defect versus other, as evaluated above), there are only three such categories with 10 or more patients (single miscellaneous chromosomal defect, two or three miscellaneous chromosomal defects, complex chromosomal defects), her ce only three such individual combinations that can be adequately individually evaluated with this sample.

To add to the problem, there are eight categories of FAB (the morphologic classification of the French-American-British Acute Leukemia Cooperative Study Group). Only three of these individual groups (M1, M2, and M4) have more than 10 subjects. These categories could be combined in 255 different ways.

Thus, to ease illustration of the method, I will develop two ad hoc scores as follows. In Table 13.3 are presented the sample size and the estimated survival times for each separate cytologic type, and for each FAB classification (combining M5a and M5 since there were only three patients in M5b with no observed deaths). Each such category

Table 13.3 Coding of the Cytologic Characteristics and FAB
Classification Using the Median Survival Times as Scores
(CYTSUR, FABSUR)

Cytology	CYTSUR
No mitoses observed	1.0
Translocation 9;22	3.0
2 or 3 misc. chromosomal defects	6.0
Normal chromosomes	6.0
Monosomy 7	8.5
Translocation 6;9	9.0
Translocation -;11	9.0
Trisomy 8	10.0
Deletion 5q	12.0
Translocation 15;17	15.5
Complex chromosomal defects	20.0
Translocation 8;21	20.0
Single misc. chromosomal defect	22.0
Inversion 16	25.0

French-American-British Acute Leukemia Study Classification

	FABSUR
M5a,b	1.5
M6	2.0
M1	4.5
M4	9.0
M2	10.5
M7	13.5
M3	15.5

SOURCE: Yunis et al. (1984)

was then given a score (called CYTSUR and FABSUR) equal to its
estimated median survival time. Then the 18 tests listed in Table 13.4
based on these ad hoc scores plus age and gender, were evaluated.

These 18 tests, of course, can be evaluated at any follow-up time
for which the sample size is sufficient. There are only 7 deaths earlier
than 1 month, and 13 deaths if a 1 month follow-up is included. Thus
the minimal follow-up time for which analysis can reasonably be
done is 1 month. For similar reasons, the maximal follow-up for
which analysis can reasonably be done is about 20 months. The
median survival time (see Figure 13.2) is about 9 months. Selected for

Table 13.4 Summary of QROC Result for Follow-up Times of 1, 3, 6, 9, 12 Months in the Yunis et al. (1984) Study (in percentages)

S(FU):	FU = 1 (0.868)			FU = 3 (0.732)			FU = 6 (0.619)			FU = 9 (0.499)			FU = 12 (0.394)			FU = 18 (0.318)		
	$\kappa(1.0)$	$\kappa(.5,0)$	$\kappa(0,0)$	$\kappa(1.0)$	$\kappa(.5,0)$	$\kappa(0,0)$	$\kappa(1.0)$	$\kappa(.5,0)$	$\kappa(0,0)$	$\kappa(1.0)$	$\kappa(.5,0)$	$\kappa(0,0)$	$\kappa(1.0)$	$\kappa(.5,0)$	$\kappa(0,0)$	$\kappa(1.0)$	$\kappa(.5,0)$	$\kappa(0,0)$
Males	12.7	1.8	1.0	5.3	1.7	1.0	4.3	2.1	1.4	3.6	2.5	1.9	2.3	3.5	7.0	3.4	5.6	15.0
CYTSUR ≤ 3	40.2	25.9	19.2	52.1	56.7	62.0	34.5	46.0	69.3	30.1	46.1	98.1	17.9	30.2	98.4	12.1	21.5	97.7
CYTSUR ≤ 6	49.5	17.9	10.9	57.6	40.9	31.7	52.4	48.7	50.5	42.6	51.2	64.1	21.2	30.5	54.1	19.7	31.0	73.7
CYTSUR ≤ 9	36.7	8.6	4.9	54.1	27.1	18.0	50.5	36.3	28.4	57.9	55.2	52.8	38.7	47.0	59.7	34.3	47.6	77.7
CYTSUR ≤ 12	21.2	3.5	1.9	42.4	15.6	9.6	51.1	28.2	19.6	62.3	47.6	38.5	54.9	56.1	57.4	51.6	62.5	79.3
CYTSUR ≤ 20	46.2	4.9	2.6	59.2	14.6	8.3	58.7	22.6	14.0	66.0	36.8	25.5	49.2	38.9	32.1	47.7	46.7	45.8
Age ≥ 35	55.1	3.1	1.6	56.9	7.7	4.1	38.0	8.3	4.7	3.2	1.1	0.6	10.2	5.2	3.5	0.5	0.3	0.2
Age ≥ 40	64.9	4.9	2.6	66.2	11.9	6.6	50.4	14.4	8.4	22.7	9.7	6.1	28.8	18.1	13.2	21.6	17.4	14.6
Age ≥ 45	76.2	9.7	5.2	54.9	15.9	9.3	35.7	15.9	10.2	25.7	16.3	11.9	24.3	21.3	19.0	16.9	17.6	18.4
Age ≥ 50	82.1	15.7	8.7	39.5	16.5	10.5	28.9	16.7	11.8	15.6	13.1	11.3	13.6	15.0	16.6	12.1	15.2	20.5
Age ≥ 55	65.7	7.1	3.8	38.9	19.4	13.0	19.0	13.6	10.7	12.6	12.0	11.5	8.7	10.5	13.4	6.6	9.2	15.0
Age ≥ 60	71.3	11.1	6.0	48.3	31.7	23.6	26.9	24.3	22.2	11.8	13.5	15.8	5.5	7.6	12.5	0.0	0.1	0.2
Age ≥ 65	55.7	27.2	18.0	30.4	27.1	24.5	16.7	19.2	22.7	9.7	13.4	21.5	3.2	5.1	12.0	2.0	2.0	2.1
Age ≥ 70	40.9	27.4	20.6	28.2	31.4	35.5	15.2	20.7	32.4	8.2	12.6	28.1	4.0	6.8	23.0	0.8	1.4	6.6
FABSUR ≤ 1.5	33.6	16.4	10.8	25.3	22.6	20.4	19.8	22.9	27.0	10.3	14.2	22.7	7.9	12.4	29.3	4.4	7.3	23.8
FABSUR ≤ 4.5	20.1	19.3	18.5	5.9	8.3	13.6	0.0	0.0	0.1	22.6	5.8	3.4	22.6	9.1	5.7	17.6	9.5	6.5
FABSUR ≤ 9	15.0	4.3	2.5	10.9	6.5	4.6	17.4	14.4	12.3	17.6	18.8	20.1	7.4	9.8	14.4	9.2	13.7	26.3
FABSUR < 9	33.6	16.4	10.8	25.3	22.6	20.4	19.6	22.6	26.7	10.2	14.0	22.4	7.8	12.3	29.0	4.3	7.3	23.6
Max	82.1	27.4	20.6	66.2	56.7	62.0	58.7	48.7	69.3	66.0	55.2	98.1	54.9	56.1	98.4	51.6	62.5	97.7

SOURCE: Yunis et al. (1984)

Table 13.5 Summary of Recommendations for the Use of Cytology and Clinical Characteristics as a Prognostic Test for Death in Patients with Adult Acute Nonlymphocytic Leukemia

FU(mos.)	Sensitivity T+	κ	Optimal: Efficiency T+	κ	Specificity T+	κ
1	Age ≥ 60	82.1%	Age ≥ 70	27.4%	Age ≥ 70	20.6%
3	Age ≥ 40	66.2%	CYTSUR ≤ 3	56.7%	CYTSUR ≤ 3	62.0%
6	CYTSUR ≤ 20	58.7%	CYTSUR ≤ 6	48.7%	CYTSUR ≤ 3	69.3%
9	CYTSUR ≤ 20	66.0%	CYTSUR ≤ 9	55.2%	CYTSUR ≤ 3	98.1%
12	CYTSUR ≤ 12	54.9%	CYTSUR ≤ 12	56.1%	CYTSUR ≤ 3	98.4%
18	CYTSUR ≤ 12	51.6%	CYTSUR ≤ 12	62.5%	CYTSUR ≤ 3	97.7%

SOURCE: Yunis et al. (1984)

presentation in detail in Table 13.4 are the results for FU = 1, 3, 6, 9, 12, and 18 months, with survival probabilities [P'(FU)] of 87%, 73%, 62%, 50%, 39%, and 32%.

These results suggest that gender and FAB classifications (at least in the ad hoc way I have used FAB classifications) play little role in defining a good test for any purpose or at any follow-up time. Age and cytologic classification, on the other hand, seem to provide prognostic information.

The summary of the optimal tests for each choice of follow-up time is presented in Table 13.5. It appears that *age* is a primary prognostic indicator of whether or not a very early death will occur. Thus Age ≥ 60 years is optimally sensitive for death prior to 1 month, and Age ≥ 70 years optimally specific and efficient. Age ≥ 40 is optimally sensitive for death prior to 3 months, but all other optimal tests are based on CYTSUR, i.e., the cytologic results.

The QROCs for FU = 1, 3, 9, 12 months appear in Figure 13.5, with the optimal tests indicated. As can be seen, the QROC for a short follow-up (e.g., FU = 1 mo) is tall and thin, that for a follow-up near the median is more symmetric around the diagonal line, and that for a follow-up that is long (e.g., FU = 12 months) is short and wide (see Figure 13.5)

For a follow-up equal to the median survival time of 9 months, for example, the optimally sensitive test is positive for those with CYTSUR

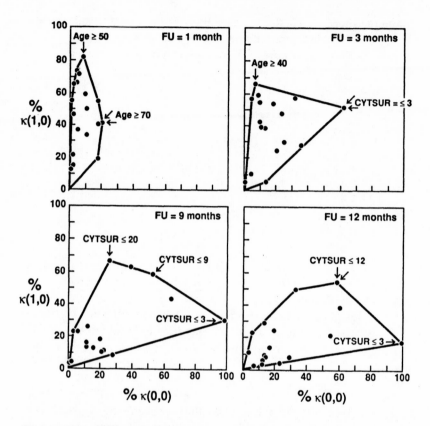

Figure 13.5. QROCs for Prognostic Test Evluations for Patients with Adult Acute Nonlymphocytic Leukemia Syndrome
SOURCE: Yunis et al., 1984.

≤ 20. Thus, within this population, a *very low-risk group* (CYTSUR > 20) with a median survival time of about 25 months includes:

Single miscellaneous chromosomal defect
Inversion 16

The optimally efficient test is negative for those with CYTSUR > 9, and hence a *low-risk group* with a median survival time of about 20 months includes:

Trisomy 8
Deletion 5q
Translocation 15; 17
Translocation 8; 21
Single miscellaneous chromosomal defect
Inversion 16

Since the optimally efficient test is positive for those with CYTSUR ≤ 9, a *high-risk group* with a median survival of 4 months includes:

No mitoses
Complex chromosomal defects
Translocation 9; 22
Two or three miscellaneous chromosomal defects
Normal chromosomes
Monosomy 7
Translocation -; 11
Translocation 6; 9

Finally, since the optimally specific test is positive for those with CYTSUR ≤ 3, a *very high-risk group* with a median survival time of about 2 months includes:

No mitoses
Complex chromosomal defects
Translocation 9; 22

Yunis et al. (1984) phrase their results in terms of identification of low-risk, moderate-risk, and high-risk groups, and these terms can now be seen to be intimately connected with optimally sensitive, specific, and efficient prognostic tests.

Patients who are negative on the optimally sensitive (PVN) tests are those who are at very low risk of the event or are likely to have the event only after a long survival time. Patients who are negative on the optimally efficient test are those who are at low to very low risk of the event or are likely to have a moderate to long survival time. Patients who are positive on the optimally efficient test are those who are at high to very high risk of the event, or are likely to have a short to moderate survival time. Finally, patients who are positive on the optimally specific (PVP) test are those who are at very high risk of the event or are likely to have very short survival times.

Such links between sensitivity, predictive value of a negative test, and identification of very low-risk patients; between specificity, predictive value of a positive test, and identification of very high-risk patients; and between efficiency and the discrimination between low- and high-risk patients clarify the necessary bonds that bring all the different methods of evaluating medical tests from different points of view into a logically coherent whole.

We have not yet, in this evaluation, considered the cost of the test. Age is "free," but no information was provided by Yunis et al. (1984) as to what the potential cost (T) of cytology classification procedures might be for these patients. On the other hand, Yunis et al. (1984) argue that the ability to identify those at low, moderate, or high risk might lead to more specific choices of appropriate and, therefore, more effective treatment. Since otherwise the outcome here is a very early death, this would suggest that the potential clinical benefit (R) is so high that the relative cost may be negligible ($t = 0$).

However, were the situation otherwise, there is no problem with incorporating the test cost and potential clinical benefit into consideration, for where $t = \$T/\$R$, $\$T$ the cost of the test, and $\$R$ the order of magnitude of the potential clinical benefit:

$$\kappa_{FU}(r, t) = [-t + PQ'r\kappa_{FU}(1, 0) + P'Qr'\kappa_{FU}(0, 0)]/(PQ'r + P'Qr')$$

and all the information necessary to calculate $\kappa_{FU}(r, t)$ at any follow-up time for which both $\kappa_{FU}(1, 0)$ and $\kappa_{FU}(0, 0)$ are available, has already been obtained.

An Alternative? Randomized Clinical Trials for the Evaluation of Screening Programs (Test + Intervention) for Prevention

It has been proposed that the value of a screening test be evaluated by use of a Randomized Clinical Trial (RCT) paradigm (e.g., Morrison, 1985), and this alternative is worth consideration.

What has been proposed here to evaluate the value of a screening test is that the population to which the results are meant to be applied be sampled, that *each* such subject be tested, and that either the entire sample be followed (Naturalistic Sampling) or randomly selected subjects in the test positive and negative groups (Prospective Sampling) be followed. The follow-up, however, was required to be done *blinded* to the results of the test. Thus the course of events in this evaluation is designed to be that which would occur in absence of testing, and the value of the screening test is determined by how accurately it predicts that course. If the test were accurate, however, this is not how it would be used in clinical practice.

Clinically, such an accurate screening test would be used to identify those at risk ($T+$) and those so identified referred for further testing, evaluation, and, possibly, treatment, to either prevent or delay the event that defines the diagnosis. If this program were followed and were successful, one would expect that the survival of those in the screening program would be enhanced. Thus, neither an inaccurate screening test nor an accurate screening test for which there is no effective intervention is ultimately of clinical value. Because of the requirement that follow-up be blinded to the results of the test, the focus in our proposal is strictly on the accuracy of the test, whereas one might well argue that the focus should encompass both the accuracy of the test and the effectiveness of the clinical response to a positive test.

Thus an alternative proposal (e.g., Morrison, 1985): Suppose we sample the population and randomly assign subjects to a test and control group. Subjects in the control group are merely followed, and consequently their survival curve is the overall survival curve: $S_0(FU)$.

Subjects in the test group are all tested, and those with a positive test ($T+$) are referred. The survival curve of those in the $T-$ group is $S_-(FU)$, but the survival curve of those in the $T+$ group is one determined not only by the accuracy of the test in identifying those at high risk [which was $S_+(FU)$], but also by the effectiveness of the further evaluation and intervention in preventing or delaying the events that define $D+$, let us say: $S_+^*(FU)$. Proposed to evaluate the value of a screening test is the comparison between the survival curves in the test and control groups:
Test:

$$Q \cdot S_+^*(FU) + Q' \cdot S_-(FU)$$

versus
Control:

$$Q \cdot S_+(\text{FU}) + Q' \cdot S_-(\text{FU}) \,.$$

The difficulty is that these survival curves are the same (Null hypothesis true) if and only if actions taken pursuant to a $T+$ are ineffective, i.e., $S_+^*(\text{FU}) = S_+(\text{FU})$. The equality of the survival curves does *not* depend on the accuracy of the tests used to define $T+$ and $T-$. Thus a statistical test comparing the survival curves is an unbiased statistical test for the effectiveness of the intervention, but biased for the accuracy of the screening test. Even random selection for labels $T+$ and $T-$, coupled with an effective intervention, produces enhanced survival in the test group. In this situation, the accuracy of the test only enhances the power of the statistical test of the effectiveness of the intervention.

That situation can be repaired, however, as follows. Once again, subjects are sampled from the population and randomly assigned to the test and control groups. Now, however, a random subsample of Q subjects in the control group are given a "pseudo" $T+$ result and referred, as are the "real" $T+$ patients in the test group, for further evaluation and intervention. All involved in dealing with the patients during the follow-up period are blinded to group assignment (test versus control), and hence as to whether the referral was based on a pseudo or a real $T+$. The survival curves now to be compared are:
Test:

$$Q \cdot S_+^*(\text{FU}) + Q' \cdot S_-(\text{FU}) \,,$$

versus
Control:

$$Q \cdot S_0^*(\text{FU}) + Q' \cdot S_0(\text{FU}) \,.$$

For these survival curves to be equal (null hypothesis), not only must the test be accurate [for otherwise $S_+(\text{FU}) = S_0(\text{FU})$ and $S_-(\text{FU}) = S_0(\text{FU})$], but also the intervention must be effective [for otherwise $S_+^*(\text{FU}) = S_+(\text{FU})$]. The statistical test is unbiased for the joint hypothesis that the screening test is accurate *and* the intervention effective.

There are inevitable objections to this design from ethical and logistical concerns. Clinicians are likely to object to having patients referred to intervention using a random pseudo-test result, ignoring the fact that an *inaccurate* real test result does exactly the same thing. Even beyond that, however, there are practical problems. If the results of the above study were to show that the survival curves were not very different, there would be no way of telling whether test accuracy or the effectiveness of the intervention or both were at fault. What direction future efforts to identify and treat high-risk patients should take would be unclear.

Separate evaluation of the accuracy of the screening test from that of the effectiveness of the intervention that would be proposed following a positive test (when accurate) seems a preferable course of action. Evaluation of the accuracy of the test would proceed along the lines here proposed. Once the accuracy of the test is established, then the effectiveness of the intervention might be established with a Randomized Clinical Trial (RCT), using $T+$ as a sample selection criterion. In that case, the sample size necessary for sufficient power to establish efficacy of intervention is likely to be far less than in either of the RCTs above, and the interpretation of its results less problematic.

Evaluating a Battery of Prognostic Tests with Variable Follow-Up Periods: Sequential Structuring

With a family of tests or a battery of tests, only Naturalistic Sampling can be used. The methods described above can be used to select the best first test for each value of r and of FU of interest. The methods for developing an optimal test sequence would then proceed exactly as described in Chapter 11.

Evaluating a Battery of Prognostic Tests Using Variable Follow-Up: Scoring a Battery with the Proportional Hazards Model

We have already defined the hazard function for patient i as $h_i(FU)$, reflecting the immediate risk of the event per unit time for a patient who has managed to survive event-free until FU. Furthermore, we have already discussed the case in which it is assumed that the hazard function is constant for all values of FU for each patient, and that all patients with the disorder were homogeneous in terms of their hazard function and all patients without the disorder were as well. I ventured the opinion that this is a tough set of assumptions to meet in real-life applications. An easier assumption is one of, not constant, but proportional hazards. If the subject's test response is x_i, which may be univariate or multivariate, each entry of which may be dichotomous (1 or 0) or scaled (e.g., three-point scales) or continuous (e.g., age in years), then the assumption is that:

$$h_i(\text{FU}) = h_0(\text{FU}) \cdot \exp(w'x_i).$$

What is being assumed is that there is some underlying shape of hazard function $[h_0(\text{FU})]$ common to all subjects in the population. If one subject has a constant hazards model, then all have. If one subject has an increasing hazards model, then all have. If the hazard is U-shaped, or J-shaped, or whatever, that shape is shared by all. What differentiates one patient from another is the height of the hazard function, not its shape. *Height* is expressed by the multiplier of the underlying hazard function; $\exp(w'x_i)$, where $w'x_i$ is a risk score.

The estimation of the weights in the proportional hazards model proceeds along the lines described in Chapter 11 and is a complex mathematical and computational problem. Once again, for the development of the model and the details of its use, more specialized and complete treatments are available (see, e.g., Lee, 1980.) The issue here is only how use of this model fits within the framework of evaluation of medical tests.

As in the models of Chapter 12, if the weights w are all zero, then all the patients have exactly the same hazard function, and, consequently, the same prevalence and survival functions. Otherwise, if we had two hypothetical patients, A and B, with the same responses on all tests except the jth one, and on that one A had a test response one unit higher than B, then the logarithm of the ratio of their hazards at any follow-up time would equal w_j, i.e.,

$$h_{A(\text{FU})}/h_{B(\text{FU})} = \exp(w_j).$$

This ratio, which we will here call the "hazards ratio," is sometimes called a "relative risk" in the medical and statistical literature. In the

Loglinear Model (see Chapter 12) the weight attached to test response *j* was related to the *risk ratio*. In the Linear Regression Model (see Chapter 12), the weight attached to test response *j* was related to the *risk difference*. In the Logistic Regression Model (see Chapter 12), the weight attached to test response *j* was related to the *odds ratio*. All of these models pertained either to the evaluation of a diagnostic test or to a prognostic test with *fixed* follow-up. Now, with the Proportional Hazards Model, the weight attached to test response *j* is related to the *hazards ratio*, not simply at a fixed follow-up time, but also, under the assumptions of the model, at any follow-up time one might specify. These are not the same model in different disguises; they are different. Generally speaking, however, if the coefficient estimated using one procedure is near zero, all are. If one is positive, all are. If one is negative, all are. Their magnitudes are not necessarily the same, nor even necessarily similar.

As stated previously, in medical test evaluation, the weight itself is important only as it plays a role in computing the best risk score. The role of a factor as a causal influence on the disorder or as a direct consequence of the disorder is not necessarily well reflected in the weight attached to that factor. Finally, the weight reflects not only the model selected to develop the risk score (Proportional Hazards, Loglinear, Logistic, Linear, Multiple Discriminant), but also what factors are included or excluded by the test evaluator. When different models are well fit using the same factors, the rank ordering of patients on the basis of what may seem very different risk scores and the test performance as indicated by the ROC, QROC, or QCROC are likely to be roughly the same.

In recent years there have been many papers in the medical literature using the Proportional Hazards Model in epidemiological studies, in clinical trials, as well as in medical test evaluation. For example, Martin et al. (1983) evaluate a prognostic test using death from any cause as one "diagnosis" and death from ischemic heart disease as another, both with a 9-year follow-up period. The population of interest here is that of patients who have survived 28 days after a myocardial infarction. The sample was naturalistic with a sample size of 666, 59 of whom were dropped for missing test responses. As the authors suggest in their report, the dropping of these subjects might introduce some small sampling bias in their results.

Nineteen test responses are proposed as "the most important variables on biological grounds or those identified in univariate analyses or past studies" (p. 962). Two separate applications of the Proportional

Hazards Model, one for all causes of death, and one for ischemic heart disease death, and those test responses (eight for all causes of death and nine for ischemic heart disease deaths) that contribute significantly to survival were identified. The results of the two analyses were quite similar, with the strongest weight in both cases applied to a history of stroke. What they called the "relative risk" and what we here call the hazards ratio, was above 2.0 (2.14 and 2.20). This means that if we had two patients, one who had had a stroke and the other who had not, but they were matched in terms of all the other test responses, the former has twice the hazard at any follow-up time of death either from any cause or specifically from ischemic heart disease. The weights for history of myocardial infarction are almost as high (2.06 and 2.15).

Estimated survival curves for those with and without a history of previous MI as well as for the total sample, were presented based on use of the Kaplan-Meier method. The crude nine-year survival rate was 52% and thus P (9 years) $\approx .48$, i.e., the maximal follow-up time in this study was approximately the median overall survival time.

The final step of such a test evaluation is to compute the risk score for each patient:

$$\text{Risk Score} = w'x_i ,$$

and use this score as a univariate test response to define a nested family of tests using different cut-off values to define a positive test, finally to compute the ROC, QROC, or QCROC to select the optimal cut points to define the optimally sensitive, efficient, and specific tests. Instructions would then be provided as to whether and how to use the prognostic test in clinical practice.

Few of the research papers using the Proportional Hazards Model report results completely enough as to so complete the process of test evaluation. Frequently little information is provided on the coefficients, and virtually none on the distribution of risk scores, or consequently the quality of the resulting battery.

Fortunately, while Martin et al. (1983) do not present any material on the range of the risk scores or the specific cut-off values that can be used, they do, in fact, provide necessary information to compute the QROC at least partially. They present the total sample divided into each quintile of risk scores, thus presenting four possible cut-off values for the risk score set at the 20th, 40th, 60th, and 80th percentiles

Table 13.6 Summary of QROC Results at FU ≤ 9 Years for a Prognostic Test for Death for 28-Day Survivors of a Myocardial Infarction (in percentages)

Quintile of Risk of Death	P	Q	κ(1, 0)	κ(.5, 0)	κ(0, 0)
> 4	47.2	19.7	15.8	24.8	57.7*
> 3	47.2	40.2	29.0	33.2*	38.6
> 2	47.2	59.6	39.4	29.7	23.9
> 1	47.2	79.6	54.3*	20.2	12.4

SOURCE: Martin et al. (1983)
NOTE: * Optimal test

of the distribution of the risk scores (Q = 0.2, 0.4, 0.6, 0.8) for a follow-up of 9 years.

In Table 13.6 are presented the estimated levels and quality indices of these four tests. All the tests used in the battery are of negligible risk and additional cost ($\$T$ = 0), since all are taken from the medical history (stroke, MI, diabetes, hypertension) or from clinical observation (sex, age, blood pressure, heart rate). The optimally sensitive, efficient, and specific tests are marked with an asterisk. Predictably, the most sensitive test gives a positive test to all but those in quintile 1; the optimally specific test only to those in the top quintile; the optimally efficient test to those quintiles where level is above the prevalence (47.2%), i.e., to quintiles 4 and 5 (level = 40.2%).

Summary

In evaluating a prognostic test where $D+$ is defined as the occurrence of an event at some future time after testing, it is inevitable that the time at which the event defining the diagnosis occurs will vary from patient to patient. It is almost as inevitably true that the follow-up times of those patients who are not seen to have an event will also differ from patient to patient, either because such patients remain event-free until the end of the study and their time in study varies, or because they drop out at various times before they experience the event. Thus, while the methods in the earlier chapters are appropriate to evaluating the value of a prognostic test when the follow-up time is fixed, such methods will not prove as useful in evaluating prognostic tests as will be methods designed to be used with variable follow-up times.

Several methods commonly used to deal with this problem in the medical research are of questionable validity. These include the simple expedient of ignoring the issue of the variable follow-up time, counting the events and survivals at whatever time they occur, and proceeding as if the follow-up time were fixed. Even more common is the tactic of counting time, not patients, as the unit of analysis: patient-years or patient-months of follow-up. Finally, the evaluator may tailor the data to fit the available and easily applied evaluation procedures by fixing the follow-up time and discarding the information about events occurring after that time or any patient who drops out before that time. Even if such an approach yielded valid results, there is a waste of information here that should be avoided. All of these approaches yield valid results under certain restricted circumstances, but the circumstances are themselves not common.

More appropriate and less chancy methods for dealing with the problem of variable follow-up time are available, namely survival methods. For the evaluation of a single prognostic test, sampling must be naturalistic or prospective (for the test must precede the follow-up). The patients are divided into two groups according to the result of the test. A survival curve is estimated for each group: $S_+(FU)$ and $S_-(FU)$. One may estimate the survival curve in the total population by:

$$S_0(FU) = Q \cdot S_+(FU) + Q' \cdot S_-(FU)$$

for Prospective Sampling, or from the total sample survival curve for Naturalistic Sampling. In any case, the Kaplan-Meier method is suggested for estimation of survival curves.

Then, since:

$$S_+(FU) = 1 - PVP(FU),$$

$$S_-(FU) = PVN(FU),$$

and

$$S_0(FU) = 1 - P(FU),$$

the quality indices (or any descriptive statistics of interest) at each value of FU can be computed.

All the quality indices as well as indices such as sensitivity, specificity, efficiency, etc., change as a function of the follow-up time. In general, evaluating a family of tests with a very short follow-up time will yield optimally sensitive but not optimally efficient or specific tests. This is a concern since many prognostic medical tests are evaluated with very short follow-up times because of the inordinate cost of long-term follow-up studies. Here what defines "short" and "long" is determined by the relationship of P(FU) to Q, the level of the test. To get the most balanced view of the qualities of tests, it was suggested that the best choice of follow-up time might be at or near the median survival time in the population studied.

With the methods of identifying the optimal test in a family, the structuring of an optimal sequence of prognostic tests is at least theoretically possible, but, given current available technology, difficult to implement.

Currently more available is a method for structuring the optimal score for a prognostic battery: The Proportional Hazards Model. Application of such a model yields a risk score with the same general properties as the risk scores discussed earlier for diagnostic tests and prognostic tests with a fixed follow-up time. The resulting risk scores should be assessed using a QROC or QCROC to ascertain the optimal cut point for the optimal tests, at any follow-up time of interest, and to evaluate their costworthiness.

Throughout this discussion a point has been made that seems a relatively new idea: The optimal test at one follow-up time is not necessarily the optimal test at another. This carries the methodological implication that the evaluation of a test at a fixed follow-up time imposes a limitation on the generalization of the results. How to identify the patients at risk of a very early event, as opposed to those very likely to have an event, but only later, may carry treatment implications that are of clinical importance.

14

Evaluation of Medical Tests: The Past, Present, and Future

Introduction: The Past and the Present

Throughout this presentation there has been recurrent worry about multiple tests, overly invasive tests, overly costly tests, risky tests, painful tests, and, above all, too many tests. The tests of concern may be unreliable, i.e., non-reproducible. They may be invalid, i.e., have little to do with the disorder they are meant to detect. They may be tests that are unnecessarily repeated, or they may be tests that should be repeated but are not. They may be tests that are easily misinterpreted, either overall or for a particular type of patient for whom the test is used. They may be tests whose results may confuse the results of other tests or whose results might be confused if other tests are simultaneously used.

Since medical tests are fundamental to medical decision making, mistakes and misunderstandings about the quality of medical tests may compromise the health and safety of the patients for whom a test is used. Any unnecessary tests, even those tests seemingly as routine and inexpensive as blood tests, must become a source of serious concern in terms of iatrogenic damage and, perhaps, even iatrogenic death.

At the same time, the basis of patient selection and classification in medical research frequently involves use of medical tests. Mistakes and misunderstandings about the quality of medical tests may provide misleading information about the etiology of disease in epidemiological studies and about the response to treatments of disorders in clinical trials.

Problems with the uncertain quality of medical tests affect all of medicine. Concern with the problems with the quality of medical tests extend beyond clinical practice and medical research. Substantial media attention has focused on the problem of testing for AIDS exposure in blood donations and of testing and registration of those positive on AIDS tests. There is consideration of requiring AIDS testing and registration of those positive on the test. There is widespread concern about testing for illicit drug use among athletes, among those in the military services, and even for employment in various industries. DNA "fingerprinting" is under consideration as definitive evidence in legal trials for identification purposes. Home diagnostic test kits, beginning with home pregnancy tests, but now extending to test kits for rectal cancer and other disorders, even for detection of illicit drug use among family members, are rapidly becoming big business items. If any of these tests are of poor quality, the repercussions will be distressing.

Notwithstanding a concern about the general public in these matters, we cannot ignore the fact that physicians may be sued for malpractice for NOT ordering a medical test that might (or might not) have disclosed a disorder that proved disabling or deadly. The standards by which legal culpability are defined concern that which is standard practice. According to Weiss (1977): " 'Playing by the rules' is, in many cases, more important than the correctness of interventions from a scientific standpoint" (pp. 580-581).

What happens as more and more tests enter the market, as the tests become more and more costly, risky, and invasive, and as the tests become standard practice in some segment of the medical community without adequate evaluation or without specific instructions for which patients and under which circumstances the test should be used? As things currently stand, it will become incumbent on clinicians to order more and more tests and more and more invasive, costly, and risky tests for more and more patients. In the absence of firm knowledge about the quality of the tests, more and more of these may be unnecessary or ill-advised. Clinicians do not have much of a choice. Practicing physicians are, in this sense, as much the victims of the inadequacy of medical test evaluations as are the patients.

In recent years there has been a great deal of finger-pointing. Many (Nash, 1985; Robin, 1984), while suggesting that part of the excessive and ill-advised use of medical tests may stem from inexperienced, incompetent, or greedy physicians and part from medical administrators concerned about balancing their budgets, suggest that patients themselves are also at fault. Patients, they point out, should be more educated and more aware. Patients should not demand tests that are of no value in their particular situation. They should ask more questions and demand explicit answers from their physicians, and be unafraid to refuse tests that do not seem well justified by their physicians.

Clearly, the physician-patient relationship is an interaction that requires the active and thoughtful participation of both patient and physician. In this case, however, where many tests have not been objectively evaluated at all, and many more have not been adequately evaluated, and for many more, the evaluations that have been done yield results in conflict with each other, the physician simply does not know the answers to the questions that might legitimately be raised by the patients. In many cases a physician's honest answer to why a test is to be done must either be: (1) We should do this test because everyone else is doing it; or (2) We should do this test because intuition says that it is an informative test. When the media report the unsupported subjective views of test proponents who are themselves physicians, how can a patient make a wise judgment as to whom to believe and not to believe? It is difficult for me to accept either the culpability of the patient or of the clinician.

How has such a situation come about? To make the question more specific, how has such a situation come about with the evaluation of medical tests, and not so much so, for example, with the evaluation of the efficacy and safety of drugs?

When a drug company wants to market a drug, the first step is usually to obtain information about that drug's performance from case histories, animal studies, in vitro experiments, and, perhaps, even small sample pilot studies. In the process the subjective opinions of scientists within the company play a role in whether further efforts for drug development are warranted. In the end, such a body of evidence is fundamental to whether or not the company undertakes a formal evaluation in a clinical drug trial. What is important to realize is that a drug cannot, by law, be marketed on the basis of information obtained from case histories, animal studies, in vitro experiments, and pilot studies. Nor can the marketing of a drug be based on the subjective opinions, no matter how expert, of the scientists involved in the development of the drug. So-called Phase 1 and 2 studies are important, because they constitute the initiation of the process of evaluation, not its end. It is here where the evaluations of medical tests fall short in comparison with the evaluation of therapeutic drugs. In medical test evaluation, studies that might be called Phase 1 and 2 studies, i.e., preliminary evaluations frequently based, to an extent, on subjective opinions, are taken as demonstrations of the quality of tests and the basis for marketing of such tests.

The subjective opinions of medical test purveyors play a very important role in such marketing of tests. This is particularly noticeable in the marketing of the most high-technology tests. Small-scale studies, comparable to those that in drug evaluation would be considered either case histories or pilot studies, are frequently given prominence in the most prestigious medical journals and are widely quoted in the popular press as "proving" the value of a medical test. It is then not surprising that patients demand from their clinicians these "proven" tests, or that clinicians might use such reports as justification for initiating widespread use of such a "proven" test.

The Federal Drug Administration (FDA) executes its mandate to protect the public from unsafe or ineffective drugs partially by setting standards for what constitutes a convincing demonstration of the efficacy and safety of a drug: randomized, double-blind, controlled clinical trials, with a convincing demonstration that the results show efficacy beyond reasonable doubt (statistical significance). The results are available to external review. Only then can the drug be licensed for marketing. Required as a result of the evaluation is a set of packaging instructions, defining how and for whom the drug should be used, any types of patients for whom the drug should not be used, any drugs that should not be used in combination, definition of the appropriate dosages, and indications of side effects. No comparable materials are generally available for medical tests. If, after FDA approval, later information documents an unexpected serious side effect, the FDA can and does rescind its approval. No such process exists for medical tests.

Much can and has been said in criticism of the FDA. Its workings are slow and ponderous. It may well be that many effective and safe drugs are inordinately slow to be approved, and during the delay patients may unnecessarily suffer or die as a result. In its zeal to avoid the Type I Error (approving an unsafe or ineffective drug), the FDA may be prone to committing Type II Errors (not approving safe and effective drugs).

Moreover, a drug licensed for one purpose (that stated in the package insert) can and is used by clinicians for other purposes. Should the patient suffer some ill effect, in these circumstances, the physician may be at risk of a malpractice suit. Whatever the faults of the system, one must keep in mind that no physician is sued for *not* prescribing Thalidomide for pregnant women, or Laetrile for cancer patients. While patients, influenced by what is reported in the media, may at times demand such drugs, and some individual physicians may advocate their use, such drugs have not gone into widespread use or become "standard medical practice," since clinical trials carry no suggestion supporting their efficacy and safety. In contrast, however, there are no standards for medical test evaluations. As we have seen, there are many different ways of evaluating a test, ways that can produce conflicting results. Proving that a test is legitimate beyond reasonable doubt for the population in question is not uniformly required for launching the widespread use of a medical test. It is frequently assumed that a test that is good for some is equally good for all. Finally, the protocol and referent of the test are frequently defined arbitrarily with no documentation of the alternatives considered and rejected. Almost universally, it seems to be believed that the referent of a test appropriate for one population or in one particular context (screening, for example) must be equally appropriate for all and in all contexts.

If there is carelessness, or, worse yet, fraud, in the presentation of results from the clinical trial of a drug, it is the drug company that is liable. Who is liable, who is responsible, for carelessness in the evaluation of a medical test? Unfortunately the answer seems to be that it is the practicing physician, who has least control over the process of drug evaluation and the incorporation of medical tests into what is "standard medical practice," and the patient whose well-being is threatened by poor testing. I have yet to hear of the investigators who advocated the use of any worthless or unsafe medical test in the medical literature called to any account at all.

Despite the controls on the testing and marketing of drugs, there remains concern that patients tend to be overmedicated. Certainly some "old" drugs have never been evaluated and some drugs that ultimately prove to be ineffective or hazardous slip through the evaluations. Physicians use the drugs in ways that they should not be used, for once licensed for one use, the drug can be used for other purposes as well. Having a standard system of evaluation is not a panacea, but, rather, it is an essential first step.

The focus of this presentation has therefore been on that first step, the development of a procedure for systematic and objective evaluation of medical tests. What is unique about what is proposed is that it does not discount any one approach currently used in medical test evaluation in favor of another. It does not favor Signal Detection methods over Bayesian methods or vice versa. It does not ignore Signal Detection methods or Bayesian methods in developing the Multiple Discriminant methods. What it does is to incorporate all that is best in each of these approaches, uses each to amplify the quality of all the other approaches, and attempts to unify the whole into one systematic, objective, and comprehensive approach.

If this approach were adopted, would useless or overly risky tests occasionally be endorsed? Yes, just as ineffective and unsafe drugs are sometimes approved by the FDA. There is a certain probability of Type I Error. Would useful tests occasionally be recommended against? Yes, just as effective and safe drugs are sometimes held up in FDA evaluation. There is a certain probability of a Type II Error. However, both types of errors would be far below current rates of either Type I or Type II Errors committed in absence of a systematic objective approach.

Will we completely avoid conflicting results in multiple evaluation of medical tests? No, not completely. However, the most common possible sources of conflict will be clarified. If two studies define the population differently; if they use a different diagnostic procedure even if for the same disorder; if they use a different test protocol, or different referents; conflicts between conclusions might be expected and explained. Such conflicts may even provide valuable information in defining what type of patients the test might best be used for, for what disorders, and in what form the test might best be used. In short, the methods help to resolve most of the conflicts.

If, on the other hand, the sampling procedure were inadequate (Pseudo-Retrospective Sampling or systematic dropout), or the statistics miscomputed (using estimation methods inappropriate to the sampling methods, for example), it may be that the results should be completely discounted, for there is then a high risk of invalid results. This is akin to non-randomized clinical trials of drugs or other treatments, where patients are selected for the treatment and control groups in a more or less systematic way, where either clinician, patient, or both are aware of which treatment (drug or placebo) is being used, and where the evaluation of response is subjective and non-blinded. Such an approach to evaluation of a drug or treatment is frequently done and the results published, but such results are known to carry such a high potential of sampling and observer biases, that when their results conflict with those of well-conducted randomized, double-blind trials, the latter are given greater credence.

Finally, the coordination of the various approaches to medical test evaluation into one single approach incorporating all, means that what is merely an appearance of conflicting results occurring only because one study used Bayesian methods, another Signal Detection Theory, and yet others various discrimination analysis methods, is eliminated.

This is far from a finished method. Before I round out the presentation by summarizing the steps in doing such a medical test evaluation, let us consider some of the weaknesses and inadequacies of what has been proposed, and some of what yet needs to be done.

The Future: Unsolved Problems

Problem: Evaluation of Monitoring Tests

The tests evaluated here have been characterized as either diagnostic or prognostic. In the evaluation, a diagnostic test is differentiated from a prognostic test by the timing of the diagnosis relative to the time of testing. If the diagnosis is obtained during the period of testing, the test is diagnostic. If the diagnosis is obtained by following the patient over some span of time (the follow-up) after the time of testing to observe whether or not some event (a presumed consequence of an existing disorder) occurs, the test is prognostic. In either case, the test is used to distinguish between those patients who have some disorder during the period of testing and those who do not.

There is another distinct and very important use of a medical test: to monitor a patient known to have a certain disorder in order to determine whether or not the disorder is in control. Such a test is designed for *repeated* use by a patient and is meant to be sensitive or specific to changes within a patient. The prime examples, of course, are the tests diabetics use on a daily basis to monitor the control of their disorder. A test that can well distinguish those who have a disorder from those who do not is not necessarily the best test to distinguish those who have a disorder kept under medical control from those who also have a disorder but not under medical control.

I will call such a medical test a monitoring test, a test of a different type from either a diagnostic or a prognostic test.

Not one word has been said to this point about methods for evaluating monitoring tests, and none of the methods described to this point are specifically appropriate to the evaluation of such a test. The model that underlies the evaluation of diagnostic and prognostic tests is a cross-sectional one, focusing on the condition of the patient at a single time, the time of testing, during which it is assumed that the patient either has the condition or does not, i.e., the clinical situation vis-à-vis the disorder is constant. The evaluation of monitoring tests requires a model appropriate to longitudinal study, requiring observation of a patient both in and out of control, to discover whether the test is sensitive or specific to such variations within the patient over a period of time in which clinical changes occur.

There seems to be only minimal statistical development of approaches to the evaluation of monitoring tests. It may have been assumed that the methods for evaluating prognostic and diagnostic tests are the same as those for monitoring tests. This is unlikely to be completely true. In any case, the methods developed here are not necessarily appropriate to the evaluation of monitoring tests. This is one methodological problem that must be left to future development.

Problem: Multicategory Responses

In the examples chosen for illustration of the methods, the broadest possible array of the types of test responses has been used. We have seen univariate as well as multivariate test responses. The responses have been natural dichotomies (e.g., gender), three-point scales (e.g., non-ischemic, probable, or definite ischemia), scales with many more points extending out to measures on a continuum (e.g., age). For measures on a continuum, the distributions have been normal, skewed, and even sometimes bimodal, U- or J-shaped. In Chapter 13 we considered an example of a test response with 17 non-ordered categories of response.

The methods here developed are designed to be very flexible in terms of the types of test data to which they can be applied. This is necessary, for the types of responses that are seen in medical tests are very varied. If it were to be required that only a univariate test response could be used, and that one response could only have a normal distribution, the scope of the method would be very limited indeed. In fact, the major objection to Signal Detection methods as they have been used in recent years is that many are based implicitly or explicitly on an assumption of a univariate test response and binormality.

However, applying these methods to full advantage when there are multiple non-ordered categories of response, is difficult. When there are k categories of response, there are at least

$$2^{(k-1)} - 1$$

possible ways of forming the referent. (If k is odd, the above formula is exact.) When there are 3 categories ($k = 3$), there are only three possible referents. When there are 5 categories ($k = 5$), there are 15. For 7 categories, the number of referents is 63; for 9 categories, 255; for 11 categories, 1,023. When, as in the Yunis et al. (1984) study, there were 17 categories, the number of possible referents was 65,535.

In the Yunis et al. (1984) study examined in Chapter 13, I "scored" the 17 categories by their median survival times. This was ad hoc and very possibly not the best way of defining the family of referents. What is the best way of dealing with classification systems with multiple categories remains a problem for future development.

Problem: Stopping Rules

Yet another area in which the methods presented here require improvement is that of defining the proper stopping rules for the evaluation of batteries of tests. The problem is one shared by all statistical procedures that are done stepwise, and is not peculiar to the problem of medical test battery evaluation. However, let us consider what form the problem takes on in this context.

When a single test is evaluated, one can test the null hypothesis that the test is not legitimate using a 2×2 Chi-Square test at whatever level of significance is deemed appropriate. Thus, for example, if the test is significant at the 5% level, there is a 5% chance of a false positive result falsely concluding that a test is legitimate when it is not (Type I Error).

On the other hand, if one scans across various referents (as one does in finding the ROC, QROC, or QCROC), selects the best referent, and then applies the usual 2×2 Chi-Square test, the rule appropriate to defining a 5% level of significance test for a single referent is not a rule appropriate to defining a 5% level of significance test for the best of a set of referents. Generally, one has better than a 5% chance of a false positive result.

The problem is compounded if the process is then repeated a second or third time, as one does in evaluating a battery of tests. The chance of a false positive result at each step is greater than 5%. At each additional step one is taking an *extra* 5% chance of a false positive result. The overall chance of a false positive result is greater than the nominal level of 5%. How much greater is generally not known. At the same time, however, as the probability of a Type I Error increases, the probability of a Type II Error decreases. What the level of Type II Error is, is also not known. Some may find this situation highly problematic, both in terms of what the probabilities of error are likely to be and the vagueness in obtaining a more specific idea of what their magnitudes are.

Fundamentally, this procedure is not meant to be a classical hypothesis testing procedure, but, rather, an exploratory and descriptive procedure. Both what would ordinarily be called Type I and Type II Errors in statistical hypothesis testing, may here be almost equally important. The usual procedure of strict control of the Type I Error (below 5% or 1%) while allowing the Type II Errors to go unchecked is here inappropriate.

Is it not then inconsistent to use statistical tests in the evaluation even if only to define reasonable stopping rules? Perhaps, but the alternatives available appear to have even greater deficiencies. In any case, this entire procedure should be regarded as exploratory. The results require subsequent validation in an independent replication study.

For the present, the best recommendation I can make to counter the problems in this arena is that a large enough sample be obtained so that the sample can be randomly split into two, the "training" sample, and the "validation" sample. Then the methods used here should be applied to the training sample, and the best formulation of the test or battery of tests obtained in that sample. The quality of the results should then be assessed on the validation sample. This would prevent inadvertently obtaining overly optimistic results. In the future others might be able to identify better defined and stronger stopping rules.

Other Problems

Working on a NIH study group at one time, I used the phrase "statistical research." A medical researcher looked befuddled and admitted that he could not grasp what was meant by statistical research. Was statistics not a "dead science" in the non-pejorative sense that Latin was a "dead language"? Was a statistical problem not ipso facto solved once it was properly identified and clearly stated? Surely all of what was to be known about statistics was known? Surely there was not disagreement from statistician to statistician or from year to year as to what the correct statistical approach to a problem should be?

While few researchers are as blunt (or honest) as this one was, it does seem as though this view is common. A medical researcher comes to a statistician to get the "right" answer, and in many cases, the honest statistician can only make a recommendation, justify that recommendation, and suggest what the alternatives there might be. The process isn't fundamentally different from what a patient gets by consulting an expert clinician.

If the researchers follow that recommendation to the letter, they may occasionally find that other statisticians (on NIH review committees for example) will disagree. No, statistics is not a dead science—it is evolving. There are always new methods under development, better than existing ones. Methods accepted some years ago are found to have deficiencies and are now recommended against.

The methods here developed contradict some of what was in the statistical literature of old, but, in turn, the methods here may be improved upon in the future.

The Present: An Overall Summary

We will end now with an overall summary of the steps involved in the systematic and objective evaluation of a medical test to serve as a check list in structuring such an evaluation or reviewing an evaluation done by others.

What Is the Disorder? What Diagnosis Is to Be Used? Is the Diagnosis Clinically Valid and Reliable?

There are many medical tests in the research literature that are proposed because they might be useful for some unspecified purpose or another. Would you accept the evaluation of a drug that might be useful for the treatment of something or the other? I would suspect not. No more should a test be proposed without a specific and well-defined purpose, and certainly a test should not be used in practice if the outcome cannot be specifically interpreted (Mold & Stein, 1986).

In What Clinical Population or Populations Is the Test Proposed for Use? How Can the Sampling Be Done so as to Obtain a Representative Sample from That Population or Populations?

One might well try out a test in a pilot sample or a "grab-sample" of patients. However, the purpose of such an informal study should be either to test the feasibility of the protocol, to gain some experience in using the diagnostic procedures or tests, or to decide whether it is worthwhile to invest the time and money necessary to do a proper evaluation of the test. Such a pilot study should not be published, or, if published, trusted as a test evaluation.

If the Test Is to Be Evaluated as a Prognostic Test, Will the Follow-Up Be Fixed or Variable? If the Follow-Up Is to Be Fixed, Fixed at What Time?

Considerable and careful thought should be given to the issue of follow-up in evaluating prognostic tests. As has been seen, the results obtained will differ from one follow-up time to another. Using a long follow-up time, whether fixed or variable, in combination with methods appropriate to a variable follow-up time, will yield these varied results and produce a much richer and more informative study. If the follow-up time is to be fixed and the methods for diagnostic test and fixed follow-up time prognostic tests are used, the follow-up time must be carefully chosen to be long enough to give the test(s) a fair chance, and then consistent with the specific medical purpose one has in mind.

Will Sampling Be Naturalistic, Retrospective, or Prospective?

The reasons for preferring one sampling procedure over another has to do with the difficulty and costs of doing the evaluation study, not with the validity of the results based on the study.

Retrospective Sampling can be used only for diagnostic tests. Prospective Sampling can be used only if there is one and only one test under consideration (not multiple referents or multiple tests in a battery). If the test is prognostic and a variable follow-up time is used, only Naturalistic Sampling will do.

Furthermore, in the case of Retrospective or Prospective Sampling there must be a screening sample first, with a *random* selection of a subset of patients thereafter to complete the procedure. If the sampling is retrospective or prospective, the estimates must be obtained in accordance with the rules governing sampling for this case. One cannot simply use the estimation procedures developed for Naturalistic Sampling—such would be miscomputed estimates and quite likely wrong.

How Large a Sample Is Needed?

The sample size must be minimally sufficient to yield at least 10 in each of the marginal positions of the 2 × 2 table for the evaluation of each single test. If multiple referents are to be evaluated, the only ones that will be considered will be those that yield at least 10 with and 10 without a positive test result. If there are multiple tests in the battery, the number of subjects must be large enough at each successive step.

The overall message is that the better the test evaluation, the larger the sample size must be. The lower the prevalence in a population, the larger the sample size must be. The more referents for a test are to be evaluated, the larger the sample size must be. The more tests in a battery of tests to be evaluated, the larger the sample size must be. A great deal of consideration, and some expert statistical consultation, should be sought in making sample size decisions before a study is begun.

How Are Dropouts and Missing Responses Avoided?

It is almost inevitable, particularly in the evaluation of prognostic tests, that there will be some dropouts. However, if the number lost is substantial, or if dropouts occur not by choice of the patient, but, rather, by choice of the test evaluator, one should begin to question the validity of the results.

Ideally, all subjects who are sampled undergo all the procedures to which they are assigned. Every patient lacking a diagnosis is omitted from the sample for analysis, and each such omission increases the risk of biasing the results. Every patient lacking a test result is omitted from the evaluation of that test result, although he might be included in evaluation of other test results in the battery if there are such. But every patient so omitted again increases the risk of bias in the results.

It is well to consider the issue of retention of subjects in the process of planning of the evaluation study.

What Are the Clinical Benefits in this Situation?

Are the benefits of accurate diagnosis primarily to those with the disorder ($r = 1$), primarily to those without the disorder ($r = 0$), or roughly equally to both ($r = .5$)? That is to say: Is the test intended for screening ($r = 1$), for discrimination ($r = .5$), or for a definitive result ($r = 0$)?

What is the overall magnitude of the benefit: Low ($\$R = \$100$), Moderate ($\$R = \$10,000$), or High ($\$R = \infty$)? Restated: Is the test to be used for a disorder that is not serious or is self-limiting and requires no treatment or to satisfy the patient's or physician's curiosity or to further the physician's education or research (low potential clinical benefit, $\$R = \$100$). If the disorder is serious, painful, chronic, or life-threatening and requires treatment, and, if so, is effective and safe treatment available to the patient upon proper diagnosis (high potential clinical benefit, $\$R = \infty$)? Is the disorder serious, but without available safe and effective treatment, or, alternatively, is the disorder moderately discomfiting and one for which safe and effective treatment is available (moderate potential clinical benefit: $\$R = \$10,000$)?

If it is possible to measure the clinical costs and benefits more exactly, one might be able to do better than the above crude categorizations of the relative clinical benefit (r) and the total potential clinical benefit ($\$R$).

In any case, in designing or evaluating a test evaluation, what the clinical benefits are should be, in one way or another, considered. If several different clinical populations are simultaneously being studied, the clinical benefits may vary from population to population.

What Are the Tests Under Evaluation—Their Protocols, Responses, and Referents? What Are the Test Costs? If This is a Single Test (a Single Fixed Cost for All the Responses) or Is This to Be Considered a Battery of Tests (Separable Costs)?

Considering the time, effort, and cost of a properly done medical test evaluation, the evaluation should be as thorough as possible. This would mean including evaluation of multiple referents, if there are such. Most commonly, obtaining the ROC, QROC, or QCROC of a family of tests is not more costly or time-consuming than evaluating a single referent for that test.

Including in a battery not only the test of specific interest, but also the tests currently most commonly used for the same disorder, may be more costly and time-consuming than evaluating a single test, but the results are more than commensurately valuable. It is such evaluations that will lead to optimal batteries of tests, that minimize the number of tests, their costs, and risks while simultaneously optimizing the overall accuracy of the test procedures.

How Are the Blinding of the Diagnosis and Test Results Assured? If There Are Multiple Tests in a Battery Under Evaluation, Are These Blinded to Each Other?

If diagnosis and test are not blinded, it will not be clear how much the bias of the diagnosticians and testers influenced the outcomes obtained. One research group positively disposed to a test procedure may find good performance, while another, seriously doubting the value of the test, may find quite the opposite. Blinding between diagnosis and test is essential.

As to the blinding of the multiple tests in the battery, the rules are less clear. It is probably best that tests in the battery having separate costs be done blind to each other's results. When the time comes, the optimal battery may require the use of one and not the other test. If the outcome of one test is used to interpret that of another, the performance of one test in absence of the other may be different than when both are done together. For this reason, the tests having separate costs in the battery might better be done blind to each other.

Is There any Internal or External Standard Provided for the Performance of an Excellent Test?

For a single test, showing that its quality, as indicated by $\kappa(r, 0)$ exceeds zero, demonstrates that the test is legitimate. Showing that $\kappa(r, t)$, where t reflects the relative cost of the test, exceeds zero demonstrates that it is costworthy in the situation in which it is proposed for use. But all this means in both cases is that the test is better than tossing a coin.

In evaluating a test with multiple referents or within a battery of tests, the best of the set of tests is identified. Yet if all the tests evaluated are only slightly better than tossing a coin, the best of these may still be a weak test.

Without some standard of excellence, however, that is all that can be done with a test evaluation. Yet there are only rare published test evaluations to date that have included such a standard. Inclusion of such a standard in future test evaluations increases the value of such evaluations, and should at least be considered.

For a diagnostic test, one might include a second independent opinion for each diagnosis as the standard. For all types of tests, one might include the best test procedures currently in use and check whether the test under evaluation compares favorably with the standard, or whether the test added to the standard produces a significantly better test result.

The preceding 10 steps are part of the planning of a study, and decisions should be made a priori. At this point the study starts, and what follows has to do with the analysis and interpretation of the results.

Was the Data Base Properly Compiled and Thoroughly Checked for Errors?

Perhaps it is superfluous to remind responsible researchers to check the data thoroughly before initiating analysis. Nevertheless, I will do so because I have had more problems with data sets in test evaluations than with data sets from other types of studies. Perhaps because data for test evaluations are frequently drawn from clinic or hospital records, or medical charts, problems of inconsistencies and minor errors are common. Weight is recorded in kilograms, except occasionally, when it is recorded in pounds; years instead of months of follow-up; Celsius versus Fahrenheit; centimeters versus inches. Added to this is the occasional slippage of a decimal point, either in the recording, in the transcription, or in the entering of the data into the computer. A follow-up of 2 months is recorded as 20 or vice versa.

The only way to avoid such exasperating errors is to check and double-check at each stage of data acquisition. The final stage is for the test evaluators to examine the descriptive statistics: the number of missing responses for each variable, the range, the mean and standard deviation, and the correlation with the diagnosis of each test response. If these do not accord with what the evaluators "know" to be true, some additional checking of procedures is in order.

For Each Single Test Under Evaluation, for Each Test in the Battery Under Evaluation, and for Each Population Under Evaluation, Have the Descriptive Statistics Been Properly Computed?

If the sampling is naturalistic, the estimates of all the common performance measures can be directly obtained: sensitivity, specificity, the predictive values, the efficiency, the average risk, the level, etc. If sampling is retrospective, the estimate of the prevalence is obtained from the screening sample, and only sensitivity and specificity can be directly be estimated. The other measures can be obtained indirectly using Bayes' Theorem. If sampling is prospective, the estimate of the level is obtained from the screening sample, and only the predictive values can be directly estimated. The other measures can be obtained indirectly using Bayes' Theorem.

If the test is prognostic, and to be evaluated with a variable follow-up time, then sampling must be naturalistic. Estimates of the prevalence and of the predictive values at each possible follow-up time can be obtained using the Kaplan-Meier method of computing the survival curves in the total population, and separately among those with a positive and a negative test result. All the other measures of performance can be obtained indirectly.

What Is the Quality of Each Single Test Under Evaluation, and for Each Population Under Evaluation (and in an Evaluation of a Prognostic Test with Variable Follow-Up Time, for Each Possible Value of Follow-Up Time)?

If there are many referents for a test or many tests in the battery, and particularly if there are many populations being studied, it is very unlikely that every single test in every single population will be looked at by the evaluator. However the process of evaluation requires that each such test be evaluated, whether explicitly examined or not. In most cases, an algorithm will be used by a computer to select certain tests deserving close perusal. Thus the first issue is whether the quality of each single test is properly considered.

The reason that different methods of medical test evaluation yield what seem to be conflicting results is that current evaluation methods are based on measures of test *performance*, not of test *quality*. Such measures as sensitivity and specificity, the predictive values, efficiency, risk ratios, odds ratios, risk differences, and many more that have not been explicitly considered in this presentation are measures of performance in that their scale shifts from population to population and from one test to another. In that sense, as measures of test quality such measures are uncalibrated measures. The foundation of the methods here proposed requires calibration of these measures so that a random test has a quality measure of zero, and an ideal test (usually an unachievable ideal) has a quality measure of one, regardless of the population and of the test.

Recalibrating the sensitivity, the predictive value of a negative test, or two of the risk ratios, we found a quality index $\kappa(1, 0)$:

$$\kappa(1, 0) = (SE - Q)/(1 - Q) = (PVN - P')/P.$$

Recalibrating the specificity, the predictive value of a positive test, and two other risk ratios, we found yet another quality index $\kappa(0, 0)$:

$$\kappa(0, 0) = (SP - Q')/Q = (PVP - P)/P'.$$

Recalibrating the efficiency, we found yet another quality index $\kappa(.5, 0)$ that turned out to be a weighted average of $\kappa(1, 0)$ and $\kappa(0, 0)$. These measures of test quality should be computed for each referent of a test, and for each test in the battery.

There are, and should be, a range of quality indices. The relative clinical importance of the two types of error, a false positive and a false negative, are known not to be identical across all the cases in medicine. If the relative clinical importance of one to the other is measured as r, the corresponding quality index of the test in that situation is given by:

$$\kappa(r, 0) = [PQ'r\kappa(1, 0) + P'Qr'\kappa(0, 0)]/(PQ'r + P'Qr'),$$

a weighted average of $\kappa(1, 0)$ and $\kappa(0, 0)$.

Thus if one is seeking a very sensitive test, one that will detect as many with the disorder as possible, $\kappa(1, 0)$ is the quality index of interest. If one is seeking a very specific test, one that will detect as many without the disorder as possible, $\kappa(0, 0)$ is the quality index of interest. If, finally, one is seeking a test that discriminates well between those with and without the disorder, $\kappa(.5, 0)$ is the quality index of interest, which is the recalibrated form of efficiency.

Graphing $\kappa(1, 0)$ versus $\kappa(0, 0)$ for each referent of each test under consideration locates the QROC, the convex hull of all such tests. A QROC should be obtained for each of the clinical populations that are of interest. In each case, those tests on the QROC between the highest (optimally sensitive test) and the one furthest to the right (optimally specific test) constitute the optimal set of tests in the battery.

The above quality indices are those appropriate when there is no cost to testing ($T = 0$), or the cost of a test is trivial in comparison to the benefits to be derived ($t = 0$, $R = \infty$). The fixed cost of a test (T) can be and should be included into consideration of test quality. When test cost for each test is included into the definition of the test quality, the quality indices become:

$$\kappa(r, t) = \kappa(r, 0) - t / (PQ'r + P'Qr') .$$

Here t reflects the cost of the test relative to the potential clinical benefit to the patient and represents a deduction from the quality that pertains when the test cost is ignored.

A graph of $\kappa(1, t)$ versus $\kappa(0, t)$ for each referent of each test leads to the QCROC. The convex hull of such tests between the highest test point (the optimally costworthy sensitive test) and the test point furthest to the right (the optimally costworthy specific test) constitutes the set of optimally costworthy tests.

In theory, one could evaluate the quality for the full range of relative clinical benefit (r) and of potential clinical benefit (R, t), but, in fact, only three values of r are of general interest, $r = 1$ for screening, $r = .5$ for discrimination, and $r = 0$ for a definitive test.

Furthermore, the value of $\kappa(r, t)$ is sensitive only to orders of magnitude of the potential clinical benefit, R. Consequently taking only a few values of R will well describe the entire range. We suggest taking $R = \$100$, $R = \$10,000$, and $R = \infty$ to represent low, moderate, and high clinical benefit.

Has the Optimal Referent for a Test, or the Optimal First Test in a Battery of Tests Been Appropriately Selected?

When there are many referents for a test or many tests in a battery, the optimal test for each value of r, R is simply the one (or ones) with the maximal value of $\kappa(r, t)$.

When the test is prognostic and evaluated for different follow-up times, the optimal test may be different for different values of the follow-up time. Presented graphically, this will give a three-dimensional QROC or QCROC (a QROC or QCROC for each follow-up time).

If There Is a Battery of Tests Under Consideration, Has the Battery Been Appropriately Evaluated?

There are two valid ways of proceeding to evaluate a test battery: sequential structuring and scoring. As we have pointed out, sequential structuring results in fewer tests and lower costs. On the other hand, scoring is much easier for the evaluator when there are many tests in the battery. However, both are valid procedures.

Sequential structuring requires that the best first test be identified. The results of this first test divides the sample (and population) into two subgroups having different clinical characteristics. The process is repeated separately in one or both of the two subgroups formed by the results of the first test. If a screening test is sought, only those negative on the first test are retested. If a definitive test is sought, only those positive on the first test are retested. If a discriminative test is sought, both groups are retested. The process is then repeated until: (1) one runs out of tests; (2) one runs out of patients; or (3) one runs out of high-quality tests.

In the scoring procedure a hypothetical model is constructed. For a fixed follow-up time, there are several models readily available: Multiple Logistic, Loglinear, Multiple Discriminant, etc; for a variable follow-up time, the Proportional Hazards Model. In either case a stepwise procedure is used to find the best first test response, then the best response in addition to the first, etc. The stepwise procedure stops when: (1) one runs out of tests; (2) one runs out of patients (not enough power to detect the quality of the remaining tests); or (3) one runs out of high-quality tests (no significant additional tests).

The score based on the estimates found for the parameters of the model are then used to obtain a score for each patient. One can evaluate the quality of the battery and find the optimal referent (cut point for the score) by using the QROC or QCROC.

References

Abbott Laboratories. Diagnostics Division. (1985, April). *Human T-lymphotropic virus type III, Abbott HTLV III EIA, enzyme immunoassay for the detection of antibody to human T-lymphotropic virus type III (HTLV III) in human serum or plasma.* (Research Rep. No. 83-1014/R2).

Are we hooked on tests? (1987, November 23). *U.S. News and World Report*, pp. 60-72.

Berkson, J. (1946). Limitations of the application of four-fold table analysis to hospital data. *Biometrics Bulletin, 2,* 47-53.

Berkson, J. (1958). Smoking and lung cancer: Some observations on two recent reports. *Journal of the American Statistical Association, 53,* 23-38.

Blakiston's Gould medical dictionary. (1979). New York: McGraw-Hill.

Bloch, D. A., & Kraemer, H. C. (1989). 2 × 2 kappa coefficients: Measures of agreement or association. *Biometrics, 45,* 269-287.

Breiman, L., Friedman, J. H., Olshen, R. A., & Stone, C. J. (1984). *Classification and regression trees.* Monterey, CA: Wadsworth & Brooks/Cole.

Brush, J. E., Drand, D. A., Acampora, D., Chalmer, B., & Wackers, F. J. (1985). Use of the initial electrocardiogram to predict in-hospital complications of acute myocardial infarction. *The New England Journal of Medicine, 312,* 1137-1141.

Bull, S. B., & Donner, A. (1987). The efficiency of multinomial logistic regression compared with multiple group discriminant analysis. *Journal of the American Statistical Association, 82,* 1118-1122.

Califano, J. A. (1986). *America's health care revolution: Who lives? who dies? who pays?.* New York: Random House.

Carroll, B. J., Feinberg, M., & Greden, J. F., et al. (1980). Diagnosis of endogenous depression: Comparison of clinical, research and neuroendocrine criteria. *Journal of Affective Disorders, 2,* 177-194.

Carroll, B. J., Feinberg, M., Greden, J. F., Tarika, J., Albala, A. A., Haskett, R. F., James, N. M., Kronfol, Z., Lohr, N., Steiner, M., deVigne, J. P., & Young, E.

(1981). A specific laboratory test for the diagnosis of melancholia. Standardization, validation, and clinical utility. *Archives of General Psychiatry, 38,* 15-22.

Chaitman, B. R., Bourassa, M. G., Davis, K., Rogers, W. J., Tyras, D. H., Berger, R., Kennedy, J. W., Fisher, L., Judkins, M. P., Mock, M. B., & Killip, T. (1981). Angiographic prevalence of high-risk coronary artery disease in patient subsets (CASS). *Circulation, 64,* 360-367.

Cohen, J. (1960). A coefficient of agreement for nominal scales. *Educational and Psychological Measurement, 20,* 37-46.

Detre, K. M., Wright, E., Murphy, M. L., & Takaro, T. (1975). Observer agreement in evaluating coronary angiograms. *Circulation, 52,* 979-986.

Diamond, G. A. (1986). Reverent Bayes' silent majority: An alternative factor affecting sensitivity and specificity of exercise electrocardiography. *Americal Journal of Cardiology, 57,* 1175-1179.

DiMaio, M. S., Baumgarten, A., Greenstein, R. M., Saal, H. M., & Mahoney, M. J. (1987). Screening for fetal Down's syndrome in pregnancy by measuring maternal serum alpha-fetoprotein levels. *The New England Journal of Medicine, 317,* 342-346.

Efron, B. (1975). The efficiency of logistic regression compared to normal discriminant analysis. *Journal of the Americal Statistical Association, 70,* 892-898.

Efron, B. (1978). Regression and ANOVA with zero-one data: Measures of residual variation. *Journal of the American Statistical Association, 73,* 113-121.

Etter, L. E., Dunn, J. P., Kammer, A. G., Osmond, L. H., & Reese, L. C. (1960). Gastroduodenal X-ray diagnosis: A comparison of radiographic technics and interpretations. *Radiology, 74,* 766-770.

Fagan, T. J. (1975). Nomogram for Bayes' Theorem. *The New England Journal of Medicine, 293,* 257.

Feinstein, A. (1985). *Clinical epidemiology: The architecture of clinical research.* Philadelphia: W. B. Saunders.

Feinstein, A. R. (1973). Chemical biostatistics XX. The epidemiological trohoe, the ablative risk ratio, and retrospective research. *Clinical Pharamacology and Therapeutics, 14,* 291-307.

Fisher, L. D., Kennedy, J. W., Chaitman, B. R., Ryan, T. J., McCabe, C., Weiner, D., Tristani, F., Schloss, M., & Warner, H. R., Jr. (1981). Diagnostic quantification of CASS (Coronary Artery Surgery Study) clinical and exercise test results in determining presence and extent of coronary artery disease. *Circulation, 63,* 987-1000.

Fisher, R. A. (1936). The use of multiple measurements in toxonomic problems. *Annals of Eugenics, 7,* 179.

Fleiss, J. L. (1971). Measuring nominal scale agreement among many raters. *Psychological Bulletin, 76,* 378-382.

Fleiss, J. L. (1981). *Statistical methods for rates and proportions.* New York: John Wiley.

Galen, R. S., & Gambino S. R. (1975). *Beyond normality: The predictive value and efficiency of medical diagnoses.* New York: John Wiley.

Garth, K. E., Carroll, B. A., Sommer, F. G., & Oppenheimer, D. A. (1983). Duplex ultrasound scanning of the carotid arteries with velocity spectrum analysis. *Radiology, 147,* 823-827.

Harrell, F. E., Jr., & Lee, K. L. (1985). A comparison of the discrimination of Discriminant Analysis and Logistic Regression under multivariate normality. Biostatistics: Statistics in Biomedical, Public Health and Environmental Sciences, ed. P.K. Sen, Amsterdam: North Holland.

Harris, J. M., Tang, D. B., & Weltz, M. D. (1978). Diagnostic tests and Hodgkin's disease. A standardized approach to their evaluation. *Cancer, 41*, 2388-2392.

Hlatky, M. A., Mark, D. B, Harrell, F. E., Lee, K. L., Califf, R. M., & Pryor, D. B. (1987). Rethinking sensitivity and specificity. *The American Journal of Cardiology, 59*, 1195-1198.

Hlatky, M. A., Pryor, D. B., Harrell, F. E., Califf, R. M., Mark, D. B., & Rosati, R. A. (1984). Factors affecting sensitivity and specificity of exercise electrocardiography. Multivariable analysis. *Americal Journal of Medicine, 77*, 64-71.

Hosmer T., Hosmer, D., & Fisher, L. (1983). A comparison of the maximum likelihood and discriminant function estimators of the coefficients of the Logistic Regression model for mixed continuous and discrete variables. *Communications in Statistics—Simulation and Computation, 12*, 22-43.

James, E. M., Earnest, F., Forbes, G. S., Reese, D. F., Houser, O. W., & Folger, W. N. (1982). High-resolution dynamic ultrasound imaging of the carotid bifurcation: A prospective evaluation. *Radiology, 144*, 853-858.

Kaplan, E. L., & Meier, P. (1980). Nonparametric estimation from incomplete observations. *Journal of American Statistical Association, 53*, 475-481.

Koran, L. M. (1975). The reliability of clinical methods, data and judgments. *The New England Journal of Medicine, 293*, 642-646.

Kraemer, H. C. (1979). Ramifications of a population model for κ as a coefficient of reliability. *Psychometrika, 44*, 461-472.

Kraemer, H. C. (1980). Extension of the kappa coefficient. *Biometrics, 36*, 207-216.

Kraemer, H. C. (1982). Estimating false alarms and missed events from interobserver agreement: Comment on Kaye. *Psychological Bulletin, 92*, 749-754.

Kraemer, H. C. (1985). The robustness of common measures of 2 × 2 association to bias due to misclassifications. *American Statistician, 39*, 286-290.

Kraemer, H. C. (1987). The methodological and statistical evaluation of medical tests: The dexamethasone suppression test in psychiatry. *Psychoneuroendocrinology, 12*, 411-427.

Kraemer, H. C. (1988). Assessment of 2 × 2 associations: Generalization of signal detection methodology. *Americal Statistician, 42*, 37-49.

Kraemer, H. C., & Bloch, D. A. (1988). Kappa coefficients in epidemiology: An appraisal of a reappraisal. *Journal of Clinical Epidemiology, 41*, 959-968.

Lachenbruch, P. A., & Goldstein, M. (1979). Discriminant analysis. *Biometrics, 35*, 69-85.

Landis, J. R., & Koch, G. G. (1977). The measurement of observer agreement for categorical data. *Biometrics, 33*, 159-174.

Lee, E. (1980). *Statistical methods for survival data analysis.* Belmont, CA: Lifetime Learning.

Maris, J. M., Evans, A. E., McLaughlin, A. C., D'Angio, G. J., Bolinger, L., Manos, H., & Chance, B. (1985). P nuclear magnetic resonance spectroscopic investigation of human neuroblastoma in situ. *The New England Journal of Medicine, 312*, 1500-1505.

Martin, C. A., Thompson, P. L., Armstrong, B. K., Phil, D., Hobbs, M.S.T., & de Klerk, N. (1983). Long-term prognosis after recovery from myocardial infarction: A nine year follow-up of the Perth Coronary Register. *Circulation, 68*, 961-969.

McNeil, B. J., Keeler, E., & Adelstein, S. J. (1975). Primer on certain elements of medical decision making. *The New England Journal of Medicine, 293*, 211-215.

McNeil, B. J., Varady, P. D., Burrows, B. A., & Adelstein, S. J. (1975). Measures of clinical efficacy: Cost effectiveness calculations in the diagnosis and treatment of hypertensive renovascular disease. *The New England Journal of Medicine, 293*, 216-221.

Melin, J. A., Piret, L. J., Vanbutsele, R. J. M., Rousseau, M. F., Cosyns, J., Brasseur, L. A., Beckers, C., & Detry, J. M. R. (1981). Diagnostic value of exercise electrocardiography and thallium myocardial scintigraphy in patients without previous myocardial infarction: A Bayesian approach. *Circulation, 63*, 1019-1024.

Menzel, P. T. (1983). *Medical costs, moral choices: A philosophy of health care economics in America*. New Haven, CT: Yale University Press.

Mogensen, C. E., & Christensen, C. K. (1984). Predicting diabetic nephropathy in insulin-dependent patients. *The New England Journal of Medicine, 311*, 89-93.

Mold, J. W., & Stein, H. F. (1986). The cascade effect in the clinical care of patients. *The New England Journal of Medicine, 314*, 512-514.

Morrison, A. S. (1985). *Screening in chronic disease*. New York: Oxford University Press.

Moskowitz, M. A., & Osband, M. E. (1984). *The complete book of medical tests*. New York: Norton.

Nash, D. T. (1985). *Medical mayhem: How to avoid it and get the best possible care from your doctor and hospital*. New York: Walker.

O'Gorman, N. V., & Woolson, R. F. (1991). Variable selection to discriminate between two groups: Stepwise logistic regression in stepwise discriminant analysis? *American Statistician, 45*, 187-193.

Olefsky, J. M., Farquhar, J. W., & Reaven, G. M. (1973). Do the oral and intravenous glucose tolerance tests provide similar diagnostic information in patients with chemical diabetes mellitus? *Diabetes, 22*, 202-209.

Oxford dictionary of quotations (3rd. ed.). (1980). Oxford: Oxford University Press.

Patterson, R., Horowitz, S. F., Eng, C., Rudin, A., Heller, J., Halgash, D. A., Pichard, A. D., Goldsmith, S. F., Herman, M. V., Gorlin, R. (1982). Can exercise electrocardiography and Thallium-201 myocardial imaging exclude the diagnosis of coronary artery disease? *American Journal of Cardiology, 49*, 1127-1135.

Pozen, M. W., D'Agostino, R. B., Mitchell, J. B., Rosenfeld, M., Guglielmino, J. T., Schwartz, M. L., Teebagy, N., Valentine, J. M., & Hood, W. B. (1980). The usefulness of a predictive instrument to reduce inappropriate admissions to the coronary care unit. *Annals of Internal Medicine, 92*, 238-242.

Press, S. J., & Wilson, S. (1978). Choosing between Logistic Regression and Discriminant Analysis. *Journal of American Statistical Association, 73*, 699-705.

Pueschel, S. M. (1987). Maternal alpha-fetoprotein screening for Down's syndrome. *The New England Journal of Medicine, 317*, 376-378.

Remein, Q. R., & Wilkerson, H.L.C. (1961). The efficiency of screening tests for diabetes. *Journal of Chronic Disease, 13*, 6-21.

Robin, E. D. (1984). *Matters of life & death: Risks vs benefits of medical care*. New York: Freeman.

Rogers, L. E., Lyon, G. M., Jr., & Porter, F. S. (1972). Spot test for vanillylmandelic acid and other guaiacols in urine of patients with neuroblastoma. *Americal Journal of Clinical Pathology, 58*, 383-387.

Ryback, R. S., Eckardt, M. J., Felsher, B., & Rawlings, R. R. (1982). Biochemical and hematologic correlates of alcoholism and liver disease. *Journal of the Americal Medical Association, 248*, 2261-2265.

Ryback, R. S., Eckardt, M. J., Rawlings, R. R., & Rosenthal, L. S. (1982). Quadratic discriminant analysis as an aid to interpretive reporting of clinical laboratory tests. *Journal of the American Medical Association, 248*, 2342-2345.

Sisson, J. C., Schoomaker, M. D., & Ross, J. C. (1976). Clinical Decision Analysis: The hazard of using additional data. *Journal of the American Medical Association, 236*, 1259-1263.

Solberg, H. E. (1978). Discriminant analysis. *Critical Reviews in Clinical Laboratory Science, 9*, 209-242.

Speicher, C. E., & Smith, J. W. (1983). *Choosing effective laboratory tests.* Philadelphia: W. B. Saunders.

Spitzer, R. L., & Fleiss, J. L. (1974). A re-analysis of the reliability of psychiatric diagnosis. *British Journal of Psychiatry, 125*, 341-347.

Stampfer, M. F., Willett, W. C., Colditz, G. A., Rosner, B., Speizer, F. E., & Hennekens, C. H. (1985). A prospective study of postmenopausal estrogen therapy and coronary heart disease. *The New England Journal of Medicine, 313*, 1044-1049.

Swets, J. A. (1982). Sensitivities and specifications of diagnostic tests. *Journal of the American Medical Association, 248*, 548-550.

Swets, J. A., & Pickett, R. M. (1982). *Evaluation of diagnostic systems: Methods from signal detection theory.* New York: Academic Press.

Theroux, P., Waters, D. D., Halphen, C., Debaisieux, J. C., & Mizgala, H. F. (1979). Prognostic value of exercise testing soon after myocardial infarction. *The New England Journal of Medicine, 301*, 341-345.

The value of diagnostic tests. (1979, April 14). *The Lancet*, 809-810.

Weiner, D. A., Ryan, T. J., McCabe, C. H., Kennedy, J. W., Schloss, M., Tristani, F., Chaitman, B. R., & Fisher, L. D. (1979). Exercise stress testing. Correlations among history of angina, ST-segment response and prevalence of coronary-artery disease in the coronary artery surgery study (CASS). *The New England Journal of Medicine, 301*, 230-235.

Weiss, L. (1977). The resurgence of biological psychiatry: New promise or false hope for a troubled profession. *Perspectives in Biology and Medicine*, 573-585.

Wetzner, S. M., Kiser, L. C., & Bezreh, J. S. (1984). Duplex ultrasound imaging: Vascular applications. *Radiology, 150*, 507-514.

Yerushalmy, J. (1956). The importance of observer error in the interpretation of photofluorograms and the value of multiple ratings. *International Tuberculosis Yearbook, 26*, 110-124.

Yunis, J. J., Brunning, R. D., Howe, R. B., & Lobell, M. (1984). High-resolution chromosomes as an independent prognostic indicator in adult acute nonlymphocytic leukemia. *The New England Journal of Medicine, 311*, 812-818.

Index

Abbot laboratories, 60
And/or rules, 20, 161-162, 166-169
Attributable risks, 66. See also Kappa

Base of tests, 23-25, 73-74
Battery of tests:
    scored, 167-169, 194-195, 199-227, 279, 285
    sequential, 165-198, 279, 285
Bayes Theorem, 3, 46, 55, 59, 90, 91, 96, 242, 282
Bayesian methods, 96-113
Benefit Threshold, 138-140
Benefit. See Potential clinical benefit
Berkson, 59, 104
Berkson's fallacy, 59
Bias in sampling, 49-53, 59-60, 171, 196-197
Bias of estimators, 35, 37-38, 44
Blakiston, 5-6
Blind Evaluation:
    among tests, 163-164, 280
    test vs. diagnosis, 28-29, 47, 232, 280
    among diagnoses, 9, 14
Block & Kraemer, 115, 186
Brush et al., 31

Bull & Donner, 218

Calibration of measures, 65, 97, 99, 103-113, 115, 283
Califano, 2
Carroll et al., 13, 18-19
Causal inferences, 170, 201
Chaitman et al., 31-32
Chi-square test, 34, 40-43, 47, 55, 57, 74, 82, 185, 274
Clinical benefit. See Relative clinical benefit
Clinical costs, 199-123
Cohen, 115-129
Collinearity. See Redundancy
Combined tests, 141, 156-161, 161-162
Constancy, myth, 43, 59-60, 91-94, 161-162, 229-230
Correlation, 21-22, 169-170, 173-176, 179
Cost of tests, 1-2, 48, 131-135, 155-161, 169-170, 279
    containment, 155, 189-193, 194-195, 209
    definitions, 131-145
Costworthy tests, 131-154, 139, 155-156, 185, 192, 203-204

291

About the Author

Helena Chmura Kraemer is Professor of Biostatistics in Psychiatry, Department of Psychiatry and Behavioral Sciences, Stanford University, School of Medicine. Born in Ansonia, Connecticut, she did her undergraduate work at Smith College majoring in mathematics, and spent a year as a Fulbright scholar in statistics at Manchester University, England. She received her Ph.D. degree in statistics at Stanford University, and joined the staff and later the faculty at Stanford.

Her primary research interest is the application of statistical methods to the study of behavior within a medical context. She has not only published many statistical papers in this area but has collaborated on research in, among other fields, psychiatry, cardiology, pediatrics, psychology, and education.

Printed in the United States
2083

9 780803 946125